JOOLZ GUIDES

RATHER SPLENDID
LONDON
PUB WALKS

JOOLZ GUIDES

RATHER SPLENDID
LONDON
PUB WALKS

A Charming Trundle through London's Neighbourhoods
via its Fabulous Drinking Houses
by JULIAN McDONNELL

Quadrille

CONTENTS

Introduction **6**
Joolz's Pub Paraphernalia Challenge **8**

THE WALKS **12**

1 A riverside ramble from Chiswick to Hammersmith **14**

2 A watery Wapping-ward walk **30**

3 A heroic pootle around Maida Vale **50**

4 A riparian route from London Bridge to Rotherhithe **64**

5 A posh perambulation from Belgravia to Knightsbridge **82**

6 A delightful dawdle through Soho **98**

7 A leafy stroll around Bloomsbury **116**

8 A Fitrovian frolic **136**

9 A circuitous crawl around Crouch End **152**

10 A Kentish Town constitutional **168**

11 A wonderful wander around Walthamstow **186**

12 The sun always shines on Sydenham **202**

13 A historical stroll from Mayfair to Westminster **218**

14 An appealing wheeling through Ealing **238**

15 An East End odyssey through Hackney **252**

16 A canter about Clapham **270**

17 Some beers in beautiful Bayswater **286**

18 A quaint saunter from Blackheath to Greenwich **300**

Acknowledgements **318**

INTRODUCTION

Pip pip! Tally ho!! Welcome to my second book, featuring 18 spiffing walks and over 100 pubs in which to slap your thigh, quaff ale, gorge upon pie and recount steamy tales of passion.

But wait! This is not a pub guide, listing opening hours and so forth; there are plenty of those already. No, this is a book of marvellous walks, with pubs *en route*! What better way to break your journey whilst exploring a new area or spending a day with friends than to discover a wonderful selection of these fine, traditional institutions filled with bonhomie and history – often boasting tremendous architecture and decor. These aren't necessarily my favourite pubs in the city – see my first book, *Rather Splendid London Walks*, for more of those – but they are all worth a visit.

As usual, the walks take you past stink pipes, coal hole covers and interesting buildings, with all nature of cultural and historical references. A pub is often the oldest establishment in a street, so why not make pubs a feature of the walks? The pubs might be good, they might be bad, they might even be ugly! But they're a part of London, that's for sure.

So what makes a good pub? Everyone you ask has a different opinion! For some, the quality of the food is paramount; others want an honest pint and a game of pool. Some people want enough TV screens to watch the big game; others seek a place to take their kids all Sunday afternoon while the parents get drunk. This variety is what I love about pubs, and what makes them such a quintessentially British cornerstone of life.

There isn't enough space here to harp on about what makes a perfect pub, but I can certainly say that what makes a perfect London walk involves stopping off at a few pubs en route. Since opinion is so divided, I have also enlisted the help of a few 'friends of Joolz Guides' to assemble some general rules which, for them at least, make for a better pub experience (see pages 166–7 and 191). Oh, and I have created Joolz's Pub Paraphernalia Challenge (see page 8) for some extra fun on your travels.

Remember to check out the corresponding videos, too (see joolzguides.com or scan the QR code at the start of each walk) – but there are plenty of juicy facts in this book which you won't find in the films!

So, it's best drinking trousers on, tally ho, and the last one down the pub gets a lick of the cat!

JOOLZ'S PUB PARAPHERNALIA CHALLENGE

Whenever you go on a London pub crawl
Be sure to hunt down at least one if not all
Of the paraphernalia that once was so common
But now is quite rare and seems mostly forgotten.
Can you spot these things whilst you're resting your legs?
A horse brass, a snob screen or fine pickled eggs?
There's no prize, as usual, it's only for fun
But find a 'lock-in' and you've definitely won!

My first book features a challenge in which you can award yourself points for spotting a range of intriguing 'street furniture': drinking fountains, cattle troughs, fire insurance plaques, old post boxes, gas lamps, cannon bollards, old street signs, parish boundary markers, wooden paving, milestones, stink pipes, torch snuffer-outers, stretcher railings, coal hole covers and cabmen's shelters… I'll still be pointing these out in this book but the world of the pub is just as fun, so this time round you can also award yourself points for spotting some of these beauties!

PICKLED EGGS

The murky world of bar snacks can cause much consternation. Ordering a packet of scampi fries or pork scratchings can either win favour amongst friends, or earn their contempt. I have a personal penchant for KP nuts. One bar snack that is becoming increasingly rare is the humble pickled egg. If you spot a pub with a jar of these you get **five points** – but only if you order one!!!

HORSE BRASSES

These are bronze amulets used to decorate the harnesses of heavy horses, such as shire horses, and were much in vogue during the 19th century. As the use of horses declined, these brasses became quite collectable and many ended up adorning pubs. If the pub is called the Horse and Groom or the Coach and Horses it's worth looking out for them; equally, though, any pub with general clutter might have a horse brass or two. **Five points** per brass.

SNOB SCREENS

A snob screen is a rather beautifully etched pane of glass in a moveable hinged frame, which would enable the middle-class Victorian patron to peek

Joolz's Pub Paraphernalia Challenge | 9

Pickled eggs

Horse brasses

Snob screens

Vintage urinals or chain flushes

Dimpled pint glasses

Bar billiards

through at the oiks on the other side of the bar without being seen themselves. I've always found them a bit ridiculous since there is a huge gap beneath them, through which one can see everything – if you are of a certain height I suppose they can prevent the age-old fight-opener: 'Were you looking at my pint?!' **Five points** if you spot a snob screen, and **ten points** if you actually use it.

VINTAGE URINALS OR CHAIN FLUSHES

Errr... Yes, sorry about this. I wasn't prepared to walk around all the toilets taking photos of them or people would think I'm weird! Obviously there are no urinals in ladies' toilets but they will sometimes have an old-style Thomas Crapper Valveless Waste Preventer. To score **points**, any toilet with a traditional flush where you pull the chain will qualify. From a gents' perspective, I must say I favour the large old urinals which these days you find mostly in the public lavatories that have been converted into cafés. You can now sit and sip coffee where gentlemen used to pee! You get **five points** as long as it's still being used as a toilet (and that doesn't mean whopping it out in a café).

DIMPLED PINT GLASSES

These traditional pint glasses (also known as 'dimple mugs' or 'dimple jugs') have existed in pubs since the 1920s. In any old photo of a bloke with a flat cap and a pint he would be holding one. Sadly, with the increasing popularity of lager, by the 2000s they had all but disappeared, as straight, handleless glasses (sometimes known as 'sleevers') replaced them, favoured due to being more easily stored and cleaned. However, dimpled pint glasses are beginning to make a bit of a comeback and there's nothing better than holding your pint of ale by the handle and putting it on a beer mat. While I'm at it, how about **points** for spotting a Toby Mug or a Landlord's Tankard, too? (Don't get a Toby Mug and a Character Mug mixed up. A Toby Mug has the whole person on it, but a Character Mug only has their face!) **Five points** if you spot any of these!

BAR BILLIARDS

This is now really rare. The game originated in the 16th century, played mostly by the French and Russian aristocracy because the tables were so expensive, and became popular in Britain in the 1930s. Every time I find one in a pub either someone has stolen the balls or the table has disappeared next time I visit. Actually, there's still a bar billiards world championship! It's really quite fun and not that easy! So you definitely get **points** for spotting these! They're so scarce I'll give you **twenty**. (Mind you, even finding a pub with a pool table is quite rare these days... and one with 'winner stays on' rarer still!)

PUB PETS

In my first book I drew attention to the cute pub cat at the Seven Stars, which always wears a ruff when on duty. Whilst pub pets are usually cats, they don't have to be. Sometimes they could have a dog – or even a parrot, like Biddle Bros in Hackney! So **five points** for spotting a cat or dog, but **ten points** if you see some other type of pub animal.

Pub pets

PUBS WITH LOCK-INS

Gosh, it's been a long time since I experienced a pub lock-in. And if you don't know what a lock-in is then shame on you! When I was young the landlord would often lock the doors after last orders and anyone left in the pub could carry on drinking. If you experience a lock-in you get **ten points**, but you'll probably have forgotten by the morning!

Pubs with lock-ins

YARD OF ALE

This type of amusingly shaped tall (or should that be 'long'?) beer glass, holding roughly 2½ pints, originated in England in the 17th century. Due to its round bottom, it's usually hung on the wall, though it's becoming increasingly rare to see one in a pub – these days yards tend to be used only for special toasts and drinking competitions. If you see one you get **five points** – but **double that** if you actually drink a full yard… Watch out for the splash-back!!!

Yard of ale

Crouch End ⑨

Kentish Town ⑩

Maida Vale ③

Bloomsbury ⑦

Fitzrovia ⑧

⑭ Ealing   Bayswater ⑰   ⑥ Soho

⑬

Belgravia ⑤   Mayfair to
to Knightsbridge   Westminster

①
Chiswick to
Hammersmith

Clapham
⑯

THE WALKS

⑪ Walthamstow

⑮ Hackney

Tower Hill to Wapping & Limehouse
②

④
London Bridge to Rotherhithe

Blackheath to Greenwich
⑱

Sydenham, Forest Hill & Honor Oak
⑫

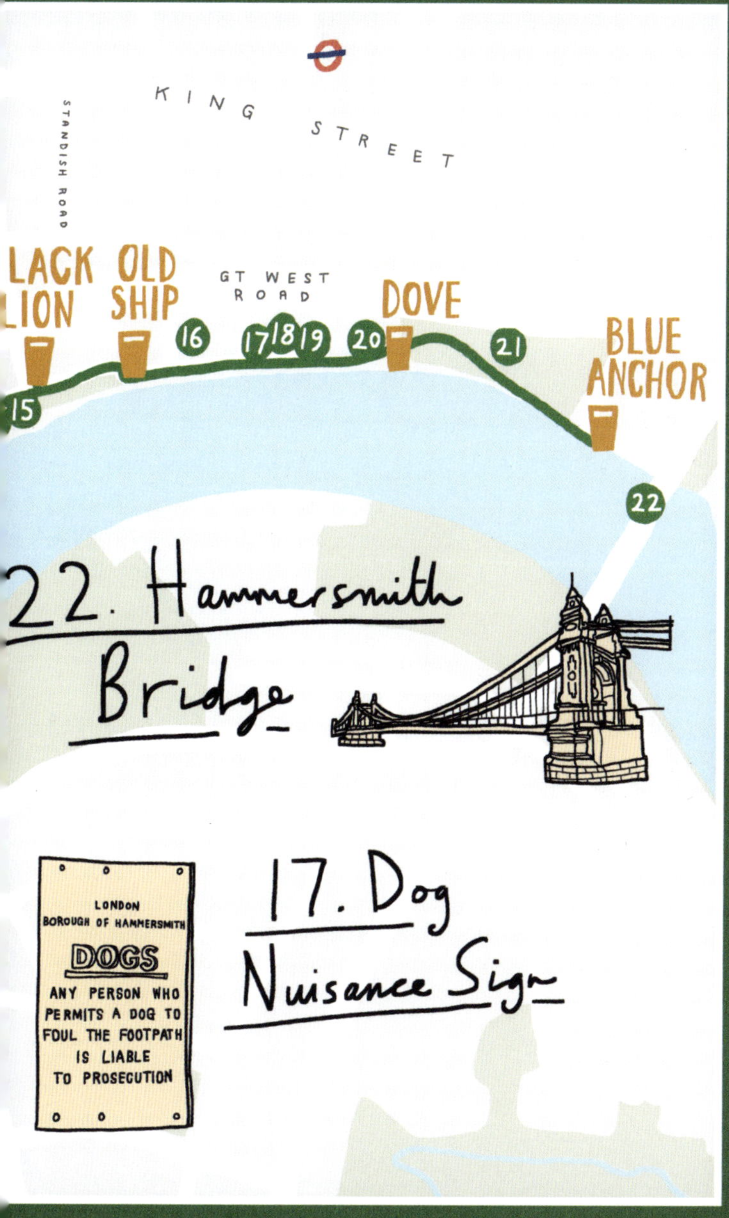

STANDISH ROAD
KING STREET
LACK LION
OLD SHIP
GT WEST ROAD
DOVE
BLUE ANCHOR
15 16 17 18 19 20 21
22

22. Hammersmith Bridge

17. Dog Nuisance Sign

I CHISWICK TO HAMMERSMITH

1 A RIVERSIDE RAMBLE FROM CHISWICK TO HAMMERSMITH

DISTANCE
3.9 km (2.4 miles)

TIME
1 hour 50 minutes
with a few pints en route

NEAREST STATION
Turnham Green

PUBS
Packhorse & Talbot; George & Devonshire; Fuller's Brewery; Black Lion; Old Ship; Dove; Blue Anchor

I say! How about we meet in the **PACKHORSE & TALBOT** on Chiswick High Road, which is very convenient for Turnham Green tube.

This former coaching inn has existed in some form here since the seventeenth century, although the present building dates to the early 1900s. I love pubs associated with ne'er-do-wells. Ever heard of Jonathan Wild, the notorious 'Thief-Taker General'? He is said to have been connected with this pub while running his ingenious criminal empire, which involved him simultaneously pretending to be some kind of public-spirited crime-fighter. He offered his expert services in recovering items which had been stolen from poor victims, taking payment for being able to get them back. However, it turned out he was the one organising the burglaries in the first place! (This all caught up with him in 1725, when he was hanged at Tyburn.) And in 1698 a group of conspirators led by George Barclay hid in the cellar here while waiting to assassinate King William III on his way back to Kensington. (The King was tipped off and Barclay had to flee.)

PUB
Packhorse & Talbot

These days it's a lot more salubrious and what I'd call a 'rugby-friendly pub', boasting a sizeable beer garden, decent food, and not a highwayman in sight.

Allow me to finish this pint of Greene King IPA, and then let's be off with us.

Turn right out of the Packhorse & Talbot, noting the statue of William Hogarth, the renowned eighteenth-century painter, who had plenty of associations with Chiswick (as we shall see shortly).

Cross over to the other side of Chiswick High Road and continue east until you reach **VILLA DI GEGGIANO** ❶. I do like this place because I came here with my mum, as you can see in the video that accompanies this walk. She was very complimentary about the truffle pasta! Much of the produce is transported directly from the Villa di Geggiano estate of the Bianchi Bandinelli family in Tuscany, who can trace their family directly to Pope Alexander III in 1160. They were also the first to import Chianti into England. I'd put it in the higher-end category of restaurants. It's the sort of place I'd go for special occasions and they do a fabulous negroni!

Cross back to the south side of Chiswick High Road and then head back the way we came briefly, before turning left into Chiswick Lane and walking all the way to the end. As you approach the Great West Road, turn right to follow Dorchester Grove to the atrocity before you, which is the **HOGARTH ROUNDABOUT** ❷. I'm sure the venerable artist would be delighted to know that his wonderful achievements led to this horrendous eyesore being named after him.

I know what you're thinking: why has Joolz taken us to this monstrous 1950s intersection? Well, around the late nineteenth century Chiswick was a country retreat for posh people who built large houses along the river. Before that it was more of a small fishing community known for its cheese farm – 'Ceswican' in Old English – where the annual cheese fair took place until the 1700s. (In the last few years this has been revived as Chiswick Cheese Market.)

Don't worry, the view will improve!! In fact, let's not spend any more time looking at the motorscape; take the underpass to Hogarth Lane, following the signs for **HOGARTH'S HOUSE** ❸.

These days we're on the busy A4, but in 1749, when Hogarth bought his country retreat here, it really was little more than a lane. Inside the house you can see some of his famous satirical works, such as *A Rake's Progress* and *A Harlot's*

Progress. One of them even references 'the ghost of Fanny Scratching in Cock Lane'. (Stop sniggering at the back!) So many people copied Hogarth's pictures that in 1735 he successfully lobbied Parliament to pass the first copyright act for visual works – so it's his fault that I can't show photos of them here!

Look out for the ingenious mechanism in his bedroom, enabling someone to open the door without having to get out of bed (the lazy so-and-so). Out in the garden, still standing today, is a mulberry tree from which his wife collected fruit to make tarts.

Head back along Hogarth Lane to the roundabout and walk via the underpass to the south side, where we'll have a drink in the **GEORGE & DEVONSHIRE** for some respite from all the traffic.

Just look at this lovely eighteenth-century Grade II-listed building. They say a pub has existed here since 1650, originally called the George, with 'Devonshire' added later. I wonder if this was to suck up to the Duke of Devonshire, who owned Chiswick House nearby?

I definitely recommend visiting **CHISWICK HOUSE** ❹. The only trouble is it's a little out of the way, as we'll be heading in the other direction, but a detour down Burlington Lane is well worth it if you have an extra half hour. The house was built in 1729 in the Neo-Palladian style by the Third Earl of Burlington and is surrounded by beautiful grounds where, in later years, Lady Cavendish entertained the Czar of Russia and had giraffes roaming in the gardens. In the twentieth century it was also used as a lunatic asylum (but only for wealthy people!) as well as being the venue for the Beatles' video for 'Paperback Writer' (near the statues of Roman figures).

If the walk to Chiswick House sounds a bit too much, you can just sit and admire the Duke of Devonshire's coat of arms on the pub sign and quaff your pint whilst doing impressions of pirates and smugglers. It's said that rum smugglers regularly used a passageway beneath the pub which led to the cottages by the river, behind the church of St Nicholas, which we will come to later.

Fifteen men on the dead man's chest
Yo ho (tally) ho and a bottle of rum
Drink and the devil had done for
the rest

Actually, it's too early for rum, so methinks I'll be having a pint of Seafarers.

Cheers!

Turn right out of the George & Devonshire and turn right again into Church Street.

From here it's as if you've stepped through a transporter: everything suddenly becomes very serene, and if it's summertime you should start to see many houses beautifully decorated with roses and hanging baskets. One of them coming up on the left is called **THE OLD BURLINGTON** ❺. This is believed to be the oldest building in Chiswick, dating from the fifteenth century, and it looks it!

More or less opposite, you should see the entrance to the church of my favourite saint, St Nicholas. Why? Because he's the patron saint of prostitutes, of course! Well, also brewers, children, pawnbrokers, repentant thieves, unmarried people and sailors (which makes sense, since this used to be a fishing village). You probably know him as Santa Claus.

It's worth having a little cruise around the cemetery here because you'll find some interesting graves. I like the pith helmet marking the **TOMB OF FREDERICK HITCH** ❻, who was one of the soldiers to earn a Victoria Cross at Rorke's Drift in 1879. You know, when the British troops (who had guns) defeated the Zulus (who had spears). You must have seen the film *Zulu*, with Michael Caine! An incredible twenty-three Victoria Crosses were awarded to the colonial forces, although you'd have to say there would have been many more on the Zulu side if they had an equivalent! Hitch returned to England and used his own horses to start a cab business, becoming the only taxi driver with a Victoria Cross. In fact, many cab drivers attended his funeral.

Another grave to look out for is that of William Hogarth, which is surrounded by railings and has rather nice depictions of easels and other artistic equipment.

Rumour has it that Oliver Cromwell might be buried here, too – because two of his daughters are, and no one really knows what happened to Cromwell's body. They'd have had a job gathering up the pieces, though, since he was posthumously hung, drawn and quartered!

Once you leave the cemetery return to Church Lane and follow it round to the left into Chiswick Mall, which runs alongside the river. This is now prime Chiswick real estate! The houses are unusual in that the residents have to cross the road to reach their gardens, some of which date back to the eighteenth century. The gardens always look terrific, so they all seem to be wonderful gardeners!

As you pass **BEDFORD HOUSE** ❼ (where the actor Michael Redgrave lived with his children, including Corin and Vanessa) look out onto the river, where you should see **CHISWICK EYOT** ❽. An eyot is a small island; when the tide is out you can even walk to this one (perhaps singing 'Islands in the Stream' by Dolly Parton and Kenny Rogers). The green post just in front of the eyot marks the halfway point in the Oxford and Cambridge Boat Race.

Roughly opposite the green post turn left up Chiswick Lane South (you might have just passed it, actually) and you will come to the **FULLER'S BREWERY** 🍺 on your left.

Now, what you might notice is that a lot of the pubs around here tend to be Fuller's pubs. This makes sense because the Fuller's Brewery is right here. I can thoroughly recommend a tour! You'll have to book in advance, but you do get some free tastings and in my opinion they have some great beers.

There's been a brewery here for roughly 400 years, going through various name changes until Fuller's took over in the middle of the nineteenth century. That's why you see Lamb Brewery and Griffin Brewery mentioned around the place. In fact, the griffin which you can see on the Fuller's logo is known as 'the guardian of treasure'. Under its right talon is a barrel of beer, which is their treasure!

PUB
Fuller's Brewery

During your tour a very interesting and friendly guide will explain all about the processes and history of brewing whilst showing you some extraordinarily large vats and tuns!

Apparently it was such hard work in the heat generated by these devices that Grand National jockeys would often come here and do a day's work shovelling out grain, in order to sweat off a couple of pounds of weight!

Whilst walking around the grounds keep your eye out for a little flower growing between cracks in the pavement. This is *Saxifraga × urbium*, or London Pride, which used to grow on bomb sites in London following the Blitz. So ever since the 1950s Fuller's have brewed a beer which they named London Pride – one of various beers you can try out in their tap room at the end of the tour.

Cheers. Ladies and gentlemen, the King!

Return to Chiswick Mall to continue your splendid promenade past yet more glorious gardens and on your left you'll see **WALPOLE HOUSE** ❾, most of which dates from the eighteenth

❶

❸

❹

❺

❻

❽

century. This was home to Barbara Villiers, Duchess of Cleveland. Often referred to as 'the uncrowned queen', she rivalled Nell Gwynn for the title of most notorious mistress of King Charles II – with whom she had five children. You really have to feel sorry for Charles's actual wife, Catherine of Braganza. I mean, it was a bit much.

Having lost her appeal and good looks, Barbara Villiers died here in 1709, but at least her children were all acknowledged and given titles, other than that of 'bastard'!

The lady next door recently told me that the place was up for sale: a snip at eighteen million quid!

Wait... **Points to me!!** (I still like to award points for all sorts of random street stuff from my first book, as well as the new pub paraphernalia challenge.)

So there are **points** for you if you spot the fire insurance plaques a few doors further along, on the wall of **MORTON HOUSE** ⓾. A couple of beauties, actually. One is for the Sun Fire Office (which was the first such company, started in 1710, eventually becoming Royal & Sun Alliance) and the other one is probably for the County Fire Insurance Co., though it's hard to be sure since a few companies used the Britannia symbol. I'm not sure why the owners needed two insurance companies. Maybe one of them expired... or maybe they just bought the plaques at an auction!

There are more **points** for spotting the **STINK PIPE** ⓫ just after Morton House, in the garden opposite St John's House. Shortly afterwards there's a **BOUNDARY MARKER** ⓬ outside Cedar House, with the date of 1931; this was to indicate the boundary between Hammersmith and Hounslow.

Even more **points** are to be had on the corner of Eyot Gardens further along, in the form of another **STINK PIPE** ⓭. This one is half-obscured by a tree which is growing around it, but don't mistake it for a lamppost – it's a piece of street Victoriana!

We soon reach Hammersmith Terrace, where yet more famous people lived. Well, you might not have heard of them – but take Samuel Moreland, for example, who invented an early version of the megaphone in 1655. The original copper prototype was twenty feet long and he boasted that it could project a voice over a mile and a half!

The terrace also seems to have been popular with printers. Number 7 is actually a sort of museum these days, the former **HOME OF SIR EMERY WALKER** ⓮. He went into business with Thomas Cobden-Sanderson, with whom he set up the Doves Press in the early twentieth century, but the pair had a falling-out. Cobden-Sanderson didn't want Walker to use his Doves typeface, so he threw all the printing blocks into the Thames! It was only 100 years later, in 2015, that they were retrieved from the river. Incidentally, the font was named after his favourite pub, which we will come to later. Emery Walker's house is decorated with wallpaper from the Arts and Crafts movement, designed by his friend William Morris.

A little further along you'll see a **BLUE PLAQUE** 15 for Edward Johnston, who developed the font used for the London Underground until the 1980s. In fact, this font is used on his plaque.

I like how, on houses like these, you see staggered windows which aren't all in line because the windows are on the landings of the staircases.

Just around the corner you will see the **BLACK LION**, which dates from the 1750s – the time of King George II. Too many pubs these days have got rid of their games, and although the Black Lion is a fine establishment, I'm sorry to report that they have followed the prevailing trend, by recently turning what was once a rare example of a skittle alley into a private function room. Why?! For the uninitiated, skittles is a bit like tenpin bowling, which it effectively spawned, but (much like pool) you're likely to encounter people making up their own rules. It seems to have so many versions, according to which part of Britain you are in, that someone is bound to try and cheat. If it's good enough for Douglas Fairbanks Jr and cricketer Bob Willis, who both played here, it's good enough for me. What a shame they got rid of it.

Get them in, my son. Mine's a large one.

Meanwhile, have you heard the famous case of the Hammersmith Ghost?

Back in 1803 there had been many sightings of what seemed to be a ghost haunting this general area, and people were absolutely terrified. One lady was literally scared to death by it, if you can believe that!

Eventually it all got so much that in early 1804 a local patrol officer called Francis Smith took it upon himself to go out one night and hunt down this ghost once and for all, and shoot it with his gun! What made him think he could kill a ghost is beyond me… Nevertheless, out he went with his pistol loaded.

Soon enough he came across a ghostly apparition in his path and took aim at

PUB
Black Lion

him, declaring, 'Damn you! Who are you and what are you? Damn you, I'll shoot you!' – whilst unloading his gun barrel into the ghost's jaw.

Well, wouldn't you know it? It wasn't a ghost, after all! It turned out to be a bricklayer called Thomas Millwood, who was on his way home from work as usual, in his white overalls and covered in dust. He was dragged into the Black Lion, where he died.

As for Francis Smith, he was sentenced to death for murder, but he appealed to the King, who reduced his sentence to one year of hard labour. This case is important in English law because it set the precedent that you are liable for your actions even if you are acting on a mistaken belief. In fact, the question of acting on a mistaken belief wasn't resolved in English law until 1984!

What's ironic is that the poor old bricklayer who was shot wearing white overalls, who wasn't the Hammersmith Ghost, is now a ghost wearing white overalls!

Leave the Black Lion and carry on along Upper Mall. **More points to me!!** The street sign here only reads 'Upper Mall W', rather than carrying the full postal code of W6, indicating that it pre-dates 1917… unless it's a replica placed there to fool me!

Right ho, time waits for no man and it's onward to the next pub, which is but a

PUB
Old Ship

stone's throw along the river. The **OLD SHIP** is a Young's pub and has been here since the 1720s, although it doesn't really look that old to me – especially on the inside, where it has been 'refurbished'. I always dread my favourite pubs being refurbished because I'm very old fashioned, but maybe not everyone likes beer-stained carpets and toothless blokes playing darts. It's nicely spruced up and the views across the river from the terrace are glorious, as with many of the pubs along here.

My friend Laura is always complaining about the lack of variety in pubs when it comes to wine, but this might be a good place for her, because their selection of wine is pretty good and goes well with their excellent dining room.

In fact, I think we'll stop here for a spot of lunch.

Right, that's better.

Let's carry on along the riverside now and past **LINDEN HOUSE** 16 (yes, yet another impressive eighteenth-century mansion). These days it's a sailing and rowing clubhouse, many of which you will have seen along here, and you will see more.

As I walk along here I like noticing the little details like the crow's nest just past Linden House, used by the Corinthians sailing club to monitor races.

Look out for the metal **DOG NUISANCE SIGN** ⓘ on a lamppost outside 42 Upper Mall. You certainly don't get these down my way! I remember we had something similar in the 1980s but they weren't as nice as this one, with its raised writing.

By the sign you'll see **LATYMER UPPER SCHOOL BOAT CLUB** ⓘ, which is next to **LATYMER PREP SCHOOL** ⓘ. Famous Latymer alumni include Alan Rickman, Hugh Grant, Heston Blumenthal and Lily Cole, although the blue plaque on the side of the boat club is for rower Andy Holmes, another old Latymerian, who won gold at the 1984 and 1988 Olympics. (Britain winning gold medals these days is a bit more common, but back then I remember it being a rarity!) Sadly, he died aged fifty-one of Weil's disease contracted from the river, where he must have been in contact with infected animals or rat urine.

Another splendid house is coming up on the left, at number 26. **KELMSCOTT HOUSE** ⓘ, built in the late eighteenth century, was once home to William Morris, best known as a textile designer, artist and social activist who was one of the pioneers of the Arts and Crafts movement. Earlier we saw the house of Emery Walker, the printer who was a friend of William Morris, and in the basement of Kelmscott House you can see lots of printing blocks and presses and other bits and pieces connected with printing and design.

Another famous occupant of this house was Sir Francis Ronalds, who created the first electric telegraph here in 1816. Oh look, another one of those excellent fire insurance plaques like the ones we saw earlier!

Gosh, I do hope you aren't too bladdered after all these pubs, because the next one is terrific: the **DOVE** ⓘ.

I love the cute little alley you have to walk down, and everything is suitably wonky once you get inside.

The pub has been here since the 1700s but is possibly even older, although it was once a coffee shop in its early days. As you enter you will pass what is thought to be the smallest bar in Britain, measuring approximately 4ft by 7ft 10in (or 1.2m by 2.4m, if you prefer).

12

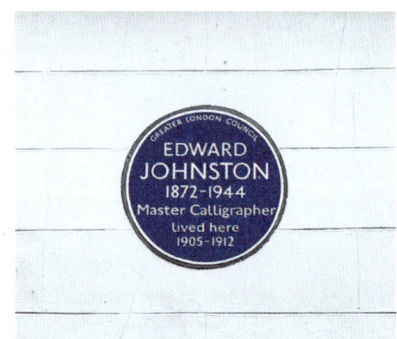

15

Black Lion

17

Dove

21

You can either sit by the fire in this cosy room in a club chair or pass through to the back, which is more suited to dining. The food is pretty good, although I always seem to end up ordering fish and chips, because I have no imagination.

On the wall you will see the lyrics to *Rule, Britannia!* (said to have been penned here by the poet James Thomson) and the Doves typeface (which, as we discovered earlier in the walk, was named after this pub; you might note the blue plaque next door indicating the site of the Cobden-Sanderson press).

My publisher has been strict about my word count, so I won't list all the famous patrons who have drunk in the Dove down the ages, but it is thought King Charles II used to entertain his mistress Nell Gwynn here. (A bit harsh on his other mistress, who lived so close by!) I love how kings drank in pubs in the old days. I guess the penalty for treason was death, so people thought twice before shouting 'Are you looking at my pint?!!' and involving him in a fracas.

Another royal connection is that of Caroline of Brunswick, who was the wife of King George IV (Hugh Laurie in *Blackadder the Third*). When he was Prince of Wales he was set up with her because he was skint and she was wealthy, but on first meeting his bride-to-be it is said that he found her so repellent that he had to call for strong brandy! He desperately tried to get the marriage annulled, but this caused various petitions to spring up in support of the Queen, one of which was started here at the Dove, because she only lived a short walk away (just beyond where Hammersmith Bridge is today). In the end George gave up and remained married to her, but when it came time for his coronation she was turned away because she didn't have a ticket! Poor Caroline sloped off home, where she died a few weeks later of an unknown illness.

I used to like King George IV, but I think that was pretty rotten.

I'll have a pint of London Pride.

As we leave the pub and continue our walk across some open green space, **FURNIVALL GARDENS** **21**, imagine that 100 years ago we would have been crossing a bridge here, over Hammersmith Creek, which flowed out of Stamford Brook – both now underground. In the nineteenth century boats could sail up here, and you can still see where the water flows out into the Thames. The creek was ultimately filled in during the 1930s; the whole area was bombed heavily in the Second World War, after which these gardens were created. Originally there was a beautiful feature consisting of a working clock in the flower bed, all adorned with flowers on the clock face. If you look carefully you might be able to see the mound where it used to be, and make out the shape.

Now, there are a couple of good pubs coming up where we could finish. I'm going to defy the Rule of Ted (see page 166) by not choosing the Rutland Arms, with its fine window boxes and hanging baskets (though as you pass, note the motto above the door reading *Multum in Parvo*, 'a lot in a little', because Rutland is the smallest county in England).

This part of Lower Mall is a popular spot for watching the varsity boat race and if you keep your eyes peeled you might spot it in the film *Bohemian Rhapsody*, or in *No Time to Die*, where Bond meets M with the bridge in the background.

Just yonder to the left you can see **HAMMERSMITH BRIDGE** ㉒. The current structure is the lowest bridge across the Thames in London, built in 1887 by Sir Joseph Bazalgette, who also designed London's first sewers. It has been targeted by Irish Republicans a few times, the first being in 1939 when Maurice Childs, a hairdresser from Chiswick, was walking home at 1.00 a.m. and spotted a smouldering suitcase in his way. He opened it up to find a bomb and quickly threw it into the river, where it exploded, sending up a sixty-foot column of water. Soon afterwards another bomb exploded on the other side of the bridge, damaging some houses nearby and weakening the bridge.

Maurice Childs was awarded an MBE for his heroic actions! But that's literally a bridge too far for us. Let's knock it on the head here with our final pub.

I suppose I'm showing my age, but I love spotting locations from the British TV show *Minder*. During the closing credits there's a montage of photos, some of which were taken around Hammersmith. I've always liked the one with Terry and Arthur sitting upstairs in the **BLUE ANCHOR** 🍺 overlooking the river. They look to be genuinely having a nice time.

This pub is also where John Hannah and Gwyneth Paltrow have a drink in the film *Sliding Doors*, and where regular Gustav Holst composed his *Hammersmith Suite*. It originally opened as the Blew Anchor and Washhouses in 1722, but I guess they gave up the laundry business.

Down the laundry hatch, then!

PUB

Blue Anchor

✦——— Quiz! ———✦

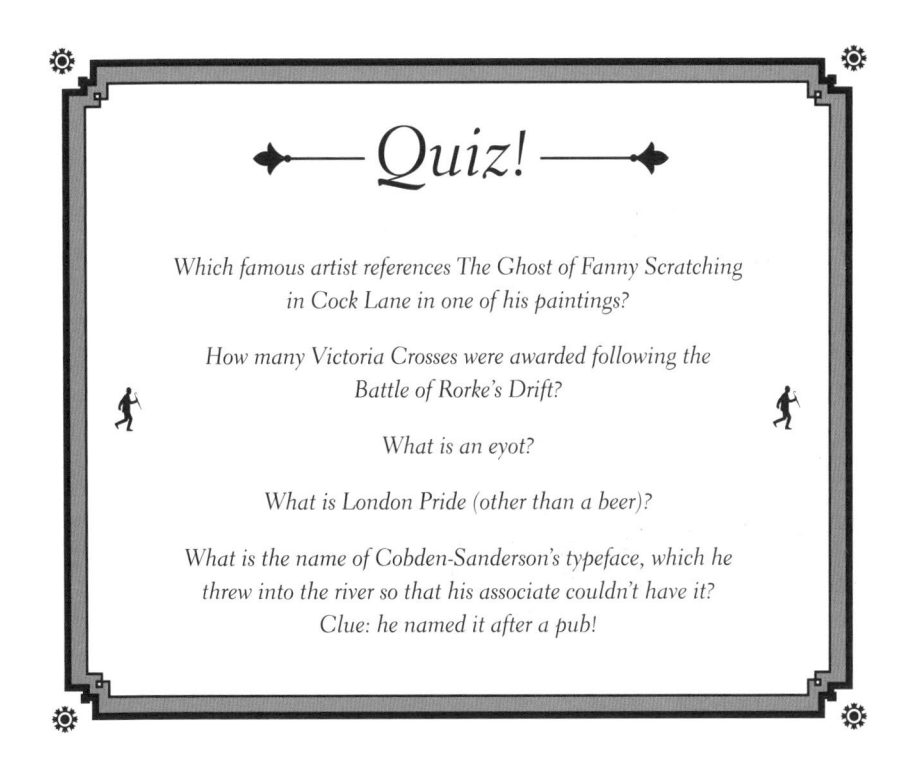

Which famous artist references The Ghost of Fanny Scratching in Cock Lane in one of his paintings?

How many Victoria Crosses were awarded following the Battle of Rorke's Drift?

What is an eyot?

What is London Pride (other than a beer)?

What is the name of Cobden-Sanderson's typeface, which he threw into the river so that his associate couldn't have it? Clue: he named it after a pub!

4. Tower Subway Entrance

A 13

20. Bascule Bridge

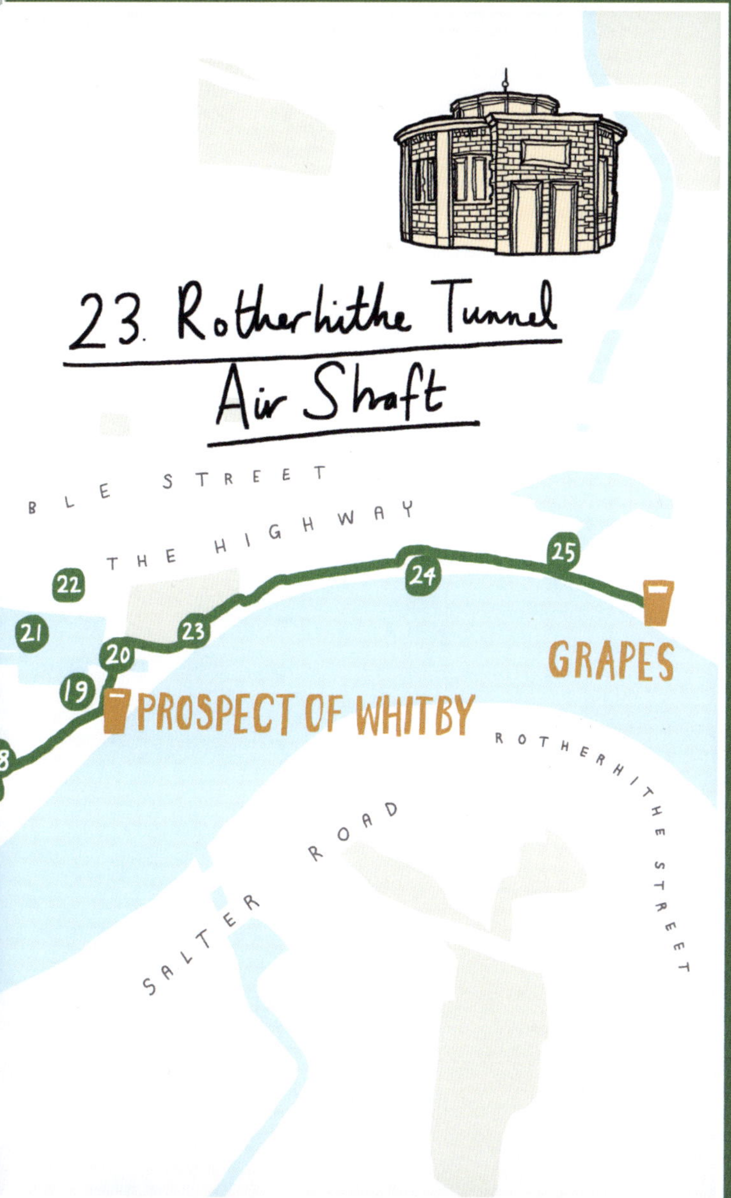

23. Rotherhithe Tunnel Air Shaft

PROSPECT OF WHITBY

GRAPES

2 WAPPING-WARD

2 A WATERY WAPPING-WARD WALK

DISTANCE
4.8 km (3 miles)

TIME
2 hours 20 minutes
with a few pints en route

NEAREST STATION
Tower Hill

PUBS
Ship; Hung, Drawn & Quartered; Dickens Inn; Town of Ramsgate; Captain Kidd; Prospect of Whitby; Grapes

What ho! Let's meet at the **SHIP**, which has a beautiful Victorian feel – it was rebuilt in 1887, on the site of the original 1802 pub.

If you're doing this walk on a weekend, unfortunately the Ship will be closed, though you can still enjoy the wonderful Grade II-listed exterior, with its painted grapevines and sea motifs; and fear not, there's another pub coming up shortly!

The interior of the Ship is pretty nice, too, with various maritime touches, and they have darts, which I'm always pleased to see. While they pride themselves on their Guinness, the selection of ales is always pretty good

– and I'm in a nautical mood, so I'm knocking back a pint of Ghost Ship before we get going.

Exiting the pub, turn right into Hart Street and then right again into Seething Lane, where you will find **ST OLAVE'S** ❶, parts of which, including the crypt, date from 1450 (other sections are more modern, following extensive damage during the Blitz). Charles Dickens referred to this church as 'St Ghastly Grim' due to the scary skulls over the entrance gate. Whilst the gate dates from 1658, it's fitting that there are so many skulls on it because this is where many plague victims were buried a few years later, in 1665 and 1666, including Mary Ramsay, often said to be the first person to have brought the plague to London.

The reason they have a bust of Samuel Pepys here is because he used to live in this street and worshipped at St Olave's with his wife. They called it 'our church' and both of them were buried here. I'm not sure what she made of him checking out the young girls in the congregation, but he certainly mentions doing so in his famous diaries.

The church is beautiful inside and contains a marvellous hidden chapel downstairs (evidently for short people who have just had some of that 'drink me' potion from *Alice in Wonderland*).

Continue south along Seething Lane. At the start of the short pedestrianised section at the end, look carefully at the building on your left and you'll see a curved ghost sign above the first arch. You might just about be able to make out 'MARK LANE STATION ENTRANCE'. That's because this building once housed **MARK LANE TUBE STATION** ❷.

The station first opened in the 1880s, with a much smaller entrance structure, which was replaced by the current building, incorporating commercial offices above, at the start of the twentieth century. If you head to Byward Street at the end and turn left, look through the metal gate across the fourth arch (after what is currently an All Bar One) and you can see some steps leading down to an old subway, which was part of the entrance system – another entrance is opposite, on the other side of Byward Street. They changed the name of the station to Tower Hill in the 1940s, before it was closed in 1967, with the replacement station (designed to cope with higher passenger numbers) opening a little to the east.

Now retrace your steps to the end of Seething Lane and continue west along Byward Street.

As you approach Great Tower Street you will see the **HUNG, DRAWN & QUARTERED** 🍺 on the other side. As I may have mentioned before, I generally find Fuller's pubs to be perfectly tolerable, with fine ales to quaff and hearty pies on which to gorge, so let's pop in here.

PUB
Hung, Drawn & Quartered

The history of the pub is fairly unremarkable, except to say that it used to be the offices for Christ's Hospital School (which was founded in 1552 by Edward VI to feed, house and educate the poor children of London). It is apt that it later became a pub named the Hung, Drawn & Quartered, since that was the fate of many a victim under Edward's father, King Henry VIII.

Back in those harsh times, if you had a slightly different view about how you should say your prayers or the amount of candles that should be lit at mass, you could easily find yourself subject to this punishment, which used to be practised near here, amongst other places.

Technically, it should be 'drawn, hanged and quartered' if you are a pedant from Pedantsville. First you would be 'drawn', or dragged, behind a horse to the place of execution; then 'hanged' (not 'hung' – you might be well-endowed, but you're not a picture!!) until almost dead; then your guts would be cut out and burned in front of you; and lastly you would be cut up into pieces. Often your head would be displayed on London Bridge…

On the outside of the pub you'll see a sign (if it's still there) noting that Samuel Pepys, the famous seventeenth-century diarist, recorded one such execution he attended, writing that the condemned man 'was looking as cheerful as any man could in that condition'.

If you're still feeling peckish after that and can't make up your mind what to have, you might like to try their tasting board of various pies. I like the steak and ale, but the chicken is also very good.

Cross the road to the church of **ALL HALLOWS BY THE TOWER** ❸, said to be the oldest in the City of London. (Strictly speaking, St Bartholomew's was outside the City walls, in case you were thinking of that one.) They claim to have been founded in 675 and there are indeed some ancient things inside. In the south-west corner there's a seventh-century Saxon arch and at the entrance to the undercroft you can see second-century Roman paving leading to an altar built from stones brought back from the Templar Church of Athlit (in present-day Israel) during the Crusades almost 1000 years ago! It's all very Indiana Jones.

Look out for the lovely model of the Roman city of Londinium, which is beautifully done. London is virtually unrecognisable from those days.

One of the people we have to thank for the church's survival is Admiral William Penn, after whom Pennsylvania is named, and who lived nearby, next to Samuel Pepys. During the Great Fire of London Penn got loads of his workers in the dockyards to come and blow up all the surrounding houses, which prevented the fire from engulfing the church.

In fact, Samuel Pepys climbed this very steeple, from which he witnessed 'the saddest sight of desolation'. (I guess the owners of the houses that got blown up were none too happy, though!)

On exiting the church turn down Petty Wales and you will come to a curious small round brick building, which is actually the **ENTRANCE TO THE TOWER SUBWAY** ❹, built in 1869. Those brave enough could be conveyed along a narrow tunnel beneath the River Thames in a small wooden cable-hauled carriage. This soon became uneconomical and they turned it into a foot tunnel; but once Tower Bridge opened in 1894 the subway became pretty redundant, and these days it just carries utility cables.

Oh, you see the **TOWER OF LONDON** ❺ over to the left? So do I, and very interesting and historic it is, too… But let's carry on along the river.

Just before reaching **TOWER BRIDGE** ❻ you might recognise the location from *Mission: Impossible – Rogue Nation* where Tom Cruise has to rescue Simon Pegg, who is strapped to bomb. I'm always amazed at the lack of police (and traffic) in those films. I got yelled at by a beefeater just for getting my camera out. They start shooting guns and no one does a thing!

As you pass beneath Tower Bridge look for the tiled alcove to the right with some stairs leading down into the river. This is **DEAD MAN'S HOLE** ❼, so called because of the dead bodies which used to wash up here in Victorian times – usually, the corpses of people who had been murdered, had thrown themselves off a bridge or met some other unfortunate end on the river. Someone would fish them out here with a long stick and leave them in this tiled area, which acted as a morgue until someone could identify them or take them away. (I wonder if any of these corpses were victims of the Kray twins, who were the last people to be incarcerated in the Tower of London for not doing their military service. Somehow this fact always made them seem slightly less macho to me, but I wouldn't say that to their faces.)

It is said that the tiles were easier to wipe clean in case of the bloated corpses exploding – which apparently did actually happen to King Henry VIII, but not here! How grim.

Continue past the bridge and into **ST KATHARINE DOCKS** ❽, where you will see many smart yachts and boats, some of which people actually live on. Hey, I can see the next pub from here!

Well, one thing's for sure: Charles Dickens never drank here at the **DICKENS INN** 🍺. That said, it was opened by his great-grandson Cedric in 1976, and it's positioned in just the sort of area where Charles Dickens would have drawn inspiration for many of his characters. Originally it was a warehouse of some sort, located slightly to the west, but was rebuilt in a style to match the surroundings, resembling one of those three-story balconied inns of the eighteenth century.

It really is a beautiful setting and very Instagrammable with its hanging baskets and charming exterior. The pub itself is just… well, a pub, and it can get quite full, but there's plenty of room for standing, while dining is available on the upper floors. I always like pubs which have a nice large pedestrian space in front of them and no motorists screaming past.

Leaving the Dickens Inn, head briefly back the way you came, with the dock to your right, and take the first left into the alleyway which leads to Mews Street. Nip to the right here and then left into St Katharine's Way. Follow St Katharine's Way east to the junction with Wapping High Street, where we're turning right.

As you continue along the river, consider what it must have been like for a young man in the eighteenth and nineteenth centuries getting a bit sozzled and staggering out of the pubs along here. Back then London was the busiest port in the world and seafaring people would hang around here trying to find jobs in pubs or warehouses, etc., but they'd have to be pretty careful because press gangs would roam the streets here looking for vulnerable drunks. If you were aged between eighteen and fifty-five and of seafaring habits, you could easily find yourself being forced into the Navy against your will!

What is definitely noticeable is how quiet it all becomes once you are past Tower Bridge and walking up Wapping High Street. You might like to go down on the foreshore to see what interesting flotsam and jetsam has washed up, but I am obliged to tell you that if you start searching for treasure you need a mudlarker's licence!

PUB

Dickens Inn

Walk 2: Tower Hill to Wapping and Limehouse | 37

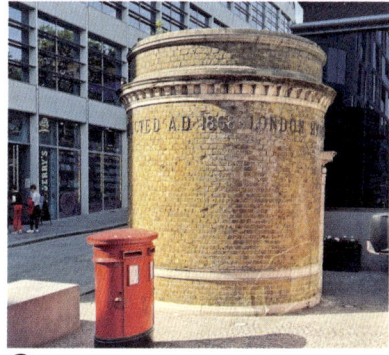

❶

❹

❼

❽

Dickens Inn

❾

Being of such strategic importance, the Port of London was heavily targeted in the Second World War, but many of the warehouses remain (although they've mostly been turned into flats). I like how you can still see the pulleys and other remnants of their original use on the outside of the buildings, quite high up.

Soon you'll come to a pair of lovely Georgian buildings facing each other on either side of a private garden, with the excellent addresses of **1-4 PIER HEAD** and **5-9 PIER HEAD** ❾. This used to be where tall ships would sail inland to the Wapping Basin. The houses were built around 1810 for the superintendents and other officials working at the docks, and the space now occupied by the garden would have been filled with water. Imagine smoking your pipe in your armchair and watching a ship sail past your window. It must have been a splendid sight.

I understand famous people live there these days but I won't name them. You know why? It's outta respect.

Time for our next pint, at the **TOWN OF RAMSGATE** 🍺. I have a particular fondness for this pub as it features in my excellent film *Take Me to Pitcairn*, which I think is my best piece of work. They say that this was the last place William Bligh had a drink with Fletcher Christian, in 1787, before they headed off on their ill-fated trip to Tahiti; there is a picture of Bligh on the wall inside.

PUB
Town of Ramsgate

I love these pubs along the river because you can sit out back and almost imagine what it was like years ago – the river full of tall ships, with merchants and sailors coming and going. It would have had quite a cosmopolitan feel to it, I imagine, but it wouldn't necessarily have been the safest place to hang out. Convicts were chained up in the cellar whilst awaiting transportation to Australia, although they weren't necessarily that nasty, given that anyone as young as ten could be transported for stealing a loaf of bread.

There has been a pub here since 1460 and it is named after the fishermen from Ramsgate who used to tie their boats here while selling their catch at Billingsgate Fish Market.

The pub itself is not huge – it's quite narrow – but has a very colourful history. In 1688 the famous 'Hanging' Judge Jeffreys was caught here after trying to flee during the Glorious Revolution. Following the Monmouth Rebellion, which was a failed plot to overthrow King James II, Judge Jeffreys had sentenced hundreds of people to death! James gratefully appointed him Lord Chancellor. Things were all very well and good whilst James remained King – but when he was finally toppled, Judge Jeffreys had to get the hell out of there because, as you can imagine, he wasn't that popular. The snivelling weasel dressed himself in rags to disguise himself as a coal miner, and shaved off his famously ferocious eyebrows!

However, a clerk whom he had once bullied in court recognised him, by his incredibly mean profile. 'Hey, it's Judge Jeffreys! Yeah, that's him! Get him!!' An angry mob gathered outside the pub to give him what for! In the end Judge Jeffreys was dragged away for his own safety, but died of kidney disease while in custody in the Tower of London.

I tend to drift off into a daydream while I'm overlooking the river here and at this point I like to replay the rumoured events of 1671, which were said to have taken place in the alleyway next to the pub, **WAPPING OLD STAIRS** **10**.

Colonel Thomas Blood (no joke, that was his name) had gained the confidence of the keeper of King Charles II's crown jewels, Talbot Edwards. At the Tower of London Colonel Blood bashed him over the head and made off with the crown and sceptre – but he only made it as far as Wapping Old Stairs, where he was no doubt intending to jump onto a boat and make good his escape, when by chance he ran into Edwards's son, who was on his way to visit his dad and had him arrested!

Colonel Blood was then imprisoned in the Tower but somehow managed to get pardoned by the King – which led many to believe the King was in on the plot and just needed to recoup some money as he was a bit skint!

Opposite the Town of Ramsgate pop through the gates to walk through the churchyard of the old **ST JOHN'S CHURCH** **11**, which was bombed by the Nazis. As you exit to the right onto Scandrett Street you will see the tower, dating from 1756, which somehow survived and has now been incorporated into a block of flats. It actually features in an episode of *Friends* – 'The One with Ross's Wedding' – when Ross and Emily come to check out the church where they're supposed to be married, only to find out it's being demolished. The church was associated with a charity school next door, which you can still see with the rather splendid figures of two pupils dressed, as usual, in blue. (There's more on this in **Walk 4** and also in my first book!) The school was founded in 1695, though the present building dates from the same era as the church tower.

On the corner of Green Bank you can see what used to be the **TURK'S HEAD** **12**, once a beautiful pub, as you can see from all the **points** you will score for spotting the signage for Taylor Walker, the old brewery connected with the pub. It's currently a French bistro and a bit posh for the likes of me, so let's hang a right into Green Bank, where you will find the **CHURCH OF ST PATRICK** 🅱 on your right. Fans of *The Long Good Friday* – the ultimate London film, and highly recommended – might recognise the interior as the location of the service where Harold Shand's mum is almost blown up, thus incurring Harold's wrath. (The exterior, though, was that of St George in the East, a different church nearby.)

After the church, turn right into Dundee Street and then left on Wapping High Street, where you'll soon arrive at **WAPPING NEW STAIRS** 🅲, next to a little garden where you can sit and contemplate life.

The next building is the **HEADQUARTERS OF THE THAMES RIVER POLICE** 🅳, officially the Met's Marine Policing Unit, which started life in 1798 as the Thames Marine Police. You've probably seen them zooming up and down the river with their sirens on.

Somewhere along this stretch of riverbank was Execution Dock, where pirates and mutineers were hanged just low enough for the tide to come and wash over them. Typically they would leave the condemned there long enough for the tide to come in three times, causing their bodies to become bloated with water. Some people say that this is the origin of the name Wapping because people passing by would exclaim, 'Gosh, that's a whopper, isn't it!!' on seeing the bloaters hanging there.

One of the most famous pirates to be hanged here gives his name to the next pub we'll stop at: the **CAPTAIN KIDD** 🍺.

Is it just something from my childhood that makes me fascinated by pirates? I mean, I'm sure they were mostly pretty scary people, but all the same, there's a certain romance connected with the lifestyle.

Captain Kidd was a Scottish sailor whose original job was to prevent piracy around the Indian Ocean – but he ended up being accused of piracy himself. In fact, the 1698 Act of Grace offered a pardon to all pirates in the Indian Ocean, but he really must have peed somebody off because he was specifically exempted from that pardon! He certainly got off on the wrong foot when sailing past a Navy yacht at Greenwich where, instead of saluting, his crew all turned and slapped their bottoms in a show of impudence!

Ultimately Kidd was captured in Boston, Massachusetts, and hanged here at Execution Dock. His corpse was displayed in a gibbet at Tilbury for three years as a warning to others!

Rumour has it that he hid some of his plunder on a Caribbean island, which

PUB
Captain Kidd

inspired stories like *Treasure Island* and *Pirates of the Caribbean*. (It's never been found, by the way.)

The pub itself was originally a coffee warehouse with three levels and only became a pub in the 1980s, but I rather like it and even had my Christmas party here one year, as they have nice little alcoves and hidden snugs.

I'll have a flagon of ale (the flagon with the dragon, not the chalice from the palace).

Bottoms up!!

By the way, do you know why we say 'bottoms up'?

In the days of people being press-ganged into joining the Navy there were some people, 'landsmen', who were exempt and they needed persuasion to volunteer. So they were offered what was known as 'the King's shilling'. A fellow like me would be offered a shilling and by accepting it I'd be enlisted into the Navy. However, a lot of people wouldn't accept it, so in order to trick people a cunning scheme arose whereby recruiters would secretly slip a shilling into your flagon of beer, and once you had drunk it someone would spot the shilling, declaring: 'Aha! You have accepted the shilling!' Then they'd cart you off to a nearby galley!!

This was in the days when beer was served in tankards, not glasses. Pubs soon got wise to this practice and decided to start serving their beer in clear-bottomed tankards, so if someone dropped a shilling inside you could see it nestling on the bottom by lifting up your beer and looking underneath. So patrons were encouraged to always check the bottom of their pint.

Bottoms up!!

After leaving the Captain Kidd, continue along to the corner of Brewhouse Lane, where you can score some **points** by spotting the old **CANNON BOLLARD** **16**. Seems like a good place for it with all this pirate talk. Then carry on and you will soon pass **WAPPING STATION** **17**, which I do like very much. It's definitely worth popping down to the platform to see Marc Brunel's excellent Thames tunnel, which we mention in **Walk 4** – a marvel of British engineering (even though he was French).

Where Wapping High Street curves to the left, meeting Garnet Street, look up above the shop on the right (currently the Sporting Club) to see that it used to be a pub called the **THREE SUNS** **18**. I do like it when they carved the signs into the actual brickwork. The amount of effort they made puts us to shame these days.

Take a right into Wapping Wall. It's extraordinary to think, as you continue along the street sticking to the river, how different it must have been before these warehouses were turned into flats. Whilst a lot of the architecture hasn't changed, they would have been a lot grubbier and more intimidating. All very *Oliver Twist*...

You will soon come to many people's favourite pub, the **PROSPECT OF WHITBY**, which has been here since 1520.

The pub, named after a coal-hauling ship that used to moor on the bank nearby, was once said to be frequented by pirates, miscreants, smugglers and other ne'er-do-wells! Hence its nickname the Devil's Tavern, and probably why I fancy a pint in there, although I don't know which of those categories I fit into!

The Prospect of Whitby is now a Greene King pub. The only genuinely ancient part that remains is the 400-year-old stone floor, but it still retains some eighteenth-century wood panelling, and from the outside it has more of a nineteenth-century look. That said, the interior is very charming, with plenty of skulduggerous seafaring pictures, references and décor. Viewers of my amazing film *Take Me to Pitcairn* might

PUB

Prospect of Whitby

also recognise the noose hanging outside the back window, a reference to Execution Dock.

In the summertime it's a wonderful place to take lunch and peer across the river. With any luck they'll have some fuchsias in the hanging baskets, because some people claim that this was the first place that this plant was introduced into Britain.

The fuchsia originates from the Caribbean, where it was identified by French botanist Charles Plumier, who named it in honour of German botanist Leonhart Fuchs. Some years later, they say, a sailor who had returned from the West Indies was in this pub when he presented a fuchsia flower to his sweetheart, who promptly put it in her window box.

Later a gardener was passing by and bought the plant off her for a noggin of rum, with the intention of planting loads of them. Whilst pumping her for further information about the flower

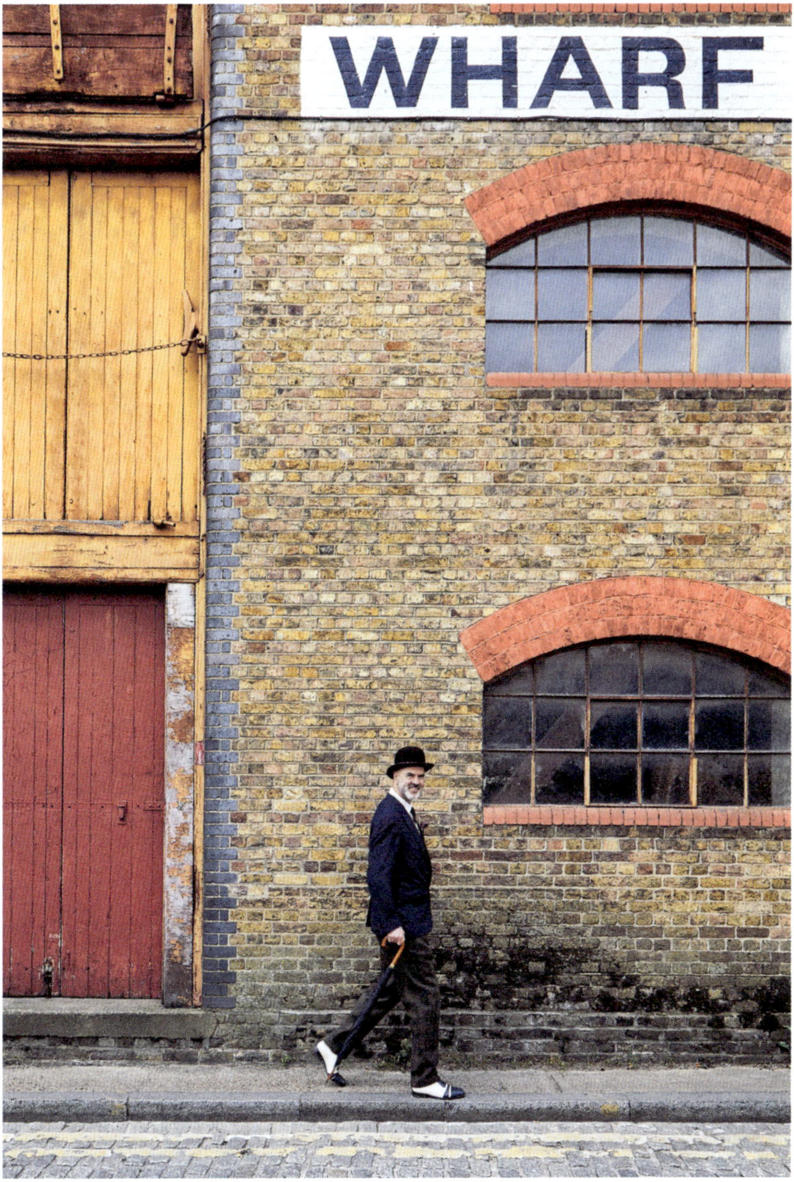
WHARF

10

11

Prospect of Whitby

20

23

24

she volunteered, 'Leonhart Fuchs!' – to which the gardener replied, 'Does he? Not as well as me, I'll wager!'

(Okay, I made that last bit up…and in fact the whole story might be a bit made up, but it's good enough for Joolz Guides!)

As you stumble, legs akimbo, out of the pub and along Wapping Wall, check out the lovely red building opposite, which today is part of the Wapping conservation area. This used to be a **POWER STATION** ⑲ owned by the London Hydraulic Power Company, which still retains its old sign on the front. No doubt it pumped water into the bridge which we are just coming up to now.

This is known as a **BASCULE BRIDGE** ⑳ and you get them on the other side of the river, too, in Rotherhithe. Water was pumped into the container at the top until it weighed down one end, so as to lift up the other end, allowing boats to pass beneath. This is a terrific piece of Victorian engineering and so interestingly juxtaposed next to these modern apartments.

SHADWELL BASIN ㉑, to your left, is another remnant of the days of the London Docks, but these days it's more for water sports. Actually, I've seen people swimming in here on hot days, but you're not supposed to! Oh, and that church you can see poking up above the houses is **ST PAUL'S**

SHADWELL ㉒, where Captain Cook used to worship. We're not going that way but it's a nice reminder of all the important seafaring characters who frequented this neighbourhood.

We're following the river and hopefully you can follow the Thames Path to your right, if it's open. This will lead you to a round brick building on the edge of the King Edward Memorial Park. This is the **AIR SHAFT FOR THE ROTHERHITHE TUNNEL** ㉓, opened in 1908. Look out for the rather splendid plaque beside the shaft in memory of the many navigators who sailed from here in the sixteenth century into the unknown.

Do your best to stick to the river, but you may have to walk around onto the main road (the Highway) if it's closed off. If so, you will pass a plaque just outside the park on a bland wall demonstrating that Captain Cook lived here, albeit in a nicer building than this one!

These days the area we are now entering is called Limehouse, after the lime kilns which used to occupy the area; but this little stretch was once a small hamlet called Ratcliff, described by Watts Phillips in 1855 as 'the head-quarters of unbridled vice and drunken violence – of all that is dirty, disorderly and debased'. Sounds like my kind of place.

Ah, look at that… They've ruined it by clearing the slums and building respectable housing…

Come on, let's keep going. Assuming you've been able to follow the Thames Path, you'll be approaching Narrow Street shortly. Just before that, if the tide is out you might like to nip down the stairs just after Keepier Wharf and onto **RATCLIFF BEACH** ㉔, which Google Maps rather optimistically labels a 'tourist attraction'. Well, that's going a bit far, but it is a nice place to stroll and take in the view. Don't stay too long, though, as the tide will come back in!!

If the Thames Path was closed and you've had to follow the Highway, you'll need to turn right into Narrow Street just before the entrance to the Limehouse Link Tunnel, and then follow Narrow Street as it turns to the left.

Don't worry, we're almost finished.

NARROW STREET

Carrying on along Narrow Street you'll eventually pass Gordon Ramsay's Bread Street Kitchen and Bar, which used to be the dockmaster's house right at the **ENTRANCE TO LIMEHOUSE BASIN** ㉕. Limehouse Basin is the end point of the Regent's Canal, built to avoid having to carry goods by road all the way from Paddington and Camden. It was still in regular industrial use until the 1960s, mostly for hauling coal, but it's much more peaceful these days, which might explain why many houseboats are moored here.

There's a nice information plaque here explaining all about the people who used to occupy the area. Dockworkers were paid daily and did jobs like rope-making or barge-loading and would have to get up pretty early, so there would be a person called a 'knocker-up', who would get up at five in the morning and use a pea-shooter to rattle their windows and get them up for work. In fact, there was even a knocker-up for the knocker-up, whose job it was to wake up the knocker-up. No wonder so many people got knocked up!

Just a little bit further along Narrow Street, score yourself some **points** for spotting the original old cannon used as a bollard on the corner of Shoulder of Mutton Alley. I love the names of the streets around here.

But hark, is that the final pub I see before me?

Goodness me, I must be getting old. That's quite enough for me for one day. And what luck that my weary legs have supported me as far as the **GRAPES** 🍺, an excellent pub which is part-owned by Sir Ian McKellen (at the time of writing). I would recommend trying to come here on a Monday for the quiz, which I won once! In fact, Sir Ian was

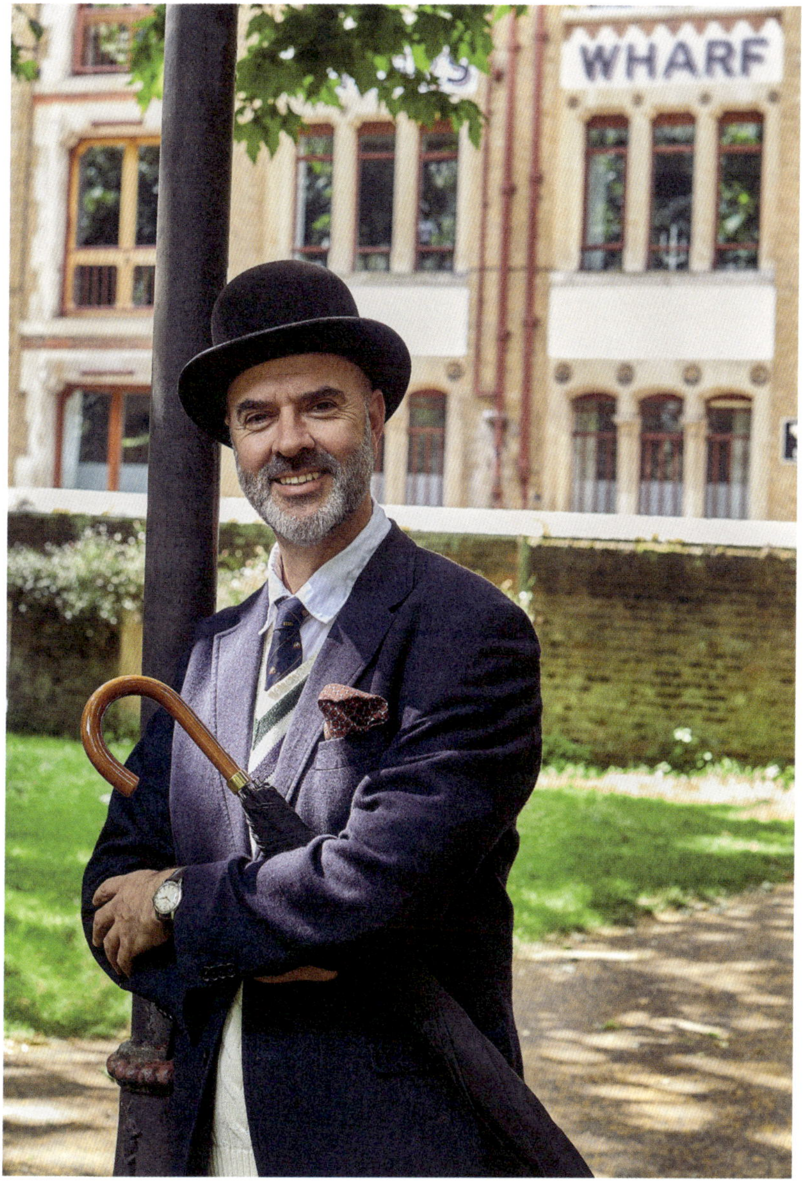
WHARF

PUB

Grapes

actually there at the time, although you don't necessarily receive his personal congratulations as part of the prize. You never know, though! You can even see Gandalf's staff behind the bar.

As with all these riverside pubs, you can sit out back overlooking the Thames, or settle in the main bar. The Grapes still retains its rickety eighteenth-century ambience, with the building dating from the 1720s. The food is pretty good pub grub and they even serve their apple crumble with custard, which earns extra **points**. (I can't stand it when pubs try to fob you off with ice cream. It just isn't the same.)

Viewers of my YouTube channel will know that I tire of mentioning Charles bloody Dickens, but that's not because I don't like him. It's just that he seems to have a connection with almost every building in London. You can't escape him! And, sure as eggs are eggs, he used to come here as a boy and entertain the patrons with his singing. In *Our Mutual Friend* he describes a pub with 'not a straight floor' based on this one, 'of a dropsical appearance' and with 'red curtains matching the noses of the regular customers'.

Apparently his godfather was a sailmaker nearby and he would bring him to this pub. It must have been a nightmare for his ex-girlfriends trying to avoid him. They weren't safe anywhere!

I'll take a flagon of ale, and be quick about it.

YOU SHALL NOT PASS!!

Sorry, I couldn't resist.

Quiz!

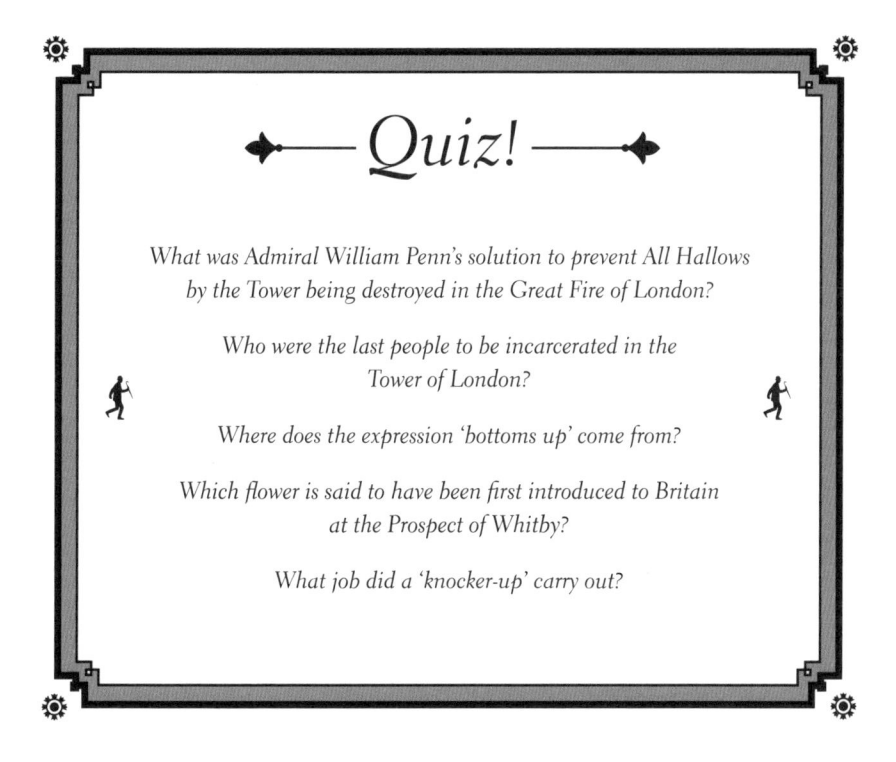

What was Admiral William Penn's solution to prevent All Hallows by the Tower being destroyed in the Great Fire of London?

Who were the last people to be incarcerated in the Tower of London?

Where does the expression 'bottoms up' come from?

Which flower is said to have been first introduced to Britain at the Prospect of Whitby?

What job did a 'knocker-up' carry out?

5. Warwick Farm Dairies

9. St. Saviour's Church

17. Lord's Telephone Exchange

3 MAIDA VALE

3 A HEROIC POOTLE AROUND MAIDA VALE

DISTANCE
5.6 km (3.5 miles)

TIME
2 hours 45 minutes
with a few pints en route

NEAREST STATION
Maida Vale

PUBS
Elgin; Carlton Tavern; Prince Alfred;
Warwick Castle; Warrington Hotel

Pip pip. There you are. I thought you'd never make it!

I thought we'd meet here in the **ELGIN** as it's just around the corner from the station. These days the Elgin has quite a modern feel inside, and last time I dropped by, mid-afternoon, I encountered plenty of people with laptops who probably describe themselves as 'digital nomads'. The pub retains some nice old features, though, and serves a rather enjoyable pint of local Elgin lager – which seems a good way to prepare for our walk.

Sláinte!

Okay, let's leave the pub and turn right, to **MAIDA VALE UNDERGROUND STATION** ❶.

Designed by Stanley Heaps, using the distinctive red-tile style introduced by Leslie Green, the station opened in 1915 after the Bakerloo Railway was extended from Paddington to Queen's Park. It's one of my favourite stations because of the wonderful original mosaic roundel which still survives inside. This version of the Underground logo was first used in 1908, but by 1917 it had changed and eventually became the more familiar red ring with a blue bar through the middle which we know today. I've seen a few similar old roundels, for example at Ealing Broadway, but this is certainly a rare survivor! The mosaics here can even be seen in Alfred Hitchcock's 1927 silent film *Downhill*, when the protagonist enters the station and goes down the escalators (this being one of the first stations to be built with escalators as opposed to lifts).

Now, we're going in the other direction but first take a quick look at numbers **124–162 RANDOLPH AVENUE** ❷, a few doors down from the station, because during the Second World War this building was Europe's biggest brothel, run by the Messina Brothers, a criminal gang from Malta. These days it's social housing, but it's ironic that it was built and funded by the church! Above the windows you can see various figures such as breadfruit plants, four-horned goats of Mendes, people with Aramaic headdress and all sorts of biblical and other mysterious themes. Perhaps there's some hidden meaning, but I'm damned if I can figure it out!

Right, let's head the other way, northwards up Randolph Avenue. Soon you'll reach the entrance to the park on your left, which is **PADDINGTON RECREATION GROUND** ❸.

It's really a rather wonderful facility they have here, with tennis courts, cricket pitches and all sorts. It's quite pleasant for a stroll, too, but I wonder if the people playing here or walking their dogs know that they've got Winston Churchill's dad to thank for these grounds. It started in 1887 when Lord Randolph Churchill started a campaign to get some money together to help the poor, as there were no social services back then. Having raised £1,800, the committee couldn't decide how best to spend it – so R. M. Beachcroft, a keen cricketer who served on London County Council, volunteered to rent eleven acres here for recreation. He stipulated that they should use the relief fund to employ people to tend the grounds and see to the drainage and fencing, but on one condition: no one was to hold political meetings or drink alcohol! (Not much use to us on this walk, then!) Anyway, that's why the gate on Randolph Avenue is named Randolph Churchill Gate.

Walk through and turn right at the

clubhouse and café, exiting the park via the north gate.

Sitting rather proudly amongst all the modern buildings on Carlton Vale is the rather beautiful **CARLTON TAVERN** 🍺. I'm so glad it's still here, with its wonderful original (or so I thought) tiles displaying the name of Charrington & Co., the brewery founded in Bethnal Green in the eighteenth century. The pub was built in the 1920s, and you'll find period décor inside. It was the only building in the street to survive the Blitz! (Maybe the Gestapo were planning on a cheeky pint here after defeating us Brits.) However, in 2015, just as Historic England were about to grant it listed status, it was demolished to make way for a housing development.

Understandably, this caused public outcry – and the developers were forced to rebuild the whole thing to the original plan! They've done a pretty good job, actually. You wouldn't know the whole thing had been flattened and replaced.

When I last visited they were playing pretty good music (well, stuff like The Smiths and The Specials) and they have comfy chairs, a beer garden and board games!

It's your round. I'll have mine in a dimpled mug. **Points**!!

PUB
Carlton Tavern

Cin Cin canarin
Quanti figli ha Turin
Ah, ne ya na'quantità
C'ha c'ha c'ha

(It doesn't seem to make much sense, but my mum used to sing it when she said 'Cheers'! I think she based it on an old Milanese riddle about a donkey.)

Okay, so let's go the nice way round by re-entering Paddington Recreation Ground. Go straight through, past the Richard Beachcroft Pavilion, and bend your steps around the far side of the running track.

Exit the park on the western side into Essendine Road and if you've gone the right way you'll notice the rather dilapidated K2 telephone box (one of only 1,500 made) and the Queen Victoria post box opposite. Both could do with a lick of paint. I mean, what would it cost?

As you walk along Essendine Road, keep an eye out for some lovely typically Victorian features above some of the front doors and the (now redundant) signs above the school entrances reading 'BOYS' and 'GIRLS & INFANTS'.

(At my old school they now have gender-neutral toilets, which shows how much times have changed. It was all boys, short trousers and school on Saturdays when I was there!)

Now, for a couple of interesting extras you can turn right at the end briefly, or you can ignore this bit and turn left.

If you turn right into Shirland Road and walk past the King George VI post box, keep going just until the next corner (Kilburn Park Road) and look up at the wall above the chemist. I rather like this **GHOST SIGN** ❹, even though it's hard to make out what it says. It looks like 'Hovis' but also seems to mention something to do with tea-dancing and dry-cleaning!

And what's this in front of the wall? A stink pipe, yay!!!! You often get these along the routes of underground rivers which have been converted into sewers, and it so happens that the River Westbourne runs along here, beneath Shirland Road.

Okay, now go back the way you came, past the end of Essendine Road, and walk straight along Shirland Road. On the other side you will see a sign on the red-brick building (now flats) reading 'J. Welford & Sons'.

In the 1840s the Welford family opened Warwick Farm near here and they started a dairy, too. They occupied this location in the 1880s, but let's walk a little further to the corner where, if you look up, you will see a lovely cow's head above **WARWICK FARM DAIRIES** ❺. Eventually, in 1915, they got sold to United Dairies, who later merged into Unigate – I remember them delivering our milk every morning!!

Now turn left along Elgin Avenue and then right into Delaware Road.

On your right, the long white building was until recently the BBC's **MAIDA VALE STUDIOS** ❻, where a great many famous musicians have performed, including David Bowie and the Beatles. It was here that Bing Crosby made his last ever recording, and where many of the John Peel sessions took place.

Fans of *Doctor Who* will be interested to know that this was the base of the BBC Radiophonic Workshop, which developed the theme music and the sound of the TARDIS (which was actually a key being scraped along piano strings).

The building started life in 1909 as the Maida Vale Roller Skating Palace and Club, and the BBC took it over in 1933. The reliefs above the doorways survive from the original building and I love looking at the windows, which also look typical of the early twentieth century to me, as my mum had the same ones in her house (built in 1912).

The BBC have moved out now and the plan was to turn it into, yes, luxury flats – but that was blocked by Historic England and now it's an independent recording studio.

Follow the street to the end and cross over Sutherland Avenue, glancing to your right to see another stink pipe as you go! Continue into Warwick Avenue and then turn left into Pindock Mews.

In August 1977 the house at **3 PINDOCK MEWS** ❼ was rented by Malcolm McLaren for Sid Vicious, bass player with the Sex Pistols, who stayed here with his girlfriend Nancy Spungen. Apparently when McLaren was told that it only had a seven-year lease, he replied, 'That's okay, he'll be dead by then!'

He was right, too. Sid Vicious died in 1979 of a heroin overdose in New York, aged twenty-one, a few months after Nancy was found dead with a stab wound in the Chelsea Hotel. Sid was accused of murder and released on bail, but died before the trial could take place.

Follow the mews to the end and then turn right onto Castellain Road and you will come to the **PRINCE ALFRED** 🍺.

Bowie alert! Bowie alert!

It is perhaps sad that the thing I like most about such a glorious pub is the fact that David Bowie filmed the *Jazzin' for Blue Jean* video here in 1984. It opens with him up a ladder outside

PUB

Prince Alfred

the front, with a plaster on his nose.

Prince Alfred was the second son of Queen Victoria. He was born in 1844, which was just a few years before this pub opened, in 1856. This explanation of the pub's name would seem to make more sense than what I was told by a bloke in this very pub: that it was named after the fourteenth child of King George III! Come to think of it, I don't suppose it really matters.

I stopped here for lunch recently and yes, I did have fish and chips. What's rather unusual is that they have all these different segregated sections with their own doors out to the street (to prevent the riff-raff interfering with the higher classes, don't you know). You can get from one section to another through the tiny little hatches, but I must say, it's tough if you're 6 ft 6!!! They were probably intended for a scullery maid, not a giant in a bowler hat!

Walk 3: Maida Vale | **57**

Now, in case you were entertaining a lady or gentleman and preferred not to be seen by the common people on the other side of the bar, you could use the 'snob screens' (score yourself **points**!), which open and close above the bar around head height, for extra privacy. It's a splendid-looking interior, very much in the style of a gin palace, with lovely carved panels and frosted glass.

I've heard that members of the Sex Pistols drank here, amongst many others, which makes sense, as it was Sid's local. I wonder if the Pistols used the snob screens… Živjeli!

Come out of the pub, turn right along Formosa Street, and right again into Warrington Crescent at the end. The building to your right has a **BLUE PLAQUE** ❽ stating that Alan Turing lived here. He was the maths genius who helped to solve the Enigma Code at Bletchley Park during the Second World War.

Soon you will come to **ST SAVIOUR'S CHURCH** ❾, which isn't to everyone's taste, but it certainly looks interesting. It was designed in the 1970s by Biscoe and Stanton architects to replace a Victorian church which was too large and expensive to maintain. It might look like a 1970s council housing estate from certain angles, but from a distance it's quite impressive, and it's worth looking inside at the hexagonal space and modern pews.

Turn right, with Warwick Avenue tube station on your left, and score **points** for spotting a **CABMEN'S SHELTER** ❿, one of thirteen remaining in London. This one is still in regular use; taxi drivers can be seen inside eating bacon sarnies, but we mere mortals have to use the hatch for our takeaway milky tea with five sugars.

'When I get to Warwick Avenue, meet me by the entrance of the tube…' Remember that song? Please don't give me a copyright strike, Duffy!

Ahead is Clifton Villas, so bend your steps thither.

Coming up on your left is a passageway leading to London's oldest garden centre, **CLIFTON NURSERIES** ⓫, which opened in 1851. Garden centres are always serene places to wander around, and a little hidden gem here is their café, which is particularly marvellous. It's almost worth getting dressed up in your best 1920s Agatha Christie outfit to sit in the wonderful conservatory. Okay, it's not a pub, but it's jolly lovely.

Come to think of it, if it's a pub you want, just come back out and turn left, then left again into Blomfield Road.

Before we get to the canal let's just turn down this cute little street called Warwick Place on the left.

PUB

Warwick Castle

A lot of the streets around here have the name Warwick because of the Warwick Farm which was here in the nineteenth century. We've already seen the Welfords' dairy; it started life here at number 4 in 1848, when cows and cow-keepers dominated the area. The **WARWICK CASTLE**, meanwhile, dates from 1846.

The whole terrace, including the pub, is listed (look out for the beautiful lamp and brackets holding the pub sign) and it has been suggested that its discreet location acted as a refuge for all the servants working in the nearby fancy houses.

I always feel one of the nice things about English pubs is that they sometimes have a local brew. If you are partial to amusingly named beers, you might try their Made of Ale. Despite the renovations the Warwick Castle has kept its Victorian features, and I always like a good fireplace. It's spacious, too.

Richard Branson used to drink here when he operated out of a canal boat nearby, and I have to mention Howard Marks, who did drug deals here. Not because I approve, but because in the film about his life, *Mr Nice*, my sister Lil' Lost Lou sings on the closing credits!

A pint of Made of Ale please, and I think I'll try some of this food, too. Looks decent!

Now return the way you came and after turning left into Blomfield Road you'll come to the canal and a little bridge.

This area has been known as Little Venice ever since it was apparently thus named by the poet Robert Browning, who lived near here.

Look out for the sign on the bridge reading 'Borough of Paddington'. It's pretty rare to see signs with 'Borough of Paddington' on them, as Paddington, along with some other boroughs, got subsumed by the City of Westminster in 1965, as you can see on the street sign for Westbourne Terrace Road Bridge.

Across the bridge is the Bridge House pub, which you might wish to visit, but we're continuing on this side of the canal by turning left.

At this point two canals actually meet: the Grand Junction Canal (which leads up towards Birmingham) and Regent's Canal (which goes to Camden and Limehouse). Cross over the next bridge, on Warwick Avenue, and look out for the **'STOP LOCKS'** 12 beneath the bridge. These were intended to

60 | Rather Splendid London Pub Walks

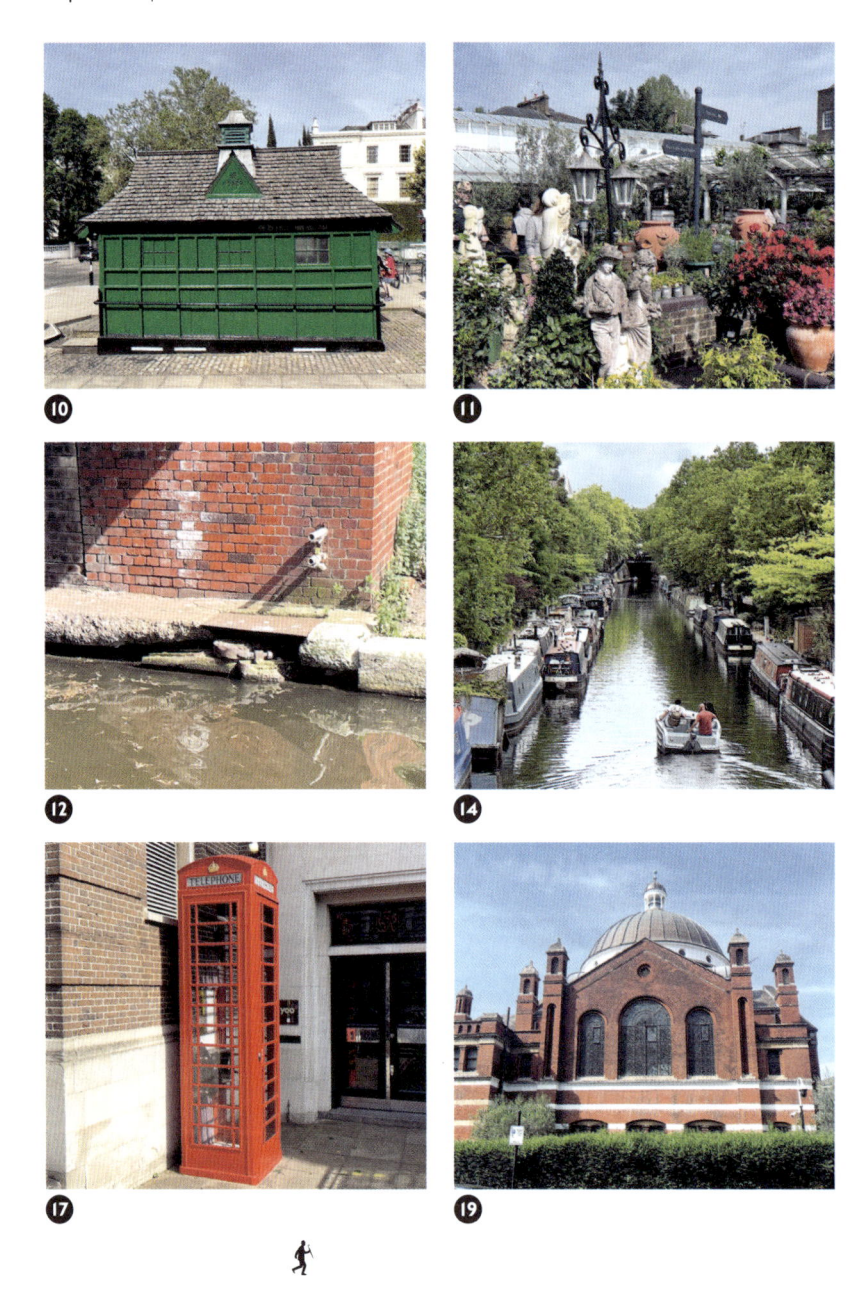

prevent people from taking water from one canal into the other, which was against the law. For some reason Regent's Canal was 15 cm (6 inches) higher than the Grand Junction Canal and the little cottage next to the bridge was occupied by the lock-keeper, who could keep an eye on things. These days it's a holiday let!

After crossing the bridge turn left into Maida Avenue, alongside the canal, and you will pass several stunning houses and apartment blocks as well as the Grade I-listed **CATHOLIC APOSTOLIC CHURCH** ⓭, built in 1891.

Several famous people lived in Maida Avenue. You might spot Poet Laureate John Masefield's blue plaque (he wrote the poem 'Sea Fever' and also a story I loved as a child called *The Box of Delights*). Further along is Arthur Lowe's plaque (Captain Mainwaring from *Dad's Army*). One person who doesn't have a plaque is John Wayne! Probably because he didn't actually live here in real life, but in the film *Brannigan* he lives in one of the apartments in Douglas House – right next to K-K-K-Ken from *A Fish Called Wanda*. Fun fact: Tony Robinson (Baldrick from *Blackadder*) plays the part of a motorcycle courier in *Brannigan*!

At the end of Maida Avenue you will emerge at Edgware Road, where we'll turn right.

In the times when people had horses to tow their barges along, boats would enter the tunnel here, which is known as **MAIDA HILL TUNNEL** ⓮. Since there's no towpath, they would unharness their horse to let it walk over the bridge and along Aberdeen Place to pick up the barge at the other end of the tunnel. Meanwhile, the captain of the barge would have to lie on his back and propel the boat through the tunnel by 'walking' along the ceiling.

Anyway, we've turned right into Edgware Road, and if you're wondering why the area is called Maida Vale, the building at number 437 can help explain. This used to be a pub called the **HERO OF MAIDA** ⓯. You can still just about make out the free-standing pub sign in the former outside seating area.

Maida is a town in Calabria, Italy; after General Sir John Stuart's famous victory at the Battle of Maida in 1806, King Ferdinand IV of Naples and Sicily bestowed upon him the title of Count of Maida. So this pub was named after John Stuart, the Hero of Maida.

Originally the pub gave the name to Maida Hill (where it stood) and Maida Vale beyond, but now the pub is no more, Maida Hill appears to have moved a mile westward! I'm not sure how you move a hill, but the tunnel here is still Maida Hill Tunnel, even if the hill is now elsewhere!

(Oh, and just to add to the confusion, in 2024 someone reopened a different pub, formerly the Shirland Hotel – back near the Maida Vale Studios where we walked earlier – calling it simply the Hero. So the connection with John Stuart continues, albeit in a different location.)

Now return up Edgware Road past the canal and turn right into St John's Wood Road, and then left into Hamilton Terrace.

Hamilton Terrace is a rather grand avenue – so wide it has parking in the middle – which has had many famous residents over the years, including Honor Blackman (Pussy Galore in *Goldfinger*), Sir Joseph Bazalgette, who designed London's sewers, and the novelist and poet Thomas Hardy. There's only one blue plaque, though, for the artist William Strang, who perhaps isn't quite such a household name.

Turn left into Hall Road. Across on your right you'll see **VALE COURT** ⑯. Back in 1973 Diana Rigg (another Bond girl, from *On Her Majesty's Secret Service*) owned an apartment here and let it to David Bowie, who was trying to escape his groupies down in Beckenham. He lived here for six months with his wife Angie and son, Zowie, before numerous complaints of excessive noise caused Diana Rigg to evict him.

Opposite Vale Court, on our side of the road, is **THE LORD'S TELEPHONE EXCHANGE** ⑰, which used to be, well…a telephone exchange, where operators would answer your call and you'd exclaim: 'I say, Operator? Give me Hampstead 2657!' Naturally it has been turned into flats, but a lovely reminder of its former existence is the ridiculously tall telephone box outside. This is surely the tallest phone kiosk in London but alas, it's not genuine. It is in fact an art installation by Philippe Starck. You can't go inside but it's great for selfies (if you're 6 ft 6 like me!)

Cross Maida Vale again and on the left you will pass the **EVERYMAN CINEMA** ⑱, which used to be a posh restaurant. You might recognise it from *About a Boy*, where Hugh Grant breaks up with his girlfriends. It's nice to see cinemas opening up for a change, instead of closing down. That's a novelty!

Continue along until the road splits into two and follow the right-hand side past the roundabout, ignoring the Warrington Hotel on your left for a moment. (Don't worry, we'll be back very shortly.) It's worth this quick stroll into Lauderdale Road, to see the rather beautiful **SYNAGOGUE** ⑲ dating from 1896, which is the headquarters of the British Sephardi community.

Okay, I'm ready for a drink now. Last one back to the Warrington Hotel's a rotten egg!

I must say, I do love these mid-Victorian pubs. For me the **WARRINGTON HOTEL** 🍺 is what pubs should look like. It's got a carpet, ornate lamps outside, intricately carved columns and a bar area with mirrors everywhere. It has a warmth to it which reminds me of how all pubs looked when I was growing up.

If you look at the ceiling you'll see some quite saucy images – probably a reference to the days when it housed a brothel known as Randy Randolph's! But perhaps my favourite thing about this pub is that it featured in an episode of *The Sweeney* called 'Night Out', where Jack Regan's ex-girlfriend lives upstairs. They sit in the pub staking out the bank next door.

For those who don't know it, *The Sweeney* was a wonderful TV show in the 1970s, all filmed on location around London – so it's fun to spot how places have changed. It's rhyming slang: Sweeney Todd = Flying Squad.

We're the Sweeney, son, and we haven't had any dinner.

I'll have a Scotch.

Cheers!

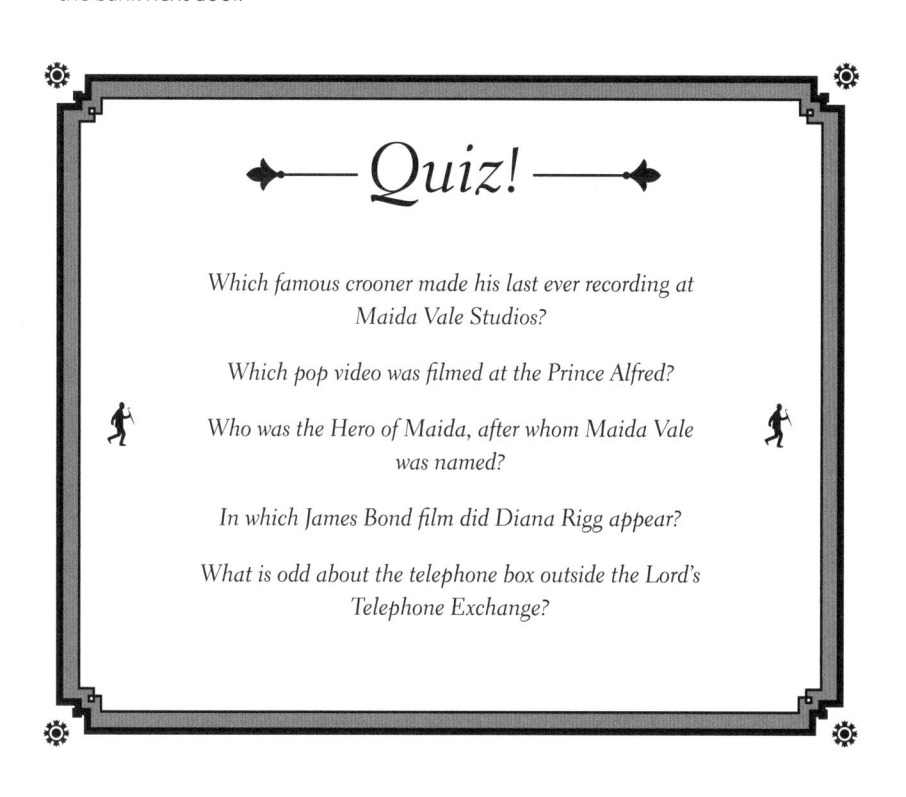

Quiz!

Which famous crooner made his last ever recording at Maida Vale Studios?

Which pop video was filmed at the Prince Alfred?

Who was the Hero of Maida, after whom Maida Vale was named?

In which James Bond film did Diana Rigg appear?

What is odd about the telephone box outside the Lord's Telephone Exchange?

2. HMS Belfast

HORNIMAN AT HAYS

ANCHOR TAP

OLD JUSTICE

WOLSELEY ST
GEORGE ROW
JAMAICA ROAD
ST JAMES'S ROAD
TOWER BRIDGE ROAD
VAUGHAN

22. Brunel Museum

THE HIGHWAY

SALT QUAY

MAYFLOWER

ANGEL

BRUNEL

SHIP

WEST LANE

SALTER RD

LOWER RD

17. St Olav's Norwegian Church

4 LONDON BRIDGE TO ROTHERHITHE

4 A RIPARIAN ROUTE FROM LONDON BRIDGE TO ROTHERHITHE

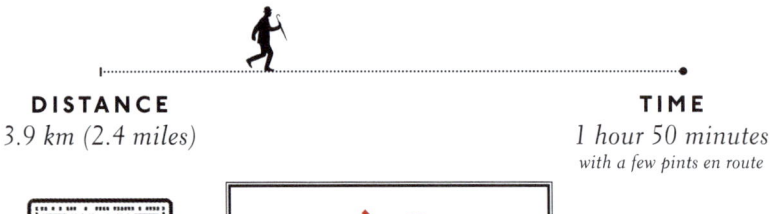

DISTANCE
3.9 km (2.4 miles)

TIME
1 hour 50 minutes
with a few pints en route

NEAREST STATION
London Bridge

PUBS
Horniman at Hays; Anchor Tap; Old Justice; Angel; Ship; Mayflower; Salt Quay; Brunel

---

Yes, yes, very funny, but the **HORNIMAN AT HAYS** isn't full of horny men (necessarily). It is actually a nice place to start our jaunt because of its wonderful location on the river, commanding spectacular views of Tower Bridge and the Tower of London.

The pub itself is modern and quite spacious, with room outside for drinking in the summer. It's named after Frederick Horniman, a nineteenth-century tea trader whose museum down in Forest Hill is one of my London favourites. And there are some rather splendid photographs of Tower Bridge, actually showing it halfway through construction, which I always find fascinating.

Let me sink this pint and we'll get going.

HAY'S GALLERIA ❶, which is the complex where the pub is situated, is named after Alexander Hay, the owner from the 1650s, when it was a brewhouse. It was converted into a wharf in the 1850s, following which it became known as 'the larder of London', since 80 per cent of London's

PUB

Horniman at Hays

dry goods were imported here (mostly tea). Eventually, by the 1960s, container ships started to drop things off further down the river and by the 1980s Hay's Wharf was transformed into a collection of shops, cafés and offices. Have a little look around before we get going. I've always liked the sculpture by David Kemp called *The Navigators*.

As with any area in central London, you could do a fun pub walk in any direction, but we have to pick one – so let's head east along the riverside, towards Tower Bridge.

On the left is **HMS BELFAST** ❷, *which isn't a battleship*, as I discovered when Mr Pedant from Pedantsville corrected me one day. It's a 'light cruiser' which saw action in the Korean and Second World Wars. Since the 1970s it has sat here as a museum that is open to the public. The six-inch (15-centimetre) forward guns can deliver a 112-pound (50-kilogram) shell up to 14 miles (23 kilometres). Back in 1971 it was decided that they should permanently be aimed at Scratchwood services on the M1 motorway (now known as London Gateway services), not for the quality of their coffee but simply because it was as mundane a location as they could think of. Bear that in mind next time you stop there for a pork pie!

Tower of London: check.

Tower Bridge: check.

You're probably admiring both these landmarks while standing near a striking bulbous building known as **CITY HALL** ❸, or sometimes 'The Onion' or 'The Glass Testicle'. Designed by Norman Foster (he's the one who, when young, told my mum that she wasn't 'shapely enough' for his architectural taste!), the building was opened in 2002 as the headquarters of the Greater London Authority (GLA). It turns out that the building wasn't owned by the GLA – they had the lease for twenty years and then as 2022 arrived they decided to decamp to somewhere out in Newham. The building is famous for containing a helical walkway, and you might recognise it from the 2015 Bond film *Spectre*. You might also remember the time when American illusionist David Blaine spent several weeks suspended in a Perspex box here with no food. It was a good effort; I just remember people throwing things at him!

As you pass beneath **TOWER BRIDGE** ❹, take a look at the lovely hexagonal Victorian post box which looks like one of the earliest models, from 1866, named after designer John Penfold.

Unfortunately they were too expensive to make and were discontinued in 1879; so, alas, this one is a replica, like many others installed at places of historic interest.

As you emerge on the other side of the bridge you'll find yourself in **SHAD THAMES** ❺, which might be named after the shad fish which was sometimes found in the Thames – or possibly it's from a corruption of St John-at-Thames, the name of the church which once stood near this spot. Who cares? What's interesting is that it's an excellent example of the type of street which was typical in London's docklands before the developers moved in. Dockers could lug barrows full of tea and spices between the tall warehouses on either side of the street via the latticed wrought-iron bridges which evoke the nineteenth century. It's unsurprising that it has been so popular in film productions, especially before the area was redeveloped in the 1980s. Scenes from *Doctor Who* were filmed down here, as well as *Oliver Twist* and *The Sweeney*.

Before we continue, just turn right up Horselydown Lane, where the **ANCHOR TAP** awaits.

I cannot tell you how joyful it makes me feel when entering this pub. It feels like finding my favourite old pair of jeans which I thought had been thrown away.

Originally it was built in the nineteenth century as a tap room for the nearby Anchor Brewery, but nowadays it's owned by Sam Smith's. They really do seem to acquire a lot of the nice old original pubs, and I must credit Sam Smith's with doing a great job of not ruining them by modernising.

When I was young it was commonplace to find dartboards and pool tables in pubs, but these days pubs are all uncomfortable wooden benches and hamburgers served on pieces of slate. The Anchor Tap, though, is a proper old-school boozer with various rooms, an open coal fire and a piano. The dim lighting and wood panels evoke the Victorian age, when hardy dockworkers would smoke in dark corners with fingerless gloves.

You might not be that familiar with the beers if you haven't been to a Sam Smith's before, but I like it here. I'll have a pint of Alpine Lager.

Turn right out of the pub and return to Shad Thames. Then find the passage leading to the river, with the curious name of Maggie Blake's Cause, which is named after a local activist who fought successfully to retain public access to the riverfront. *Brava!* (That's the feminine version of *bravo*, in case you're wondering.) Continue alongside the river, passing various new-looking brasseries, until you come to a bridge which crosses the **RIVER NECKINGER** ❻.

Sometimes cargo would remain on ships here for weeks before being unloaded, attracting thieves and pirates, and if you were caught stealing something you might be hanged here, at St Saviour's Dock. The noose used for hanging pirates was referred to by Cockneys as 'the devil's neckerchief' or 'the devil's neckcloth', which is how the river got its name.

The area on the far side of the Neckinger was worse than slum dwellings in Victorian times, when it was known as Jacob's Island. It's amazing how upmarket the area has become, when you consider how Charles Dickens described it in *Oliver Twist*:

> *The houses have no owners; they are broken open, and entered upon by those who have the courage; and there they live, and there they die.*

It was just over there that Bill Sikes met his end, hanged by his own rope whilst trying to escape over the rooftops above Folly Ditch. It is much changed these days, and it's thought that Dickens' description of the place contributed to the authorities deciding to do something about it:

> *Every repulsive lineament of poverty, every loathsome indication of filth, rot, and garbage; all these ornament the banks of Folly Ditch.*

Dickens was apparently so accurate that they were actually able to locate the exact place he described; although nowadays no one can quite agree on the precise location where Sikes would have met his fate. (It was a work of fiction, after all…)

Cross over the excellent bridge and just ahead is the building where, in *A Fish Called Wanda*, John Cleese hangs upside down outside the window, today known as **NEW CONCORDIA WHARF** ❼.

Go through the little tunnel and you'll find yourself at a corner.

Turn right and head up Mill Street. I simply never tire of walking past these converted warehouses. When you reach Jamaica Road turn right and you will come to an excellent viewing point for the River Neckinger. From here you can really get a sense of Bill Sikes and Oliver Twist! It's easy to find because, wait for it, it's just before a **STINK PIPE** ❽ at the corner with the end of Shad Thames.

Opposite here, on the wall above 144 Tanner Street (a Vietnamese restaurant called Tre House at the time of writing) is a **PARISH BOUNDARY MARKER** ❾ with 'St. M.M.B.' on it… Can you guess what it is yet? St Mary Magdalen Bermondsey.

Now, if you wanted to turn this walk into an all-dayer, you could follow Tanner Street round to the **BERMONDSEY BEER MILE** ❿, all along the railway arches. Actually, there are more like *two* miles of cool, groovy brewery bars and tap rooms, plus you can stuff your face with excellent food at **MALTBY STREET MARKET** ⓫, which is not to be missed on a weekend.

My constitution isn't what it once was, however, so I'm heading back the way we came along Mill Street and when you get to the corner where you came out of the tunnel, turn right along Bermondsey Wall West.

In a moment you come to an open space on your left – head to the wall and look over at the **HOUSEBOATS** ⓬.

These houseboats are actually much bigger on the inside than they look. If you have a friend who lives here you might manage to get invited to some of the little concerts they do from time to time, or cool events with Tower Bridge forming an enchanting backdrop as the sun goes down.

Continue along Bermondsey Wall West until you reach East Lane – turn right here, and then turn left into Chambers Street. Follow Chambers Street to the end and turn left into Bevington Street.

Ahead of you is **FOUNTAIN GREEN SQUARE** ⓭. It's aptly named: it's square, it's got green grass, and there's a fountain in the middle, commemorating one Philip Stewart. Philip Stewart was a magistrate and judge and also worked for the East India Company, as if you cared – but that's the point. I like how these fountains have seemingly random names on them in memory of someone that no one really remembers. Why they chose here is a mystery, since Stewart died and was buried in Brighton, though he had lived in London… There! We remembered a man we wouldn't have otherwise thought about. Don't you feel great now?

Anyway, this is the site of a former dry dock, called Fountain Dock, and there is some confusion among historians as to whether the dock was named after the fountain, or whether the fountain was moved here after the dock was filled in, to keep a 'fountain' connection going.

While you're pondering fountains and docks, I'm heading over to the right, to the **OLD JUSTICE** 🍺.

I do like it when the council steps in to stop something beautiful being destroyed – as opposed to doing the destroying themselves! In 2017 this lovely building, dating from 1933, had been acquired by an offshore developer who tried to turn it into flats, despite its listed status. Luckily, after they started to rip out the beautiful interior, Southwark Council intervened and made them pay to restore it. It was closed for six years whilst renovations took place, but it's finally open again, much to the joy of many local residents.

The pub featured in Paul McCartney's video for 'No More Lonely Nights', and more importantly in *The Sweeney* (which I love almost as much as *Columbo*).

The back room has board games and a TV projector for sport. The prices were pretty reasonable when I was last here for – yes, you guessed it – their pub quiz…which we won! (Hear the team name 'Universally Challenged' and tremble.)

PUB

Old Justice

Leave the pub and continue alongside the river, following the Thames Path until you reach a little area called **CHERRY GARDENS** ⓴, where the famous diarist Samuel Pepys used to buy cherries for his wife. This all sounds very romantic until you discover that it was usually on his way home from Deptford, where he had been having rumpy-pumpy with one Mrs Bagwell, wife of a ship's carpenter!

This is also said by some to be the location from which J. M. W. Turner observed the scene he depicted in *The Fighting Temeraire*. In the old days if a boat wanted Tower Bridge to be opened up, they would toot the boat's horn when they reached this spot.

Right, now carry on along Bermondsey Wall East until you see an open green space on your right, with some barely noticeable ruins.

This was a fourteenth-century **MANOR HOUSE** ⓯ built by King Edward III; you can just about make out where the moat would have been. It was also occupied by King Henry IV when he was suffering with leprosy in 1412, a year before he died.

I also rather like the **SCULPTURES** ⓰ next to the river here of Alfred Salter (a much-loved MP from the 1920s till the 1940s) and his family. Originally he was a doctor but he entered politics in order to improve living conditions for poor people living in slums. His wife, Ada, was the first female Labour councillor in London. Here she is carrying a spade because she campaigned to get various

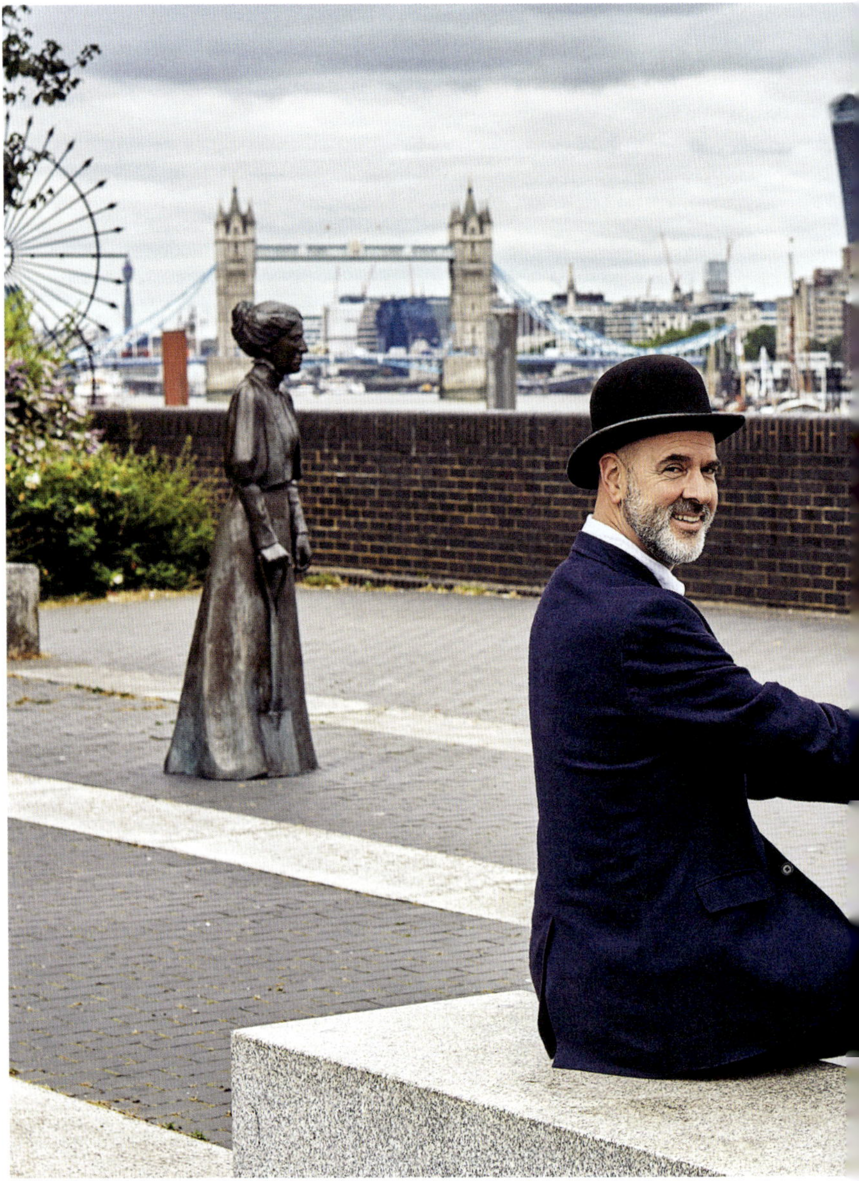

Walk 4: London Bridge to Rotherhithe | **73**

public spaces turned into playgrounds for children. Their daughter is also represented here; she died of scarlet fever. It is said that her death could have been avoided had they moved her to a posh school elsewhere, but they wanted to show solidarity with the local people so remained living amongst the slums here.

As for the cat…that's just their cat. Nobody knows its political persuasion.

Ah…what a lovely pub I see.

Now, anywhere that Captain Cook drank is good enough for me and the **ANGEL** is certainly a fine pub with excellent views. In fact, the views are so good that the famous hanging Judge Jeffreys, whom I spoke about in **Walk 2**, used to sit here and watch people being hanged at Execution Dock opposite (the sadistic git). They say that smugglers used the trap doors beneath the pub to avoid having to pay the hefty import charges in the London ports.

There was originally a pub here in the fifteenth century, owned by the monks of Bermondsey Abbey, but the current incarnation is from the nineteenth century and is in good condition. These Sam Smith's pubs usually are.

If you like, you can take the back stairs down to the foreshore when the tide is out and kick pebbles around. I often do.

Now head up Cathay Street, past the ruins, and turn left at Paradise Street.

Walk past the church and take the path across the green diagonally to your right.

Turn left and soon you will see, on the other side of the horrible busy road, **ST OLAV'S NORWEGIAN CHURCH 17**. It has one of my favourite weathervanes on top, featuring King Olav II, who helped Ethelred the Unready to retake London (which had been conquered by the evil Danish King Sweyn Forkbeard). Together they sailed up the Thames, tied ropes around the supports of London Bridge and pulled it down… giving rise to the song 'London Bridge Is Falling Down'… or so a bloke told me down the pub.

We'll stay on this side of the road. Turn left down Saint Marychurch Street and you'll come to the **SHIP**.

Time for a bit more of a salt-of-the-earth-type pub, methinks. All those picturesque riverside pubs with wonderful views are great and all, but

PUB

Angel

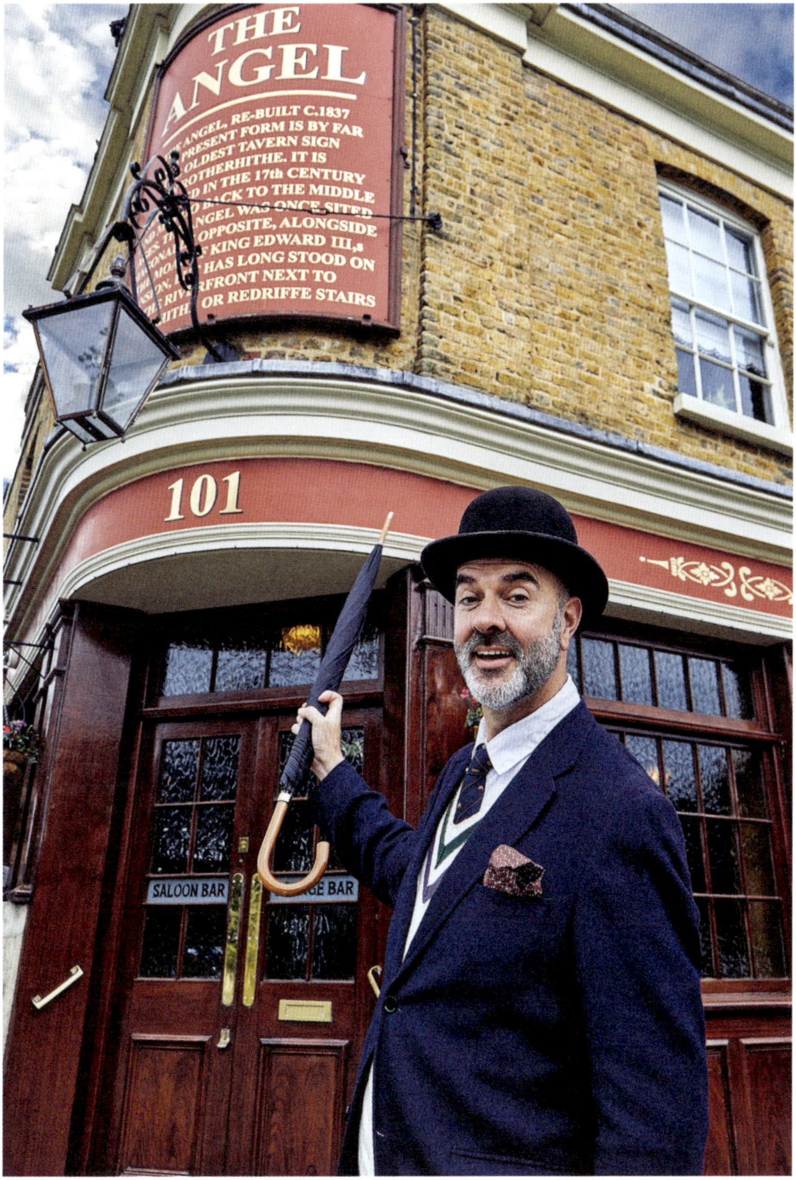
THE ANGEL
101
SALOON BAR

76 | Rather Splendid London Pub Walks

③

⑤

⑥

⑫

㉑

㉒

PUB

Ship

sometimes you just want to go to a boozer full of locals.

Well, when I first walked into the Ship I got the distinct feeling that everyone turned around and stopped their conversations for a moment, whilst a metaphorical piano-player stopped playing and the barman said, 'What'll it be, stranger?'

In fact, I found it very friendly and I loved the nautical-themed 'publicalia'. (Is that a word? I use it to describe pub memorabilia and décor.)

There's been a pub on this site since at least the early nineteenth century, though the current building dates from the early twentieth century. It's a lovely building, actually, sitting proudly on its own amongst the surrounding housing estates. This would be my sister's favourite pub on this walk.

Until 1985 the Ship had the curious accolade of being one of the few pubs in England with two names. On one side was a sign reading 'The Ship' and on the other 'The Great Eastern', which was Brunel's famously huge steamship.

They have a nice little garden out the back, but I'm rather enjoying my drink here, sitting out the front watching the locals come and go.

Now turn left out of the pub and continue along Saint Marychurch Street, past the old nineteenth-century **FIRE ENGINE HOUSE** [18] and you'll come to **ST MARY'S CHURCH** [19], where Christopher Jones is buried. He captained the *Mayflower*, which took the Pilgrim Fathers to America in 1620; many of them were Rotherhithe men. It was also in Rotherhithe that Jonathan Swift got the idea for *Gulliver's Travels*. He described Gulliver so well in the book that locals swore that they actually knew the man in person! On a somewhat darker note, it was outside this church that the corpse of Jack 'the Hat' McVitie was dumped, wrapped in an eiderdown, after he was murdered by the Kray twins in 1967.

Opposite the church is a **CHARITY SCHOOL** [20], founded in 1613 by two seafarers so that their fellow sailors' children could be educated. You can recognise this as a charity school because of the two figures in blue school uniforms above the door. It was a cheap option to dye the clothes blue. The school stood next to a **WATCH HOUSE** [21], which was used before we had police to keep an eye on miscreants getting up to no good, like snatching bodies from the graveyard and selling them for medical research!

After the church turn left and you'll come to the **MAYFLOWER** 🍺. I'll award **points** for spotting the parish markers on the side of the pub, reading 'ST. M. R.' (St Mary Rotherhithe).

You can see why this pub is so popular – especially with Americans – and I must say, I love coming here too. With its dark atmospheric wooden beams, mugs hanging from the bar surrounded by plants and cosy fireplace, it's the sort of place you don't want to leave once you've sunk a few pints. As you can see in the photo opposite, I have scored **points** for my dimpled pint glass!

There has been a pub on this spot since at least 1780, when it was known as the Ship Inn, and subsequently the Spread Eagle and Crown. In 1957 it was renamed the Mayflower, after the famous ship which lived out its final years rotting away on the riverbank nearby. It is said that some of the ship's timber was salvaged and used in the construction of the pub. In fact, if you can prove you are descended from the original Pilgrim Fathers who set sail from Rotherhithe in 1620, you are invited to say so in their Mayflower Descendants Book.

They have a decent menu (I like their fish and chips!) and a good selection of beer; but since the nineteenth century customers have been able to come here for a different purpose. Because sailors might not have had much time in port, the pub also operated as a post office. The postal hatch can still be seen at the left side of the bar, although it's not really used any more. They do still carry a licence to sell British and American stamps, though!

Further along Rotherhithe Street is Brunel's Engine House, which is now the **BRUNEL MUSEUM** ㉒.

In 1824 Marc Brunel started work on the first tunnel in the world to pass beneath a river. He died before it was finished, so his son, Isambard Kingdom Brunel, completed it in 1843. This engine house stopped the tunnel flooding. These days you can attend concerts and other events in there, as well as finding out more about the tunnel, which we will see in a moment.

From April to October you can enjoy home-made botanical cocktails, locally brewed beer, wines and soft drinks in the Midnight Apothecary garden on top of the Brunel Museum tunnel shaft. All of the ingredients used for the syrups and cocktails are foraged locally, or sourced from the garden itself. On a summer's evening it's a beautiful place to enjoy a campfire drink under the stars and gather around the central fire pit, toasting marshmallows (if you're into that sort of thing). Toasting kits are available! It feels like you've been transported to a beachside bar in Thailand.

If you want to see yet more riverside views you can continue along

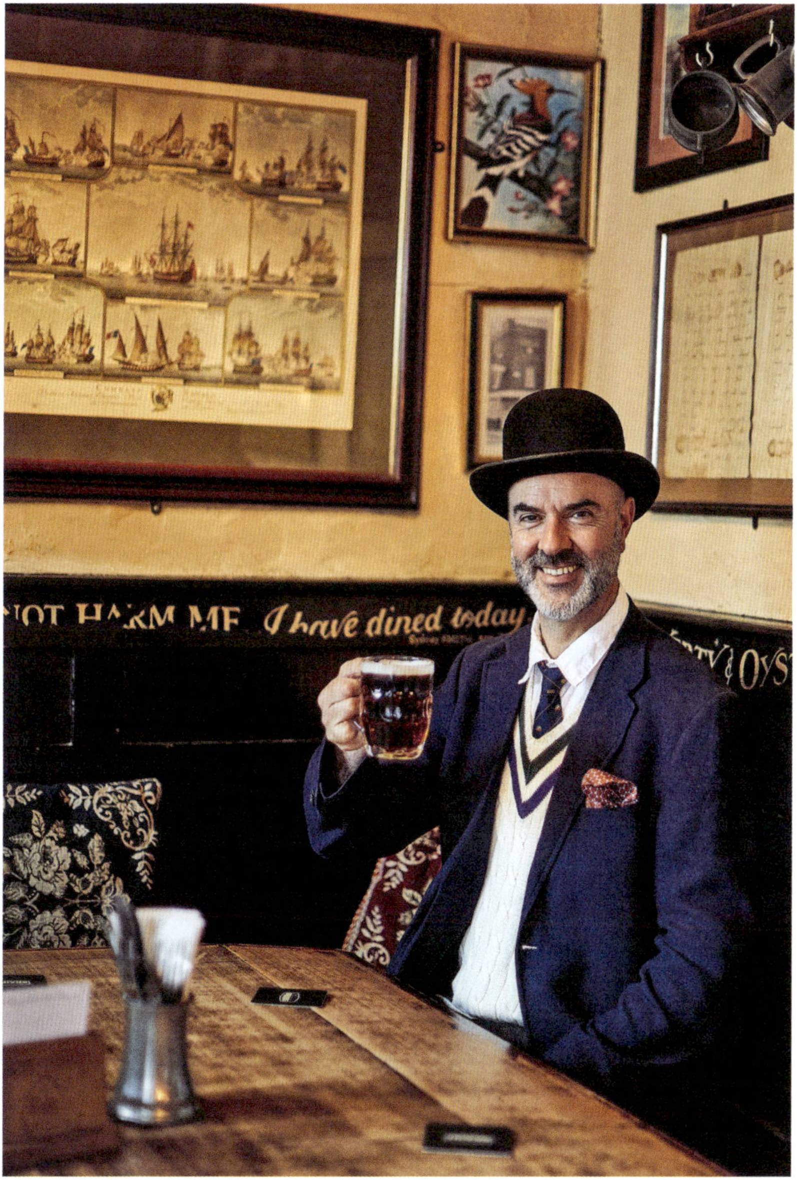
I have dined today

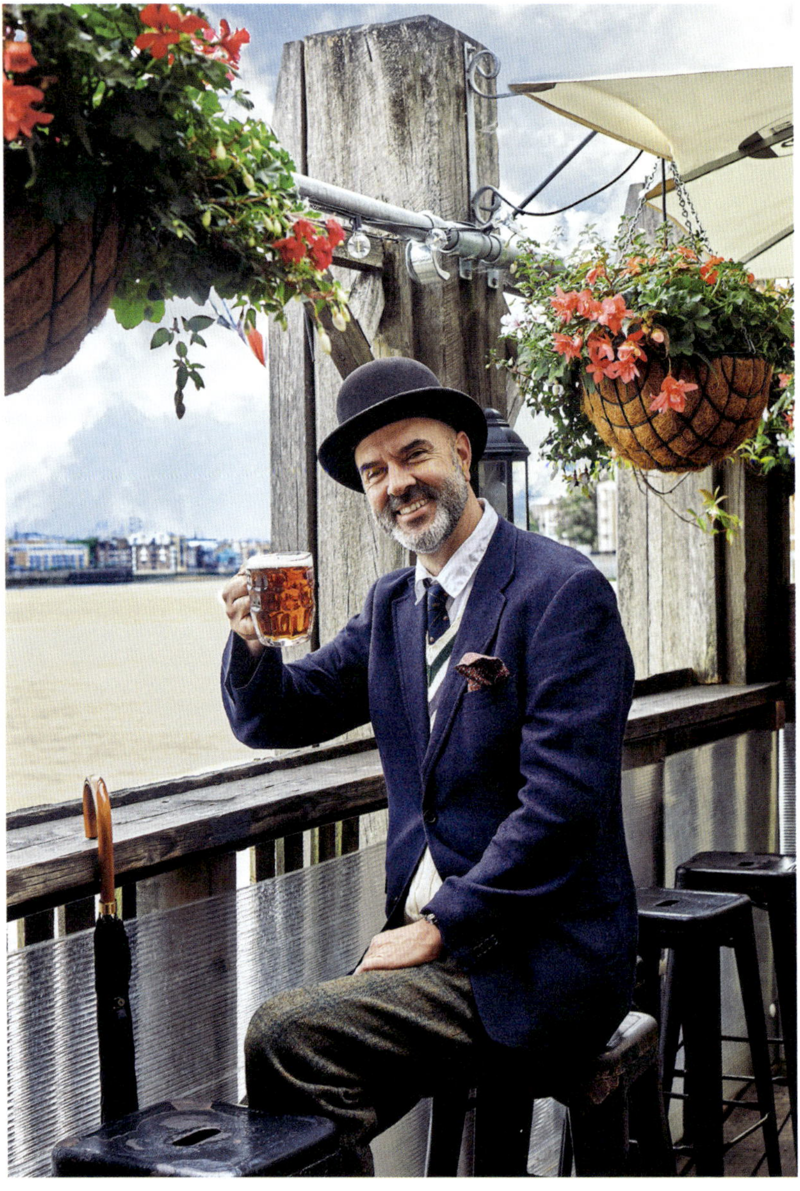

Rotherhithe Street until you come to the **SALT QUAY** 🍺, which is positioned in front of one of those bascule bridges which we saw in Wapping (see **Walk 2**). The pub has a large terrace overlooking the river where you can watch the sun go down. But we're going to finish our walk at a different pub, near the Windrush Line Overground station.

From the Brunel Museum walk down Railway Avenue and you'll come to **ROTHERHITHE STATION** ㉓. This is one of my favourite railway stations because from the platform you can see the original tunnel built by the Brunels, now used by the trains. Originally it was a foot tunnel but it ended up attracting prostitutes, thieves and, worse still, street hawkers and pedlars (like me) selling their wares under dim gaslight; so in 1865 it was taken over by the railway company. You can still see the wonderful brickwork and feel the dampness of the river seeping through.

Turn left at the station and you'll find the **BRUNEL** 🍺. It's not particularly historic, but it's brilliant for events – there's always something new…drag shows, karaoke, live music and the like.

There's a dog-friendly beer garden, too. Woof woof!

I'm drinking rum. Yo ho ho, me hearties!

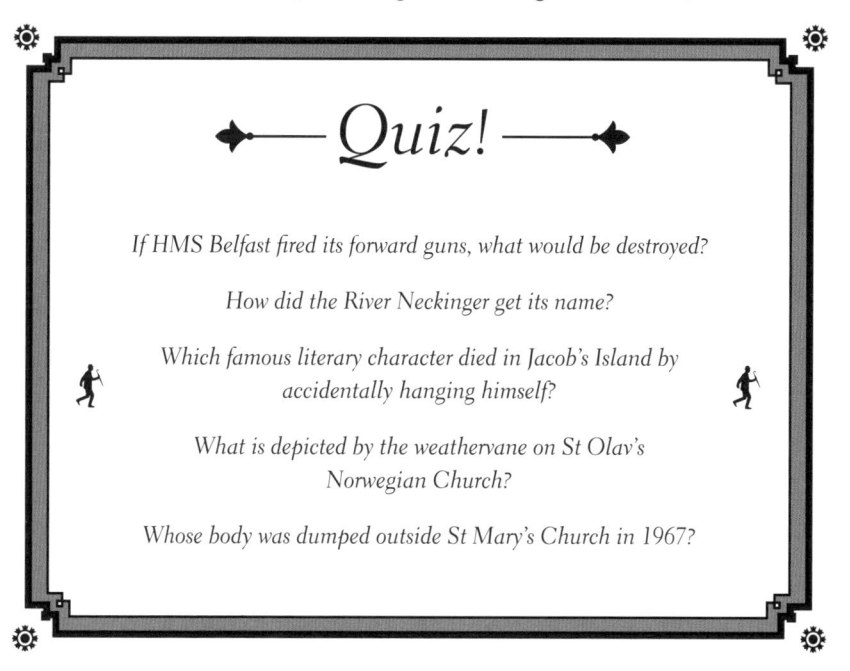

✦ — *Quiz!* — ✦

If HMS Belfast fired its forward guns, what would be destroyed?

How did the River Neckinger get its name?

Which famous literary character died in Jacob's Island by accidentally hanging himself?

What is depicted by the weathervane on St Olav's Norwegian Church?

Whose body was dumped outside St Mary's Church in 1967?

18. Mortimer House

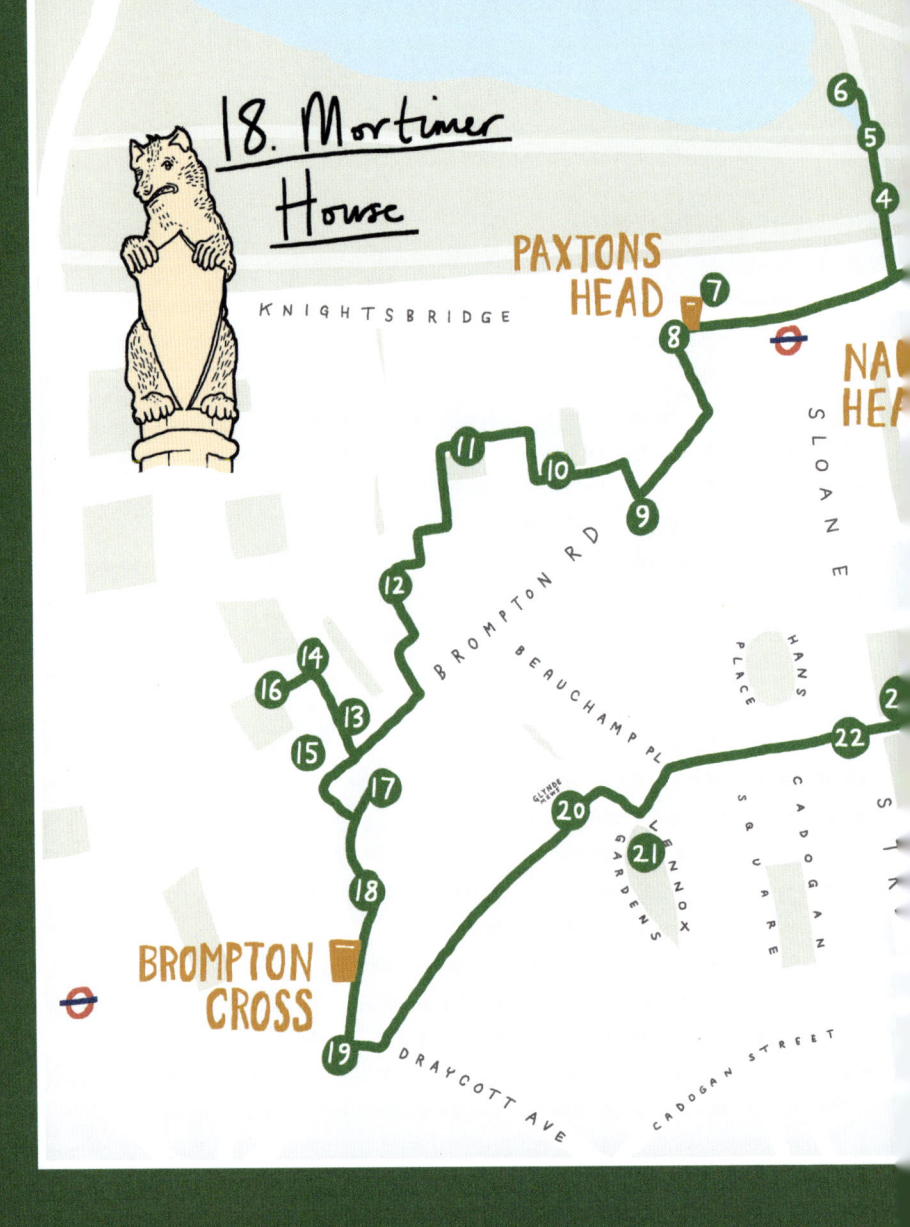

PAXTONS HEAD

KNIGHTSBRIDGE

BROMPTON RD

BEAUCHAMP PL

SLOANE

HANS PLACE

CADOGAN SQUARE

LENNOX GARDENS

BROMPTON CROSS

DRAYCOTT AVE

CADOGAN STREET

5 BELGRAVIA TO KNIGHTSBRIDGE

The GRENADIER

- GRENADIER
- WILTON CRESC
- STAR TAVERN
- HORSE & GROOM
- PLUMBERS ARMS
- EATON PLACE
- EATON SQUARE

3. Cabmen's Shelter

5 A POSH PERAMBULATION FROM BELGRAVIA TO KNIGHTSBRIDGE

DISTANCE
6.8 km (4.2 miles)

TIME
3 hours
with a few pints en route

NEAREST STATION
Victoria

PUBS
Plumbers Arms; Horse & Groom; Grenadier; Paxtons Head; Brompton Cross; Star Tavern; Nags Head

PUB
Plumbers Arms

I say, jolly spiffing, what? Belgravia is certainly one of the poshest parts of London, with properties here worth millions and owned by some of the uppermost echelons of English society. It makes sense, therefore, to start in the **PLUMBERS ARMS**, which dates from the middle of the nineteenth century. On 7 November 1974 Lady Lucan ran into this pub – screaming and covered in blood – claiming that her husband, Lord Lucan, had murdered their nanny a few doors away.

Let's chin down this pint and we'll go and take a look.

Come out of the pub and turn right, stopping at **46 LOWER BELGRAVE STREET** ❶, the scene of this bloody murder. Richard John Bingham was the Seventh Earl of Lucan, an aristocrat and professional gambler. (He was known as 'Lucky Lucan' due to his good fortune in the casino, even though he didn't seem that lucky to me – he was always skint!) His relationship with his wife Veronica, née Duncan, was fractious, to say the least – it involved bitter custody battles and fights, and Lord Lucan trying to get her certified insane. On the night in question the children's nanny was found bludgeoned to death in the basement. Veronica was also attacked and accused her husband of being the perpetrator.

Lord Lucan then went missing. His car was found abandoned in Newhaven, with bloody lead piping in the boot, sparking one of the greatest mysteries to ever capture the imagination of conspiracy theorists and historians for years, although it was widely accepted that he had probably drowned. My mother was obsessed with Lord Lucan and was convinced he was innocent. She even came down here once to spy on his wife. (This is so typical of her. I miss my mum.) She was also convinced, as many people were, that he was still alive! There were numerous reported sightings of him, some claiming he was living in Africa!

I wonder if he's read my first book, or is reading this one??

Continuing straight, you will pass **EATON SQUARE** ❷ on your left, said to be the largest square in London.

The Belgravia area used to be called 'the Five Fields' and was renowned as a place of vice, highwaymen, ne'er-do-wells, beggars, thieves and prostitutes…and then they went and ruined it, by getting Thomas Cubitt to build all these swanky houses!

Back in 1784 the Chevalier de Moret, a doctor and total quack, charged admission to the public to see him ascending from the Five Fields in a hot air balloon (which was a bit of a craze at the time, known as 'balloonamania'). Sixty thousand people arrived to witness the display, but it was a spectacular failure, and the crowd got angry and made for him! Fortunately de Moret narrowly escaped with his life, having been rescued by some kindly gentlemen, whilst the mob destroyed what was left of his balloon and car.

(It should really have been called 'balloonacy'. Some people have no imagination…)

Continue along Upper Belgrave Street and turn right into Chapel Street.

24 CHAPEL STREET ❸ is where Brian Epstein, manager of the Beatles, lived and died. He hosted some epic parties here, including the launch party for *Sgt. Pepper's Lonely Hearts Club Band*, but sadly in 1967 he was found dead in his bedroom on the first floor, having overdosed on barbiturates.

Take the next right into Groom Place and then turn right again, where you will find Epstein's local, the **HORSE & GROOM**.

I suppose the name of this pub makes sense when you consider its location in a mews, next to what was once Bryant's Depot, where – according to a nineteenth-century *Sporting Chronicle* advertisement – one could buy 'Horse Clothing', 'Harnesses' and, most appealing of all, 'Soiled Saddlery' (that's my favourite type of saddlery).

Despite the date reading '1698' above the pub door, both buildings (along with many of those in Belgravia) were constructed around the 1830s. The year 1698 refers to the establishment of the Shepherd Neame brewery, Britain's oldest. However, that's not the reason we're here. We're here because this is where the Beatles used to come and have meetings with Brian Epstein, who could probably have hopped over his garden wall to come in the back door!

It's not the largest of pubs but on a warm day that doesn't matter so much, as at least there isn't loads of traffic whizzing past outside, which allows for relatively peaceful drinking al fresco.

I'll have a pint of Spitfire – the Bottle of Britain!!!

PUB
Horse & Groom

Chin chin.

Retrace your steps to Brian Epstein's house and then back down Chapel Street the way you came. Now turn right into Belgrave Square.

At the north corner of the square continue straight across the junction, into Wilton Crescent, before turning right into Wilton Row. Follow it round until you come to the **GRENADIER**.

Now, I know we've only just stopped at the Horse & Groom, but I do love a well-hidden pub! This one exudes special charm. It started life in 1720 as the officers' mess of the First Regiment

PUB
Grenadier

of Foot Guards, whose barracks were nearby. It became a pub (the Guardsman) in 1818, later being named in honour of the Grenadier Guards' heroics at the Battle of Waterloo.

They have a hearty menu (the Beef Wellington being a favourite) and, would you believe it, a ghost! Yes, who'd have thought it? Yet another pub with a ghost.

The poor fellow in this case was a junior officer beaten to death for cheating at cards, which might explain why there are playing cards and bank notes all over the ceiling. Keep your eyes open and you might spot the one placed there and signed by me! **Extra points** if you do!!

It's unsurprising that the Duke of Wellington drank here, since it was his local! Other famous patrons have included Prince William, Madonna and King George IV (who seemed to spend a lot of time in pubs).

Mine's a lager.

Turn left out of the Grenadier and follow Old Barrack Yard to the end and then around until you reach Knightsbridge. Turn left and walk as far as the junction with William Street, where you can cross over to the other side of Knightsbridge into Albert Gate. Pass the French Embassy on your right and the Kuwaiti Embassy on your left as you head into Hyde Park.

HYDE PARK

Keep walking straight and you will come to a dirt track intended for horses. Score some **points** by spotting the horse trough (one of the few which could well still be used, since horses still use this road). Before it on the left, and after it on the right, you can find sets of mounting blocks, which look like three kerb stones, to help riders get onto their horses. Behind the mounting block on the left look for a pair of **BOUNDARY STONES** ❹. (If you squint very carefully, or take a photo and then zoom in, like I did, you'll see a tiny plaque on the 'S.M.W.' marker advertising the fact that it is made of 'grano-metallic stone', as if you cared.) These mark the boundary between the old parishes of St Margaret Westminster and St George Hanover Square.

This road, **ROTTEN ROW** ❺, used to be known as the Old King's Road to Kensington, until they built the New King's Road to Kensington alongside; but who cares, we're crossing over it towards the little **WATERFALL** ❻ on the other side.

The whole of the Serpentine Lake beyond is actually part of the River Westbourne, which flows down from

Hampstead. Nowadays the river is almost entirely underground (and passes through a pipe above the platform at Sloane Square tube station), all the way to the Thames at Vauxhall. In fact, two knights once fought a duel at this point on a bridge over the river – which is how Knightsbridge got its name. These days the waterfall is the only part of the Westbourne you can still see flowing.

Now retrace your steps to the French Embassy and turn right along Knightsbridge.

After the tube station take the right fork. We're now in one of the most extravagant shopping districts in Britain. The modern glass building on the right is **ONE HYDE PARK** ❼ where, in 2010, the most expensive flat in the world was sold (supposedly to a Qatari prince), for £140 million. Some of the flats are worth even more now – but the building looks like a prison from a science fiction movie, if you ask me!

Perhaps the prince visited **SAMER HALIMEH** ❽ over the road on your left, with the rhinoceros above it. Mr Halimeh is known as 'the Red Carpet Jeweller' because he provides all the bling for people like Angelina Jolie and Elton John at the Oscars. It's the most heavily fortified jeweller in London and once had a diamond ring for sale worth £20 million.

PUB

Paxtons Head

Crossing over Knightsbridge, just before Samer Halimeh there's the **PAXTONS HEAD** ❾, if you fancy another drink.

Hey. I like karaoke, and if liking karaoke is wrong then I don't wanna be right! But don't worry – they don't have karaoke *every* night.

This rather splendid Victorian gin palace was rebuilt in 1851 on a site where pubs have existed since the 1600s. It's named after Jospeh Paxton, who designed the Crystal Palace for the Great Exhibition, which took place in Hyde Park in that same year of 1851.

They show sports and do Sunday roasts here, too; and if you like original oak panelling and etched mirrors with red-brick walls and Victorian architecture, you'll probably want to have a pint or two in here.

I might go for some of this food while we're at it. Some Good Olde English Fayre.

Greene King IPA for me!

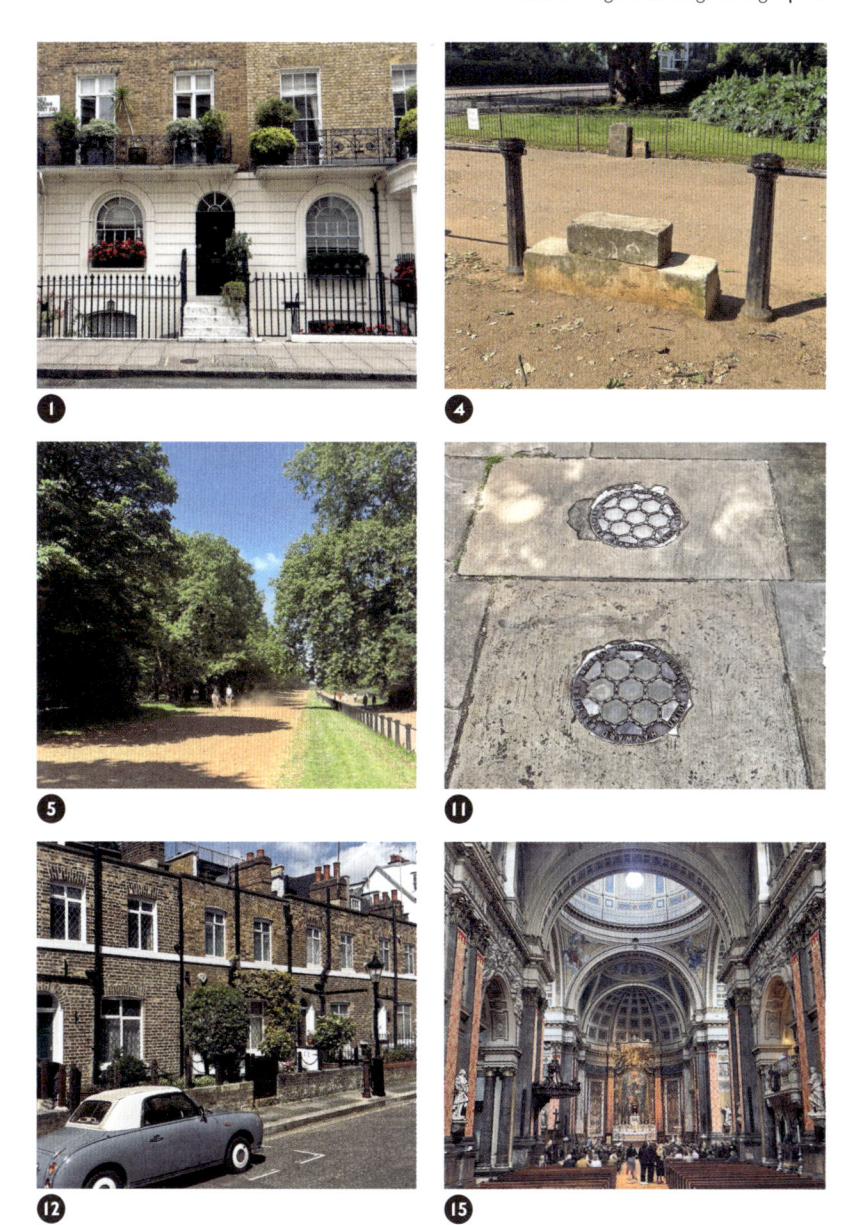

Walk 5: Belgravia to Knightsbridge | **89**

Turn left out of the pub and then left again into Knightsbridge Green. Then at the end turn right into Brompton Road. Over the road you will see **HARRODS** 9, which is so famous I won't use up my word count describing it! It's amazing how it's grown since Charles Henry Harrod, a tea merchant, opened his small grocery store in 1834 in Stepney. Until the First World War you could buy 100 per cent pure cocaine here!

Turn right into Lancelot Place and left into Trevor Square, noticing the pinkish-red-brick building ahead with the words 'Harrods Ltd' on it: this was once the **HARRODS WAREHOUSE** 10, with tunnels leading to the main store. Now it is – you guessed it – luxury flats.

Continue past Trevor Square and follow Trevor Place round to the right, before turning left into **MONTPELIER SQUARE** 11.

We're going this way because the streets are so charming around here and it's much nicer than walking along the main road. In fact, every house on Montpelier Square is Grade II-listed. In this square you'll also see some very nice coal hole covers. Look out for the ones made of glass by Haywards of Borough, a most prestigious brand. Edward Hayward patented this invention because the light would refract through the glass into the space below. **Points** to me!!!

Enter Sterling Street, in the south-west corner of the square, and then turn

MONTPELIER PLACE

right into Montpelier Place, spotting some more nice coal hole covers. Some of them will have the old postcodes (without the numerical subdivisions), indicating that they most probably predate 1917.

Turn left into Montpelier Walk and right into Rutland Street, following it around the corner and past some cute **COTTAGES** 12 built in 1830. They must be worth a fortune these days, but in the nineteenth century there were thirty of them and they were considered slums!

Continue to the end of Rutland Street and turn right into Cheval Place, eventually going round another corner and emerging back on to Brompton Road.

Across the road is the Bunch of Grapes if you're thirsty again – it contains some beautiful back-painted mirrors and 'snob screens' (more **points**!) – but I'm continuing west on this side of Brompton Road, past Brompton Square.

Turn right into Cottage Place, where you'll pass the disused **BROMPTON ROAD TUBE STATION** 13. The red tiles are typical of Leslie Green, who designed this and many other stations. After Knightsbridge station was modernised in the 1930s, Brompton Road was deemed surplus to requirements, so it was closed and later used as the Royal Artillery's anti-aircraft operations room. Last I heard, it had been bought in 2014 by a billionaire Ukrainian, who wanted to turn it into flats.

At the end of Cottage Place is **HOLY TRINITY CHURCH** ⑭ – which is easily missed, due to the huge domed **ORATORY** ⑮ overshadowing it. Look for the statue of **ST FRANCIS OF ASSISI** ⑯ in the garden.

According to Oleg Gordievsky, a Russian double-agent in the 1960s and 1970s, this spot was used as a drop by spies at the height of the Cold War. Russian agents would be notified, by a chalk mark on a lamppost in Mayfair, that a package had been left; they would come here, walk around Harrods until they got dizzy, to make sure they weren't followed, and then look behind a tree next to the wall behind St Francis! (And you reckon it's unsafe when your Amazon delivery is left unattended outside on your doorstep!)

Now head back to Brompton Road. You simply must look inside Brompton Oratory (also known as the London Oratory, or simply the Oratory), which is the huge church that looks like it ought to be in Rome.

An oratory is a group of Catholic priests who live together in a community (they actually live in the building next door to the church). The community moved here from Charing Cross in the 1850s, with the church building itself being consecrated in 1884. It's a truly magnificent structure, full of beautiful sculptures and religious art. Spies also used to leave packages behind the two pillars next to the First World War monument in here – I guess it was useful in case it was raining!

Cross over Brompton Road and walk into Egerton Place. Turn left briefly to take a look at **44 EGERTON GARDENS** ⑰, which was where Ruth Ellis lived with David Blakely. After shooting him outside a pub in Hampstead in 1955 (see my first book) she became the last woman to be hanged in Britain.

Head back the other way, passing the end of Egerton Place, to follow Egerton Gardens round to the next junction. Then turn left, past more coal hole covers, and then turn right at the little park, taking you into Egerton Crescent.

This is one of the most expensive streets in Britain. I particularly like the red-brick **MORTIMER HOUSE** ⑱ on your right, built in 1868 for Edward Palmer, the Governor of the Bank of England. It has some terrific sculptures on top, typical of Victorian buildings. Look out also for the street sign reading 'Egerton Crescent SW' (without the number). Could this be over 100 years old? It is, unless it's a replica!

And what's this? **Points**!!! Just a little further along on the right is a stink pipe!

Turn left onto Brompton Road and you'll soon see the **BROMPTON CROSS** 🍺 on your left.

I very much enjoy the look of pubs like this, built in the 1930s. This was once the Hour Glass, which had been going since 1852; but its 1930s style is a nice change from the others we have visited on this walk. I particularly like the fact that they have retained the Charrington Brewery features, with the excellent mosaic sign above the door and the Toby Ale tiles. Look out also for the original lanterns outside.

The original features continue inside; perhaps I should have worn my spats and 1930s suit.

In here it feels a bit more like a locals' pub where you can get a Scotch egg and watch the footy.

Come on, you *!#&$@£ – oops… I almost let on who I support there!

A pint of Timothy Taylor Landlord for me.

Turn left out of the pub and continue along Brompton Road until you see **MICHELIN HOUSE** ⑲.

I was recently asked which is my favourite building in London, and whilst I went with a different one, I must say

PUB
Brompton Cross

I was tempted to pick this. It was built in 1911 as the UK headquarters of Michelin Tyres, but these days it's a restaurant – which kind of makes sense, when you consider that they invented the Michelin Star system (so they can give themselves a couple of stars for this place). Originally the *Michelin Guide* was a book (compiled since 1900) which offered motorists advice on where to eat, or which hotels to stay in, when driving around Europe. Inside the building you can see some wonderful scenes of early motoring depicted on the tiles.

Now briefly head back up Brompton Road the way you came and turn right into Draycott Avenue. Turn left into Walton Street and walk all the way along until you get to Glynde Mews (don't worry, Walton Street is very pleasant, full of cute boutiques and nice cafés). More or less opposite Glynde Mews, you'll see the former **WALTON STREET MAGISTRATES' COURT** ⑳, which is now flats. Originally built in 1850 as a school, it used to have signs on the entrances reading 'Boys' and 'Girls' – but although the signs survived all the years that it spent as a courthouse, for some reason the developers decided that people wouldn't want them on their flats. Shame.

A bit further along is Lennox Gardens. Turn right here, and then turn left once you get to the little private garden. This used to be where the **MARYLEBONE CRICKET CLUB** ㉑ played – although it didn't last too long because there was an ice-rink nearby for posh ladies, so batsmen were encouraged not to hit the ball too hard in that direction! Not much use if W. G. Grace (who played here) needed to reach his century! The MCC moved to Lord's in St John's Wood shortly after that.

On entering Pont Street, turn right and admire the beautiful red-brick houses built in the 1870s. This sea of red is referenced in a poem by John Betjeman about the **CADOGAN HOTEL** ㉒, which is coming up on the right.

In 1895 it was here, in room 118, that Oscar Wilde was arrested for gross indecency. He was actually encouraged to leave the country, but fell into a lethargy and was imprisoned, ultimately leading to his ill health and demise.

Betjeman writes of the street:

To the right and before him
Pont Street
Did tower in her new built red,
As hard as the morning gaslight
That shone on his unmade bed.

And of the arrest:

A thump, and a murmur of voices –
('Oh why must they make such a din?')
As the door of the bedroom
swung open
And TWO PLAIN CLOTHES
POLICEMEN came in:

'Mr. Woilde, we 'ave come for tew
take yew
Where felons and criminals dwell:
We must ask yew tew leave with
us quoietly
For this is the Cadogan Hotel.'

He rose, and he put down The
Yellow Book.
He staggered – and, terrible-eyed,
He brushed past the plants on
the staircase
And was helped to a hansom outside.

Poor old Oscar. :(

Continue along Pont Street and, after crossing Cadogan Place – when you can score some **points** for spotting a **CABMEN'S SHELTER** ㉓ – it will eventually lead you into Chesham Place. Then turn left up Belgrave Mews West, and you'll come to the **STAR TAVERN** 🍺.

Ah, here's yet another pub hidden away in a little mews. I do love these. It was built in the middle of the nineteenth century and has been included in the *Good Beer Guide* for at least the last fifty years.

94 | Rather Splendid London Pub Walks

⓰

⓲

⓳

⓴

㉒

㉔

These days it's a Fuller's pub, which usually means you can get a decent pie; but it was in the 1950s and 1960s that it achieved notoriety for being a place where highlife met lowlife. The upstairs room was generally where the rogues and ruffians would hang out, whilst more genteel patrons drank downstairs.

It was here, in the upstairs room, that the Great Train Robbery was planned (unless it wasn't; see **Walk 8**) by Bruce Reynolds and Buster Edwards in 1963. Reynolds' Aston Martin could regularly been seen parked outside.

Fifteen members of Reynolds' gang held up a mail train and made off with over £2.5 million, although they didn't get away with it for long…except for one gang member. Ronald Biggs managed to escape from Wandsworth Prison by making a rope out of bed sheets and eventually made it to Brazil, where he ended up making records with the Sex Pistols!

Bing Crosby popped into the Star Tavern for a pint, as did Princess Margaret and Peter O'Toole, whilst John Profumo was said to have secret meetings here with Christine Keeler.

The landlord, Paddy Kennedy, was also quite a character, once telling Elizabeth Taylor to 'Move your fat arse!' so that his friend could sit down. Apparently she complied!

Ale for me. Cheers.

PUB

Star Tavern

Leave the pub and turn left, continuing up Belgrave Mews West, which leads you into Halkin Place. Turn left into West Halkin Street and then right into Lowndes Street. Next turn right into the pedestrianised Motcomb Street, with its rather smart cafés and restaurants.

The huge impressive building on the left is the **PANTECHNICON** **24**. These days it's a restaurant with a posh roof terrace, but from 1830 until the 1970s it was a warehouse specialising in art and furniture removals. Its name derives from the Greek *pan*, meaning 'all', and *techne*, meaning 'art'. They were the first company to develop what we know as the modern removals van. They had horses, of course, but the main van was pretty similar to today's, and until not that long ago people referred to these vans as 'pantechnicons'.

Carry on and then turn left at the Alfred Tennyson into Kinnerton Street. Keep going until you see a pub with

'Kevin Moran' written outside – which is actually the **NAGS HEAD** 🍺, where we can rest our weary bones.

This sure is a bit of a tiddler, ain't it? It must be one of London's smallest pubs, but also one of its most characterful. In any direction your eye will fall on some interesting piece of clutter. If you have the right coins you can even play the vintage arcade game.

In the old days it would have catered to stable hands and other members of the working classes in the service of the larger houses in the area. On a nice day drinkers may spill out into the quiet alleyway, whence you can see the house at **44 KINNERTON STREET** ㉕ where (*allegedly*) Prince Andrew attended a party and was photographed with his arm around Virginia Giuffre's waist (*allegedly*). Who knows if it's true, but the whole debacle led to some pretty uncomfortable interviews and denials.

My favourite thing about the Nags Head, though, is that it is run by the father of the actor who played Pogo Patterson!! (Pogo was a character from *Grange Hill*, the much-loved children's TV show about a school.)

Anyway, I wouldn't bring it up. He must be tired of hearing it.

Now, I've got a straightforward shooting party to attend, so let's be having you.

Mine's a lager.

PUB

Nags Head

✦ —— *Quiz!* —— ✦

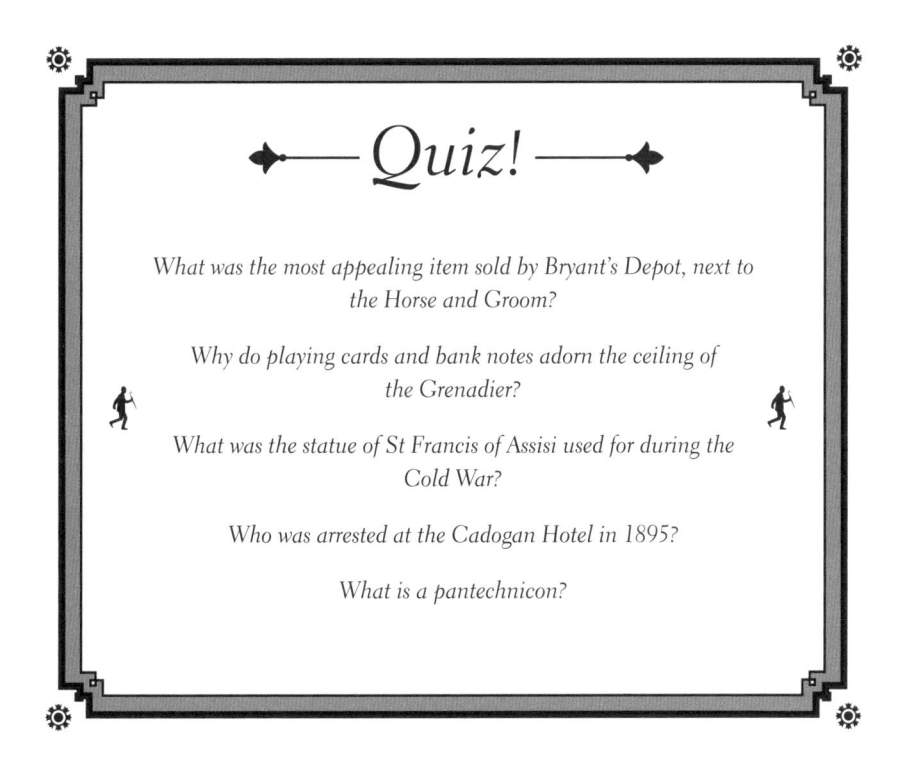

What was the most appealing item sold by Bryant's Depot, next to the Horse and Groom?

Why do playing cards and bank notes adorn the ceiling of the Grenadier?

What was the statue of St Francis of Assisi used for during the Cold War?

Who was arrested at the Cadogan Hotel in 1895?

What is a pantechnicon?

29. Water Pump

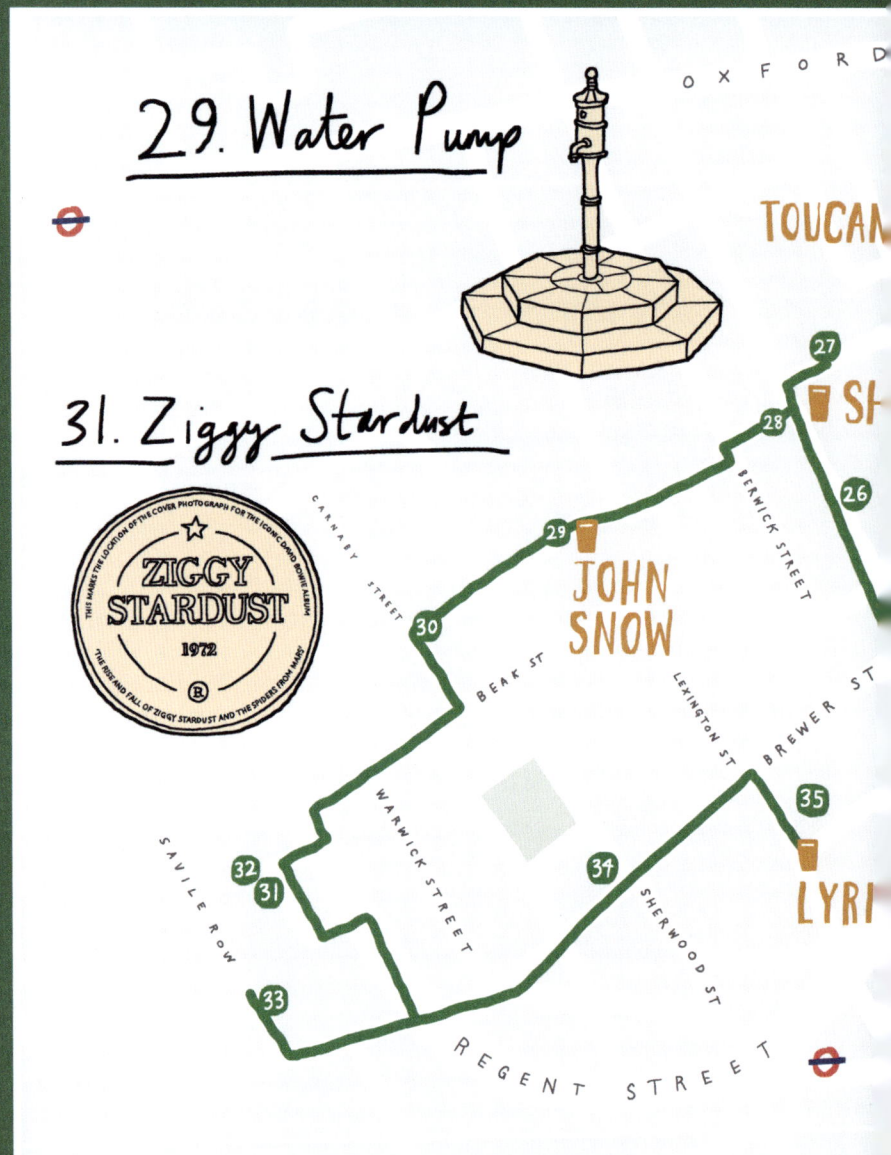

31. Ziggy Stardust

ZIGGY STARDUST 1972
THIS MARKS THE LOCATION OF THE COVER PHOTOGRAPH FOR THE ICONIC DAVID BOWIE ALBUM "THE RISE AND FALL OF ZIGGY STARDUST AND THE SPIDERS FROM MARS"

6 SOHO

ANGEL

COACH & HORSES

FRENCH HOUSE

THE FRENCH HOUSE

French House

6 A DELIGHTFUL DAWDLE THROUGH SOHO

DISTANCE
3.2 km (2 miles)

TIME
1 hour 30 minutes
with a few pints en route

NEAREST STATION
Tottenham Court Road

PUBS
Angel; Coach & Horses; Toucan; French House; Ship; John Snow; Lyric

---

Let's start this musical romp at the **ANGEL**. (If music isn't your thing, don't worry – I'll be pointing out some 'normal' stuff, too!)

There's been a pub or coaching inn here since at least the 1540s, although the current incarnation was extensively refurbished in Victorian times. It has what you expect from a Victorian pub: polished brass, dark wood panelling, beautifully decorated glass and, most importantly for me, a carpet and fireplace! Old school. Love it.

The reason we're starting here is that, in medieval times, this was on the route from Newgate Prison to the gallows at Tyburn (where today's Marble Arch stands). The wagon with the condemned prisoner on it would stop here for a rest, while the churchwardens from the church of **ST GILES IN THE FIELDS** next door offered them one last merciful drink. This was known as 'taking the St Giles Bowl' – or having 'one for the road' – according to some bloke I met in this very pub… so it must be true!!

PUB

Angel

Occasionally a prisoner would be rescued by his criminal pals who frequented the rough area nearby, known as the Rookery because people were packed in like roosting birds – full of thieves, beggars and ne'er-do-wells.

> *Where misery clings to misery for a little warmth, and want and disease lie down side-by-side, and groan together.*

That's how the area was described in a quote attributed to Keats…and 'attributed' is good enough for me!

If the prisoner wasn't rescued, someone might offer him a second beer, to which the reply would come: 'No, he can't have another. He's on the wagon!' And it was off to the gallows with him – which is why teetotallers are referred to as being 'on the wagon' (according to some other random bloke in the pub).

Turn left out of the pub and walk past St Giles in the Fields, named after the patron saint of lepers, following the founding of a leper colony here in the twelfth century.

Now enter Denmark Street.

The first building on the left is currently Thirteen, a cocktail bar linked to the Chateau Denmark hotel, but in the 1970s and 1980s it was a **JOB CENTRE** ❷ where the notorious serial killer Dennis Nilsen worked. It's said that for their Christmas work party one year he prepared the food using the same pot that he used to boil one of his victim's heads!

Denmark Street was one of the most important streets in Swinging Sixties London. Anyone who was anyone would be spotted here; it was like a Mecca for up-and-coming musicians, and there are so many places of interest I shall have to list them!

REGENT SOUNDS ❸ at number 4 was once a recording studio where the Rolling Stones recorded their first album and Black Sabbath recorded their first two albums. It was here that during the recording of the Kinks' 'You Really Got Me' that Dave Davies' girlfriend said the song 'didn't really make her want to drop her knickers' – so he decided to slash the speaker of his guitar amp, creating what some people call the first heavy metal sound.

Originally 'It's Not Unusual' was intended to be sung by Sandie Shaw, but when they recorded the demo version here they used an unknown young singer called Tom Jones. A keyboard player was required, so they went up the street to La Gioconda café and a bloke called Reg Dwight offered to play on it. Anyway, it was so good that Sandie Shaw rejected it and suggested Tom Jones sing it himself, creating my favourite karaoke song of all time! (Reg went on to change his name to Elton John.)

Numbers 6 (No. Tom Guitars) and 7 are actually listed **SEVENTEENTH-CENTURY TOWNHOUSES** ❹; Denmark Street is unusual in having preserved seventeenth-century properties on both sides of the street. It's funny to think that the outbuilding behind number 6 is where the Sex Pistols once lived and where John Lydon drew caricatures of the band on the wall. (According to the official Historic England listing, they survived the refurbishment, but they don't exactly invite you in to check!) Steve Jones said that he used to smash windows and steal guitars next door!

On the other side of the road is number 20, formerly **MILLS MUSIC PUBLISHERS** ❺, where Elton John had a job making the tea in 1965. It's said that Bernie Taupin was sitting on the roof one night, waiting for Elton to get back from an evening out, and was so bored he started kicking the moss off the tiles – giving birth to the line 'I sat on the roof, and kicked off the moss' in 'Your Song'.

Mills were also the publishers who turned down Paul Simon's 'Homeward Bound' and 'The Sound of Silence', saying they weren't commercial enough. Idiots!

Opposite is number 9 (currently a Flat Iron steakhouse). This used to be the aforementioned **LA GIOCONDA** ❻, where Marc Bolan, the Small Faces and many other musicians used to hang out. David Bowie used to sleep outside in his van!

The last building on the right, at the corner, once housed the offices of music publishing mogul **DICK JAMES** ❼. One story says that the Beatles came to Denmark Street with Brian Epstein, intending to have a meeting with a new publisher, but the silly fool decided not to show up – so they duly knocked on Dick James's door instead. He presumably couldn't believe his luck! Whether that story is true or somewhat embellished, Dick James certainly played an integral part in the Beatles' story, helping to establish Northern Songs, which published the work of Lennon and McCartney.

Another story tells of the time Lennon and McCartney were walking past here when they spotted the Rolling Stones in a cab on their way to a recording studio. They hopped in and the Stones asked if they had any songs they could use. Lennon and McCartney replied, 'Yeah, we've got one we were writing for Ringo, called "I Wanna Be Your Man". You can have that if you like!' It went on to be the Stones' second single and their first hit record!

At the end of Denmark Street turn left into Charing Cross Road, cross over to the other side, and you'll find **FOYLES BOOKSHOP** ❽.

This used to be St Martin's School of Art, where the Sex Pistols played their first ever gig. They were supporting Bazooka Joe, who had Stuart Goddard on bass! (That's Adam Ant, by the way.)

Carry on past the Montagu Pyke, a Wetherspoons pub which used to be one of the later locations of the **MARQUEE CLUB** ❾. The Marquee had passed its heyday by this stage, but in the 1990s I did see a band called The Trudy here – they were excellent!

This is Soho we're talking about, so there's no shortage of pubs. Next you'll come to one of three in the area called the Coach & Horses; but we'll shortly be going into a different one instead. (I remember them always having drag shows in this one before Covid-19…I haven't spotted them lately, but these are certainly changing times.)

Before that, though, I need to issue a legal disclaimer stating that the next point of interest is optional and viewed entirely at your own risk! Outside the Coach & Horses you can cross very carefully over to the little traffic island with a boring-looking metal grille. Peer down through the grille and award yourself **points** for spotting a couple of very old street signs, for **LITTLE COMPTON STREET** ❿; that was once the name for the eastern end of today's Old Compton Street. Some will try to tell you that you're looking at a lost underground street, but in fact you're looking at a utility tunnel, and these signs would have told workers where in the subterranean network they were.

Over on the east side of the road you'll see a McDonald's. This is the site of the bookshop at **84 CHARING CROSS ROAD** ⓫, immortalised in the memoir made up of letters between the writer Helene Hanff and bookseller Frank Doel, later made into the film starring Anne Bancroft and Anthony Hopkins.

Continue down Charing Cross Road until you reach the **SPICE OF LIFE** ⓬ on your right. In the 1950s it was known as the Scots Hoose and had London's first folk club upstairs, where legends like Bob Dylan, Cat Stevens and Leonard Cohen all played. These days they still do live music in the basement, where another legend, Lil' Lost Lou, has also played. (She's my sister!)

Turn right into Romilly Street and you will come to another **COACH & HORSES** 🍺.

Well, one really can't pass this pub without popping in for a quickie. It's not quite what it used to be; it was once one of the most notorious pubs in London. The current building dates from the 1840s, but in the twentieth century it became a favourite of actors, gangsters and general nutters. The landlord of over sixty years, Norman Balon, was known as London's rudest landlord –

PUB

Coach & Horses

hence the title of his memoirs, *You're Barred, You Bastards: The Memoirs of a Soho Publican*.

Famous patrons have included the Beatles, John Hurt, Peter Cook, Tom Baker and one Jeffrey Bernard, a writer for *The Spectator*. However, he was frequently so drunk after spending time here that his column would get cancelled with the excuse that 'Jeffrey Bernard is unwell'. This resulted in the pub's interior being recreated on stage in the hit play *Jeffrey Bernard is Unwell*.

He drank vodkas, so I guess I'll have one, too.

Cheers, Jeffrey.

Next door is the oldest French café in London, **MAISON BERTAUX** (13), dating from 1871. It's rather cute inside and good for your Instagram with all their cakes and nice crockery, but we're supposed to be on a music pub crawl, so instead let's turn left down Greek Street and then right into Shaftesbury Avenue.

Looking across to the other side of Shaftesbury Avenue, just to the right of the red door marked 116 (Egmont House), you can see where **DRUM CITY** (14) used to be in the 1960s – this is where Brian Epstein came with Ringo Starr in 1963 to buy a drum kit. Ivor Arbiter, the store owner, hastily designed a Beatles logo to go on the bass drum, and that's what they stuck with for ever after. Arbiter didn't get any money for it except the price of the drum kit – which recently sold for around $2 million. (But he *was* responsible for introducing karaoke to Britain, so he's a hero to me!)

Turn right up Frith Street, past the Curzon cinema.

Cross over Old Compton Street (Balans on the corner does a decent brunch, by the way) and stop outside **RONNIE SCOTT'S** (15).

Do you like jazz? I love 1920s and 1930s jazz, but at Ronnie Scott's – London's most famous jazz club – you will see outstanding performers playing jazz of all eras and genres. In 1970 Jimi Hendrix played his last ever gig here, after which he returned home and choked on his own vomit while intoxicated with barbiturates.

Opposite is **BAR ITALIA** (16), which has been here since 1949 and is a very

Walk 6: Soho | 105

③

④

⑬

⑱

Toucan

French House

useful pit stop on your way home from a night out, since it's open until 5.00 a.m. (That's a rarity in London, I can tell you!) If you want a cappuccino made with an original 1950s Gaggia machine, until recently I'd have pointed you here – but when I last visited they had replaced it. They told me it was just being repaired, but let's see… Italian immigrants and refugees first settled in Soho in the 1860s and then more arrived after the First World War. High rents have slowly driven them out, but you can still see a few surviving Italian businesses clinging on for grim life.

Upstairs is where John Logie Baird bribed a teenage-looking 'office boy', William Taynton, to come up and be filmed on his newfangled device called a television, thereby achieving the accolade of being the first person ever to be transmitted on TV! I always find it amusing, because these days, if you offered a fifteen-year-old boy to come upstairs to your dingy office in Soho, saying 'I'll give you a fiver, I just want to film you,' you'd either get a slap or a visit from the police! Actually, it turned out that the 'office boy' was twenty. That's perfectly acceptable, then!

Oh… Apparently some bloke called Mozart stayed a couple of doors further along – look for another **BLUE PLAQUE** **17**.

At the end of the street is **SOHO SQUARE** **18**, where you might want to look for the memorial bench of Kirsty

PUB

Toucan

Maccoll, who was sadly killed in a boating accident, far too young. 'One day I'll be Waiting There, No Empty Bench in Soho Square.' Cheers, Kirsty.

On the south side of the square stood the seventeenth-century mansion, Monmouth House, home to the Duke of Monmouth (he of the Monmouth rebellion). He was the oldest illegitimate son of King Charles II and it's said that he used to have a hunting cry to call off his harrier dogs. It went like this:

Sohooooooooooooooooooo!!!!!

Which is how the area got its name.

On the western side of the square is **MPL COMMUNICATIONS** **19**, which is Paul McCartney's company. Having sold the rights to the Beatles' music through a terrible error of judgement, he did regain the rights to some of the songs, at least. For a while they were owned by Michael Jackson!

Turn left into Carlisle Street and you'll come to the **TOUCAN** .

Although it looks quite old from the

outside, the Toucan has only existed since 1994. Back in the 1960s the downstairs bar ran a disco called Knuckles, organised by the drummer from the Pretty Things, Viv Prince. After Chas Chandler (bassist from The Animals) brought Jimi Hendrix here in 1966 it started to be the place for up-and-coming musicians to get noticed. Upstairs was a sandwich bar until the 1990s, but the new owners got frustrated by the lack of places to get a good pint of Guinness in London – so they started the Toucan. These days you're likely to hear a rendition of 'Danny Boy' or 'The Wild Rover' randomly breaking out, though every time I've been it's been so full it's had people spilling out onto the street. Must mean it's very popular.

Let me think. I'll have a Guinness, and I don't mean a can of Guinne'ss. That said, if one can do what a toucan can, think what two can do!

Sláinte!

Continue along Carlisle Street and turn left into Dean Street.

Joolz Guides Challenge!!

Somewhere along here, outside one of the shops on the left side of the street, is a nose!

The seven noses of Soho were once thirty-five and modelled on the nose of their creator, Rick Buckley, who protested that there were too many CCTV cameras looking at us all the time and that the government were nosey parkers. So he placed these noses around Soho; it is said that if you find all of them you will become very rich!! (Don't count on it, though. My friend Kai found them all and he's skint!)

Don't mistake these noses for the big one on Meard Street, which you'll come to on your right. That's a red herring!

Actually, the building on the corner of Meard Street is where the famous **BATCAVE CLUB** [20] used to be in 1982, when goth culture kicked off in London. The entrance was the second door on the right just down Meard Street. Musicians like Siouxsie Sioux, Nick Cave, Robert Smith from the Cure and Marc Almond were regulars.

Continue along Dean Street and cross over Old Compton Street again, passing Prowler, where my accountant buys his panties.

Ahead of you is the **FRENCH HOUSE**. Even if you're not ready for another drink yet, we're popping in.

Now, I do like this pub, but I wish it were a little more spacious. I'm sure it's fine for normal people – but I'm two metres tall and often find myself crammed into some uncomfortable corner, or standing with my head poking up above everyone else because we're all so close together.

That said, the French House has an enormous amount of charm. It was opened in 1891 by a German, but at the outbreak of the First World War it was sold to a Belgian, whose son, Gaston Berlemont, was born in the pub in 1914 and continued to work there until 1989.

During the Second World War Charles de Gaulle escaped to London and held meetings of his newly formed Free French Forces upstairs here. To this day it still feels very Continental, with its obsession with only serving half-pints of beer.

I guess I'd better have a half, then, whilst I peruse these photos of famous people who have visited down the years. If you do insist on a whole pint, try coming on 1 April, when you might see Suggs from Madness pulling the first pint of the day!

Santé.

Now return to Old Compton Street and turn left past the **ALGERIAN COFFEE STORES** ㉑, where I buy my coffee. You should pop in, if only to inhale the lovely aromas. They have all sorts of wonderful blends and varieties.

Next on the right is the **ADMIRAL DUNCAN** ㉒.

Many of the pubs and bars around here are popular with the LGBTQ+ community. This one was targeted in 1999 by a right-wing extremist, who set off a nail bomb here, killing three people and injuring eighty-three more. He'd also set off bombs in Brixton and Whitechapel that same month. Look for the plaque outside, in memory of those who died in this shocking and senseless act of violence.

Further along on the left you'll come to **COMPTONS** ㉓, a pub that has been one of London's favourite venues for the LGBTQ+ scene since 1986. It started life in 1890 as the Swiss Hotel. A fellow once told me that it was in here that Cliff Richard decided to change his name from Harry Rodger Webb. It does sound cooler, I suppose.

This claim about Mr Webb does sound pretty likely, because next door is **POPPIES** ㉔ – a fish and chip shop

PUB

French House

Walk 6: Soho | 109

21

Ship

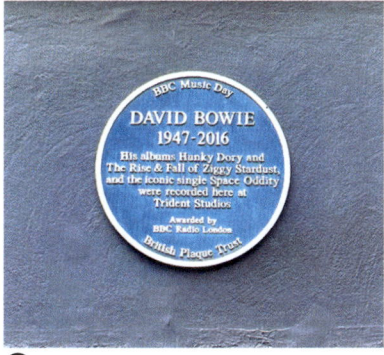

27

29

31

32

which used to be the 2i's Coffee Bar, where the London rock 'n' roll scene started in the 1950s. Cliff Richard was discovered here, and other famous musicians were regulars, including Hank Marvin, Tommy Steele and Ritchie Blackmore. Peter Grant, the manager of Led Zeppelin, was a bouncer here and Lionel Bart (who wrote Cliff Richard's hit 'Living Doll' and the musical *Oliver!*) was a waiter!

They still have some charming photos on the walls of how it used to be.

Carry on past number 61, the site of the recently closed **I. CAMISA & SON** ㉕, a delicatessen that was part of the golden age of Italian Soho – it might have reopened elsewhere by the time you read this! – and turn right into Wardour Street.

I can't help singing 'The London Boys' by David Bowie at this stage:

> Bright lights, Soho, Wardour Street,
> You hope you make friends with the
> guys that you meet.

Wardour Street is not like it used to be in Bowie's time, but just before number 100 you'll see Soho Lofts, which used to be the **MARQUEE** ㉖ in its heyday. One of the most important clubs in British rock history, the Marquee started life in Oxford Street (where the Rolling Stones played their first gig in 1962) but from 1964 to 1988 this site saw some of the greatest bands perform. The very long list of artists to have played here includes David Bowie and the Manish Boys, The Who, Dire Straits, The Police, Status Quo, The Damned, Jimi Hendrix, The Cure, Joy Division, the Sex Pistols, the Stranglers, XTC… So basically everyone… except the Beatles.

It looks ugly these days, so carry straight on until you reach the **SHIP**.

Sometimes the artists appearing at the Marquee would perform under pseudonyms, to avoid too many screaming fans showing up; but if you wanted to know who was playing you could always pop into the Ship, which was a famous rock 'n' roll pub. Because the Marquee didn't have a licence to sell alcohol, most of the musicians would come and get drunk here first – people like Syd Barrett (from Pink Floyd) and John Lennon. Keith Moon was famously barred for letting off a smoky cherry bomb, and the barman was telling me all about some shenanigans that Jimi Hendrix used to get up to in the toilets with the girlfriends of other famous bands' members! He's known to have fallen down the stairs here after some high jinks, too! According to one ex-girlfriend, Linda Keith, Hendrix 'really had no interest for anything other than music and women'.

As with most rock 'n' roll pubs, someone will have a story about something and you'll probably meet other punters here who recall 'the good old days'. But if you're lucky you might spot someone famous even today, like Jason Momoa or Harrison Ford, both of whom have been in for a pint.

Come out of the Ship and turn right. Then turn right again, into St Anne's Court.

Stop when you see the plaque on your left and *bow your head... We are not worthy!!!*

Worship in the presence of the very studios where two of the greatest albums of all time were recorded!!! In fact, not only did Bowie record *Hunky Dory* and *The Rise and Fall of Ziggy Stardust and the Spiders from Mars* here; **TRIDENT STUDIOS** ㉗ also saw the recording or mixing of countless classic songs over the years, including 'Hey Jude', 'I Don't Like Mondays', 'Carolina in My Mind' (my favourite song), 'You're So Vain' and many, many more!

Go back to Wardour Street, cross over to your left and then turn right, into Broadwick Street.

On your left is Sounds of the Universe, which used to be the **BRICKLAYERS ARMS** ㉘. In 1962, when Brian Jones held an audition here for his new R&B band, Mick Jagger decided to show up, with his mate Keith Richards. Yes, this is where the Rolling Stones were effectively born! It's always sad to see a closed-down pub, but at least it's still a record shop, I suppose.

Carry on along Broadwick Street to the junction with Berwick Street. You're at the exact point where the photo was taken for the front cover of the Oasis album *(What's the Story) Morning Glory?* (look to your left).

Keep going ahead, along Broadwick Street, and it's time for a pint at the **JOHN SNOW** 🍺.

As long as you like Sam Smith's beers you should like this pub. It's another one of those Victorian pubs from the 1870s with different sections divided

PUB

John Snow

by panels. To get from one to another you need either to be a hobbit or to do the limbo.

Before going in, just take a look at the **WATER PUMP** ㉙ outside, which is a replica of one which stood a few feet away in the 1850s.

John Snow was an epidemiologist and physician, who famously administered Queen Victoria with anaesthetic when she was giving birth… She was the first monarch to submit to chloroform – rather brave of him (and her), if you ask me. However, Snow's greatest accomplishment came in 1854, when there was a cholera epidemic in Soho.

The received opinion was that cholera was spread by airborne particles – but Snow noticed something. There was a bunch of men on a construction site nearby who seemed to be completely fine; after watching them for a while, he noticed that they only ever drank beer from the pub, whereas all the other locals were coming to this water pump and getting ill. He immediately had the handle removed from the pump and, hey presto, the epidemic cleared up (even though people still weren't convinced for some time after this). I always said beer was good for you!

Well, okay… The builders couldn't have been drinking at this precise pub, because it only opened in the 1870s. So maybe it was another pub, but it makes the story nicer. Back then it was called the Newcastle-upon-Tyne, but a century after Snow had the handle removed they renamed it to the John Snow in his honour – even though he didn't drink!

Better get me a pint of Alpine Lager, before I contract any hideous diseases.

Chin chin.

Now continue along Broadwick Street all the way to the end, where you'll reach Carnaby Street.

Just before turning left, look at the **MURAL** ㉚ on the wall above your head. It shows most of the famous people who've lived in the area down the years. It's a pity the clock hasn't worked for a while, because when it does, every hour Casanova blows a kiss whilst Teresa Cornelys winks back and Karl Marx sips his drink.

Carnaby Street is just a shopping street these days, but it was the coolest place to hang out in the Swinging Sixties and where Mary Quant invented the miniskirt (or so we like to claim in England).

In the Kinks' 'Dedicated Follower of Fashion' this is the location referred to when Ray Davies sings: 'Everywhere the Carnabetian army marches on, each one a dedicated follower of fashion.'

Turn left into Carnaby Street and then right at Beak Street. At the end, cross

Regent Street while turning left and then turn right into Heddon Street.

Again, prostrate yourself! You're about to reach the scene of the photo from the **COVER OF THE ZIGGY STARDUST ALBUM** ③. It's a restaurant now but outside number 23 is where you want to stand to recreate the picture.

The actual photo was taken in black and white, and later coloured in, giving it that weird look. All the bars named in David Bowie's honour are a recent addition since he died. I remember the day well and I actually came to this very place, where many other distraught fans had also congregated, just standing around in slight bewilderment. We never thought the day would come.

By the way, the **PHONE BOX** ③② around the corner is no longer the same one that he used for the back cover. If you look carefully he is in a K2, but it was replaced with a K6. I suppose it's cool in a way that no one can properly recreate that moment any more. Some things are sacred.

Walk to the end of Heddon Street and back onto Regent Street, turning right.

Quickly turn right onto Vigo Street and right again into Savile Row.

Number 3 is Abercrombie & Fitch today, but it used to be the location of **APPLE RECORDS** ③③, where the Beatles played their last-ever live gig on the roof – much to the annoyance of local businesses, who called the police on them and had them shut down! Fools. In Peter Jackson's TV series *Get Back* you can see passers-by congregating on the street to watch.

Now go back to Regent Street. Cross the road and head into Glasshouse Street, before bearing left into Brewer Street. On your left you'll pass the Crown, which is the site of the **HICKFORD ROOMS** ③④, a concert hall where Mozart gave a recital at the age of nine. On your right you'll pass another pub (we're not going into this one, either), the Glasshouse Stores, which I only mention because it still has a bar billiards table…but on my last few visits they've said they have no balls left to play on it, because they keep getting stolen, which is a pity.

Keep going until you reach Great Windmill Street (thus named because of the big windmill which used to stand nearby until the 1690s) and turn right there.

Coming up on the left is Be At One, which used to be the **RED LION** ③⑤ where, in 1847, the Communist League held its second conference, when Marx and Engels submitted their communist manifesto proposals. But we're not going in there…nor are we going to the famous Windmill strip club!

Instead, let's finish opposite, in the **LYRIC** 🍺.

In the eighteenth century this used to be the Ham, which gave its name to Ham Yard. It changed its name in the 1890s to match the name of the theatre around the corner.

With so many pubs owned by the same old breweries it's hard to find a selection of unusual beers in central London, but if you're a lover of ale this is a good place to finish. They have over twenty craft beer and cider taps, at least eight changing beers, and many more bottles.

I have fond memories of hanging out with Woody Harrelson upstairs, after he had appeared in a West End show and invited us up to join him. (Ahem… Did I mention I used to play football with him?) Some sort of altercation broke out, which I won't go into, but it was caused by a fan who had perhaps had a few too many. No harm was done, but my friend and I often laugh about 'Our night out with Woody.'

Cheers, Mr Harrelson. I'll have a Harvey's Sussex Best.

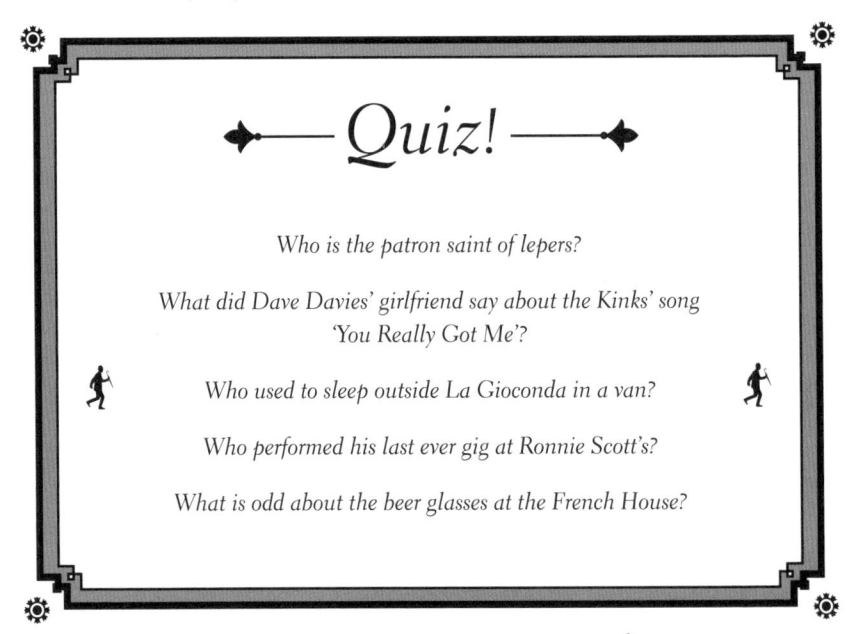

PUB

Lyric

— Quiz! —

Who is the patron saint of lepers?

What did Dave Davies' girlfriend say about the Kinks' song 'You Really Got Me'?

Who used to sleep outside La Gioconda in a van?

Who performed his last ever gig at Ronnie Scott's?

What is odd about the beer glasses at the French House?

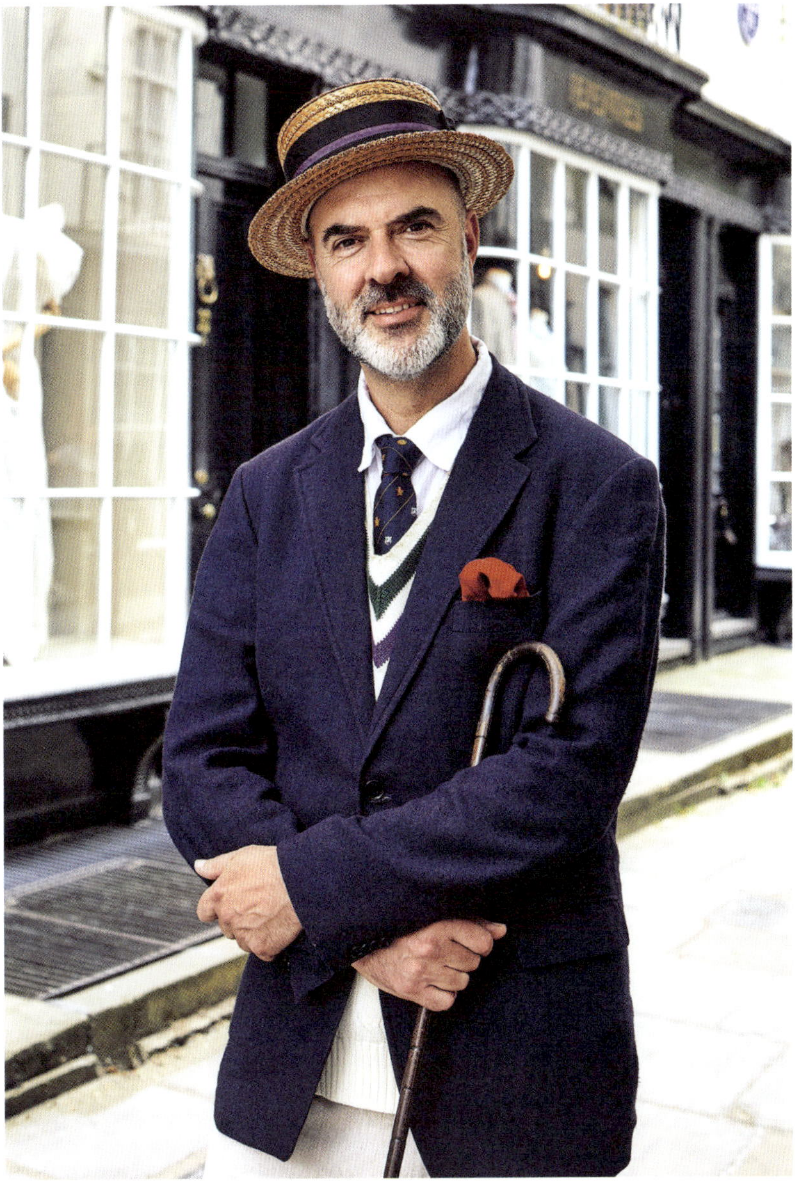

8. Grant Museum of Zoology

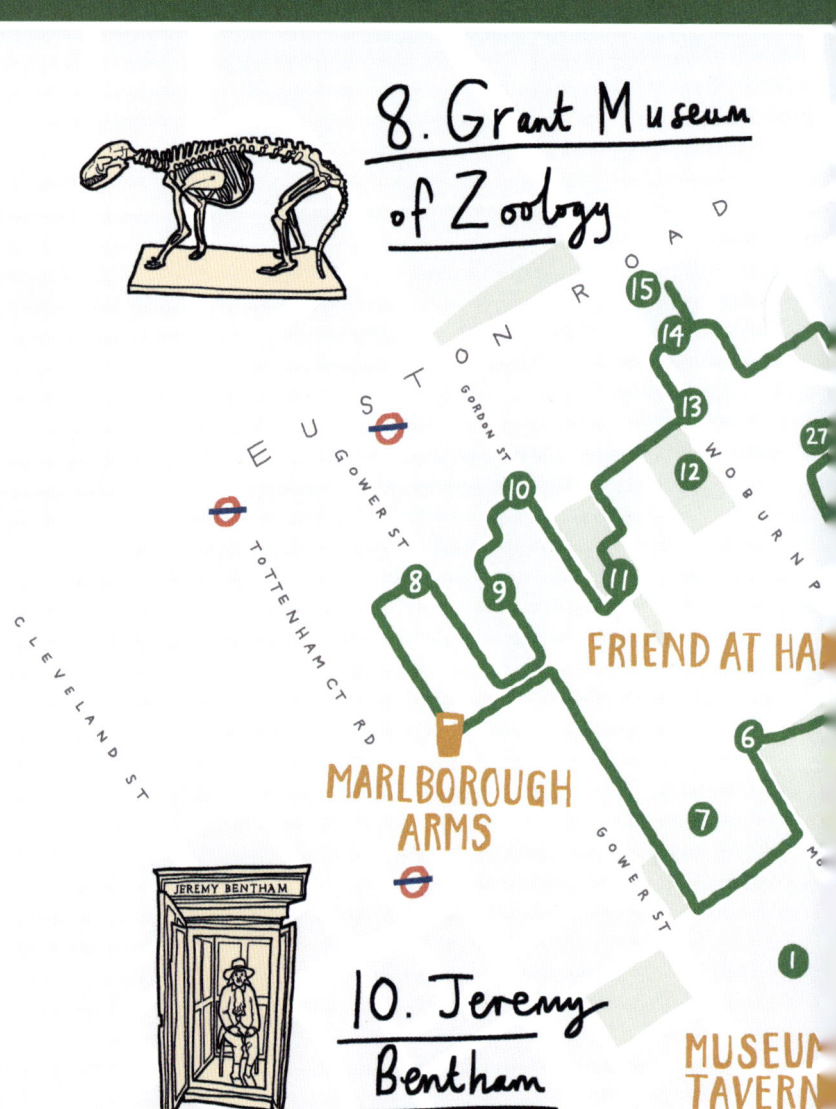

15
14
13
27
12
10
8 9 11

FRIEND AT HA[ND]

EUSTON ROAD
GORDON ST
GOWER ST
TOTTENHAM CT RD
CLEVELAND ST
WOBURN P[L]

MARLBOROUGH ARMS

GOWER ST

6
7
1

10. Jeremy Bentham

JEREMY BENTHAM

MUSEUM TAVERN

NEW OXFO[RD]

20. Baby Things, Mitten

7 BLOOMSBURY

7 A LEAFY STROLL AROUND BLOOMSBURY

DISTANCE
7.9 km (4.9 miles)

TIME
3 hours 45 minutes
with a few pints en route

NEAREST STATION
Tottenham Court Road

PUBS
Museum Tavern; Marlborough Arms; Boot; Friend at Hand; Queen's Larder; Duke; Lamb

PUB
Museum Tavern

What ho! Let's meet at the **MUSEUM TAVERN**, since it's near enough to several tube stations (Holborn and Russell Square are almost as close as Tottenham Court Road) – and it's also where Arthur Conan Doyle used to drink. In fact, in his Sherlock Holmes story *The Adventure of the Blue Carbuncle* this is most likely the Alpha Inn, since he describes its location. (Although some claim it's the Plough on the next corner; from the description in the story it could be either.)

Karl Marx drank here, too, and there are pictures of him inside the pub. This was probably brief respite from his studies in the reading room of the **BRITISH MUSEUM** ❶ opposite, where numerous other celebrities were members too. They still have Lenin's membership pass! The British Museum is superb, by the way, and free to enter; but you probably knew that already.

Let me chin down this Estrella and we'll get going.

Turn right out of the pub and walk along Great Russell Street, with the museum to your left. When you reach the Scotch Shop (at the junction with Bury Place), stop to admire **66-71 GREAT RUSSELL STREET** ❷, which were the first buildings in London designed by John Nash. He was King George IV's favourite architect and designed many of the famous buildings and streets you know, including Regent Street and Marble Arch. Not bad work if you can get it!

Carry on until **BLOOMSBURY SQUARE GARDEN** ❸ where, in 1694, a twenty-three-year-old Scot, John Law, killed Edward 'Beau' Wilson in a duel for which he was incarcerated. However, he managed to escape from prison and absconded, eventually to France – where he was made controller of finances under King Louis XV! Maybe he didn't include the killing part on his CV… or maybe he did, and that's what got him the job!

Turn left into Bedford Place, and walk to the end, where you'll reach **RUSSELL SQUARE** ❹.

The Russell family were the Dukes of Bedford. They owned a lot of land in Bloomsbury, which is why right now you're probably looking at a statue of one of them, called Francis. There's an entrance to the gardens just to the right.

In the summertime this is a jolly pleasant place to eat your sandwiches. Oh, and it features in the first episode of *Sherlock*, where Watson is persuaded by a friend to consider meeting Holmes and moving into 221B Baker Street.

The lovely terracotta building overlooking the square is the Kimpton Fitzroy London Hotel, built in 1898 as the **HOTEL RUSSELL** ❺. The original dining room was designed by Charles Fitzroy Doll and used as the blueprint for the one on the *Titanic*! For some reason they've removed it now, but you can still see a gold-coloured (but actually bronze) dragon on the staircase inside, called Lucky George, which was one of two designed by Fitzroy. The other one (Unlucky George) is lying at the bottom of the Atlantic, in a watery grave with the rest of the *Titanic*.

Exit Russell Square at the north-west corner and earn some **points** for spotting the **CABMEN'S SHELTER** ❻, a nicely preserved and functioning one, if I may say so.

120 | Rather Splendid London Pub Walks

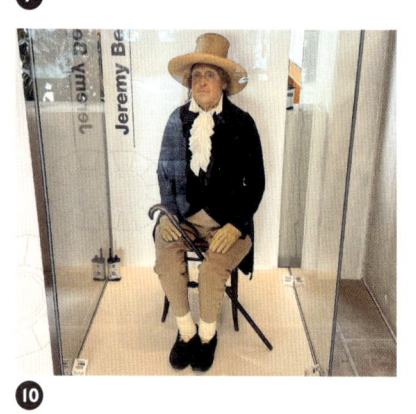

PUB
Marlborough Arms

Turn left alongside the square and then turn right into Montague Place, before turning right again, into Malet Street.

The tall white building on the right is **SENATE HOUSE** ❼, which you may have seen in films like *Batman Begins*, *The Dark Knight Rises*, *No Time to Die* and *1984* (the adaptation released in, er, 1984). In fact, George Orwell's wife used to work here during the Second World War when it was the Ministry of Information, responsible for propaganda, which is what inspired the Ministry of Truth in his novel. They say Hitler was intending to unfurl one of his banners down the side of Senate House after he defeated Britain, and would have done so had we not given him a damned good hiding!

Continue to the end of this leafy street (which is lovely in the autumn, by the way), and turn left at Torrington Place. This is supposed to be a pub walk, so continue along to the corner with Huntley Street and let's nip into the **MARLBOROUGH ARMS** 🍺 for a quickie.

This pub is named after the Duke of Marlborough, John Churchill. During the 1960s and 1970s it was a favoured drinking spot of various exiled members of South Africa's anti-apartheid movement, including Joe Slovo, Dulcie September and Thabo Mbeki (who later became the second president of South Africa).

It so happens that I rather like the ambience in here. A good mixture of tourists, locals and students – who get a 20 per cent discount if they have the right app! It's spacious and has some traditional features like wood panelling and a big painting of soldiers, which looks suitably worn. These Greene King pubs often have sports on the TV, especially rugby and cricket, which isn't to everyone's taste, but I'm fine with it. The sound of leather on willow, polite applause, endless discussions about the LBW laws. Marvellous.

Now cross the road and head north up Huntley Street. When you reach University Street turn right and look for the **GRANT MUSEUM OF ZOOLOGY** ❽.

These little museums are tremendous and often missed.

Robert Edmond Grant was the first Chair of Zoology in England and taught Charles Darwin, who got a lot of his ideas about evolution from Grant! It's a fascinating place with exhibits including dodo bones (apparently humans used to eat dodos!!!), a quagga skeleton and their famous jar of moles!

As if that wasn't enough, there's an equally wonderful little museum around the corner.

Turn right out of the Grant Museum, then right again into Gower Street and then left into Torrington Place, which we came down earlier.

TORRINGTON PLACE

You will now have to enter UCL (University College London) by turning left into Malet Place and asking for the **PETRIE MUSEUM** ❾, which is on your left. (A security guard might try to stop you, in which case you have to state that you are going to the museum.)

The museum is named after the prolific archaeologist William Petrie, although it was founded thanks to his mentor Amelia Edwards, 'the Godmother of Egyptology', who bequeathed her collection to the university upon her death in 1892. It's full of household Egyptian artefacts and some beautiful extant paintings of people from ancient times. My favourite item is the Tarkhan Dress, the oldest woven garment in the world – over 5000 years old! – complete with sweat stains under the armpits. (I guess it must have belonged to a geography teacher.)

Come out of the museum and turn left.

The next bit of the route is hard to describe, so follow the signs through the tunnel and round to the UCL Student Centre, or ask a friendly student where you can find **JEREMY BENTHAM** ❿.

Bentham was a great philosopher and social reformer of the eighteenth and nineteenth centuries. Known as the father of utilitarianism (a doctrine that right and wrong is measured by 'the greatest happiness of the greatest number'), he called for the abolition of capital and corporal punishment. My favourite Bentham quotation is when he described people having natural rights as being 'nonsense upon stilts'!

In his will Bentham asked for his body to be preserved and displayed at the university – so you can actually see him sitting here in a glass box! It's not as creepy as it used to be: students kept stealing his head and playing pranks on their friends by hiding it in their drawers, and eventually it got so leathery and decayed that it was decided to replace it with a fake head. The rest of him is real, although I can't say whether he has anything on under his trousers. In some circles it is suggested that Bentham invented underpants! However, while he did favour a form of 'boxer shorts' and

Walk 7: Bloomsbury | 123

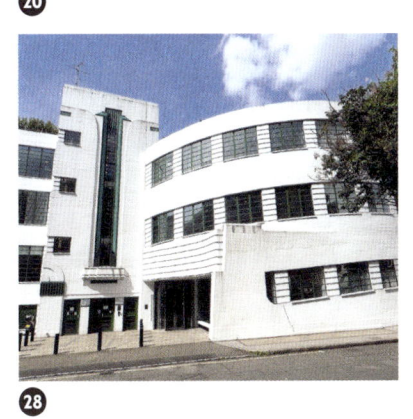

was one of the first to popularise them, the actual invention of underpants is perhaps nonsense upon stilts!

Exit the Student Centre and turn right, following the side of Gordon Square. Turn left at the end and walk into the small **GARDEN** ⓫ within Gordon Square, which is very pleasant. There is an information board here which will tell you all about the Bloomsbury Group of intellectuals, writers and artists who lived in Bloomsbury around the start of the twentieth century. They included E. M. Forster, Virginia Woolf, Vanessa Bell, John Maynard Keynes and Duncan Grant. Demonstrating how low-brow I am by comparison, I should point out that in the 2001 film *The Mummy Returns* this is also where you see a bus hurtle down the east side of the square, pursued by the undead!

Close by, in Boswell Street, Ezra Pound, Robert Frost and Edward Thomas were encouraged to browse in a bookshop where some of them even took lodgings and were visited by Wilfred Owen. 'What passing-bells for these who die as cattle…' The poor fellow died in the last week of the First World War. He would have made it if it weren't for the pesky Hun!

Exit the garden on the east side of the square and turn left. At the northeast corner of Gordon Square turn right into Endsleigh Place and pass Tavistock Square, which has a **STATUE OF MAHATMA GHANDI** ⓬ in the centre.

On the east side of Tavistock Square you'll find the site of (yawn) the **LAST LONDON RESIDENCE OF CHARLES DICKENS** ⓭ – who I really like, but I'm bored of mentioning. (Actually, the houses opposite, on the west side of the square, are still well preserved and his would have looked something like those.)

It is moving to recall that it was here, on 7 July 2005, that a terrorist bomb on a bus killed thirteen people, whilst other bombs were detonated elsewhere in the capital.

Head north into Upper Woburn Place and then turn right into Woburn Walk.

WOBURN WALK

Speaking of Dickensian times, this is a beautifully preserved street from the 1820s which gives a good feel of what shops were like in those days. Funnily enough, this street was tucked away in a discreet corner so as not to disturb the wealthier residents of the Bedford Estate. Looks pretty nice to me! In later times the poet W. B. Yeats (known to locals as 'the toff what lived in the buildings') used to hold meetings here in his rooms at **5 WOBURN WALK** ⓮, attended by the likes of Ezra Pound, T. S. Eliot and John Masefield.

Walk 7: Bloomsbury | 125

At the end it's worth nipping left briefly along Duke's Road, to look at the caryatids (sculptures of ladies holding up buildings in place of columns) adorning **ST PANCRAS NEW CHURCH** ⓯. These date from the same time as Woburn Walk and were based on the Temple of Athena on the Acropolis. St Pancras New Church was the most expensive church to be built since St Paul's Cathedral, which is why it's funny that these ladies look slightly out of proportion. The sculptor, Charles Rossi, spent three years on them – and then discovered they were too tall! So he had to remove a section of their midriffs! I think he's done an okay job of it, but it's still noticeable.

Now return along Duke's Road and follow it round to the left, before turning right into Burton Street.

Then head left into Burton Place and walk across the pleasantly green Cartwright Gardens.

Turn right as you come out of the gardens, and then turn left into Leigh Street.

One of the buildings on the right was where the enslaved Mary Prince was staying in 1828, at the house of slave-owner John Adams Wood, before fleeing and going on to write one of the most important narratives in Black history: *The History of Mary Prince, a West Indian Slave. Related by herself*. Although other slave narratives existed, this was the first to be written by a woman. It was so harrowing and shocking that even the people who supported her had trouble believing her story.

At the end of Leigh Street turn left into Judd Street and then right at Cromer Street. Since this is supposed to be a pub walk, I propose that we – to use a word Dickens (not him again) would like – repair to the **BOOT** 🍺, where there is good company and strong liquor!

What a delight it is to enter a pub that has a dartboard *and* a pool table... and even a yard of ale – **points** to me! The place feels instantly welcoming and whilst it looks like a pure locals' establishment, it has a good mixture of punters. There's been a pub here since 1724 and... am I mistaken, or is Charles Dickens about to feature yet again? Yep, bingo! That ubiquitous man who seems to have lived in every street in London *also* seems to have drunk in every pub. In his novel *Barnaby Rudge* he describes the Boot as being 'a very solitary spot', 'quite deserted after dark' and 'approachable only by a dark and narrow lane'.

> PUB
> # Boot

Thankfully, these days there is less chance of being abducted en route here. Back in 1780, though, it is where plans for the Gordon Riots were hatched. I can just imagine it standing alone in the woods 200 years ago, at the end of a dingy lane with some plotters doing some good old plotting.

Fast forward a couple of centuries and you might have seen Kenneth Williams approaching by the same route, except this time surrounded by student cafés and bookshops. He lived around the corner, as we shall see, and could often be seen playing the piano here.

The staff are lovely, so I'll be back.

There's all sorts of eclectic decoration, including Irish flags and hurling sticks – so I guess I'll have a Guinness.

Cheers.

Return to Judd Street and turn left.

On your right you will pass a blue plaque for **ALEXANDER HERZEN** ⓰, who founded the Free Russian Press here in 1853. London seemed to be a hotbed of Russian activists at the time, and Herzen set up the publishing company to give them an 'uncensored voice'.

When you get to Tavistock Place, head left until you reach **REGENT SQUARE** ⓱. This is where Vladimir Lenin first came to live with his wife, in 1902, before moving to various different addresses in the area. He seemed to like Bloomsbury, as did many of the editorial board who worked on *Iskra*, his revolutionary newspaper.

Just after Regent Square, look on your right for a small gated alleyway; head down this into **ST GEORGE'S GARDENS** ⓲. In the eighteenth century these were created as adjoining burial grounds for two churches, both called St George's (in Bloomsbury and in Holborn) – hence the name. By the end of the nineteenth century they had been converted into a single public park.

Stroll through the gardens to your right and emerge onto Handel Street. At the junction with Hunter Street turn left, and then left again (by the UCL School of Pharmacy), along the top of Brunswick Square, and you'll come to the **FOUNDLING MUSEUM** ⓳, which charts the history of Britain's first home for abandoned children.

In the eighteenth century Thomas Coram, a master mariner, was appalled by the number of children abandoned by their parents. He campaigned for seventeen years until King George II let him open the Foundling Hospital here, in 1739. The museum contains some wonderful artwork and very interesting artefacts, the most moving of which is the collection of tokens which desperate mothers would leave as mementos when leaving their children here, so they could be identified if ever they came back to reclaim them. Oliver Twist had one such token in Dickens' novel: a locket with a picture of his mother, which is stolen from him. The composer George Frederic Handel – whose street we just walked down – held numerous fundraising concerts for the Foundling Hospital, including an annual performance of his Messiah, and was made a governor of the institution as a result.

Outside the museum look for the cute art installation titled **BABY THINGS, MITTEN** ⑳ on the railings. It's easily missed because it just looks like an abandoned child's mitten. It was created by Tracy Emin (who doesn't only recreate her unmade bed with dirty knickers strewn across it).

Return back to Hunter Street. Opposite you is the huge **BRUNSWICK CENTRE** ㉑, which wasn't popular in the 1970s when it was completed, though I've warmed to it. It actually has some pretty cool flats upstairs, as well as a cinema, shops and restaurants.

We're going to walk through it – but before we do, head down to the left to cast your eye at the building on the corner of Grenville Street and Bernard Street. The **J. M. BARRIE BLUE PLAQUE** ㉒ shows the site of the writer's flat at 8 Grenville Street, which is the location he had in mind for the scene where Peter Pan flies in through Wendy's window.

Barrie actually donated the copyright for his *Peter Pan* play and novel to the nearby Great Ormond Street Children's Hospital and they still benefit from it financially today.

Walk through the Brunswick Centre, either from Bernard Street or from where we were on Brunswick Square, and head towards the western exit onto Marchmont Street, which is to your left as you approach the Waitrose supermarket.

Turn right, and as you walk, look at the ground and spot the little metal trinkets embedded in the pavement. These were placed here by artist John Aldus, to represent the **TOKENS** ㉓ left at the Foundling Hospital. I think they're cute.

I really like this street, full of cafés, bookshops and young students full of spunk and enthusiasm for life… The opposite of me, basically.

There are many blue plaques along here including, at 57 Marchmont Street, one for **KENNETH WILLIAMS** ㉔, who lived above his father's barber shop until he was thirty. I like the fact that there is still a barber's downstairs.

Keep going, and on the right you'll pass **GAY'S THE WORD** ㉕, London's first LGBT bookshop, founded in 1979.

Turn left into Tavistock Place, where you will pass a couple more blue plaques. One marks another of Lenin's abodes, at **NUMBER 36**㉖, and the next shows where Jerome K. Jerome (who wrote *Three Men in a Boat*) lived, at **NUMBER 32** ㉗.

Turn left into Herbrand Street.

HERBRAND STREET

After a tall chimney thingy near the junction with Coram Street you'll see a beautiful Art Deco building on your right. This was built in 1931 as the **DAIMLER CAR HIRE GARAGE** ㉘… basically a car park! They certainly don't make them like they used to. Now it's just offices.

Continue straight ahead, crossing Bernard Street.

I know what you're thinking: how come we haven't come across any pubs which are haunted? Fear not, dear reader, as we are about to nip into the **FRIEND AT HAND** for a very swift half.

This has been here since 1735, when that big horrible Marylebone Road was being built to ease congestion along Oxford Street, and yes, Charles *bloody* Dickens drank here, as did Prime

PUB

Friend At Hand

Minister William Pitt the Younger. Apparently, Pitt was prescribed alcohol as a baby and was a raging alcoholic by the age of twelve. The sign on the wall says he drank so much that by the age of twenty-four they made him Prime Minister!

Oh – the ghost? The poor barman, William Thornton, who was nursing a sore head from too much overindulgence, sent the barmaid to fetch more booze (like that's going to help!) and when she returned she found his throat slit! Somehow the coroner recorded the death as suicide. Well, haunting pubs was all the rage, so he didn't want to be left out, I suppose; and if you wait long enough you might see him.

Turn left out of the pub and at the end of Herbrand Street turn left into Guilford Street, noting the **PRESIDENT HOTEL** ㉙. The cover of the retrospective Beatles album *On Air – Live at the BBC*

Volume 2 used a photo of the Fab Four taken at this spot.

Take the next right, down a little alley by the car park ramp, and walk across Queen Square, which contains a **STATUE OF QUEEN CHARLOTTE** 30 (you can get into the gardens about halfway down). At the end of the square, on your right, you'll come to the **QUEEN'S LARDER**.

Sharp, sharp! The king, the king!!!

What a nice little cosy pub this is, set in a listed eighteenth-century house on a pedestrianised street. It officially became a tavern in 1799 but sold ales well before that. The reason it's called the Queen's Larder relates to when King George III began to suffer with mental illness and was staying in this square under the care of Dr Willis. The king's wife, Queen Charlotte (who sounds like a lovely person) rented the cellar beneath this pub, where she stored all sorts of goodies and nice food to spoil her husband and nurse him back to health. When they turned it into a proper tavern they decided to call it the Queen's Larder in her honour.

A swift lager, methinks. What what, hey hey.

Exit the pub and cross Queen Square, passing the **WATER PUMP** 31 which was closed down during the cholera epidemic in the 1850s. Continue into Great Ormond Street, past the hospital. Keep an eye out for the lovely

PUB

Queen's Larder

SIGN 32 on the right at Barbon Close, for G. Bailey & Sons, Horse and Motor Contractors. Turn right into Orde Hall Street, which will lead you to Dombey Street.

It's hard to believe we didn't have council tower blocks until after the Second World War. On your right is **BLEMUNDSBURY** 33, which was one of London's first ten-storey residential social housing tower blocks, built in 1949. It is named after William de Blemund, who in 1201 bought land here – an estate which had originally been granted to Westminster Abbey by Edward the Confessor! Eventually Blemundsbury, meaning 'fortified place or settlement of Blemund', became Bloomsbury.

Turn left into Dombey Street and then left again into Lamb's Conduit Street.

This is a lovely street with a very Continental villagey feel about it. You may wish just to hang out here in the cafés or pubs – but time waits for no man, so lead on, Macduff!

Walk 7: Bloomsbury | 131

㉜  ㉝

Duke 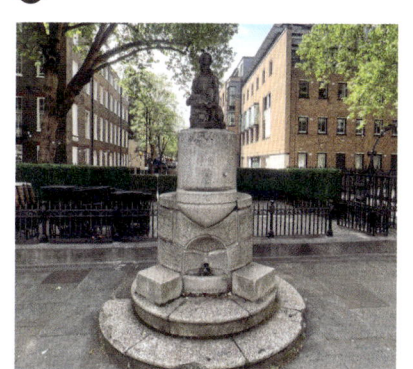 ㊲

㊳  Lamb

On your left is the funeral director **A. FRANCE & SON** (34). This is a 400-year-old business descended from France of Pall Mall, who arranged Nelson's funeral; hence the model of HMS *Victory* and baby Nelson coffin in the window. Well, I guess hairdressers have photos of famous footballers whose hair they've cut, so why shouldn't undertakers advertise whose funerals they've arranged? I see they also do embalming – not that it was necessary in Nelson's case, as he arrived pickled in rum anyway, to preserve him on the route home! Crew members secretly syphoned off a sip here and there, giving rise to the phrase 'tapping the admiral'.

RUGBY STREET

Turn right into Rugby Street and you will pass **NUMBER 18** (35), which was where the poets Ted Hughes and Sylvia Plath spent their wedding night, after getting married at St George the Martyr (opposite the Queen's Larder) in 1956. The only guest was Sylvia Plath's mum, while the groom wore his black corduroy jacket, so it sounds like it was a real jolly affair! Pure romance, folks.

'We came together in that church of chimney sweeps with nothing but love and hope and our own selves,' wrote Plath. Rather more depressingly, she committed suicide a few years later. Gosh, and I'm writing this on Valentine's Day…

On your right you will pass what is claimed to be the narrowest street in London, Emerald Court. Well, a few places make that claim, but in its favour Emerald Court doesn't smell of urine, so I'm backing it.

There are lots of good pubs around here so you can take your pick. I'm going to put in a bit more legwork before my next drink, so I'm turning right at the Rugby Tavern and then left into Northington Street. This will lead you to the Lady Ottoline, a pub named after the society hostess and aristocratic patron of the Bloomsbury Group intellectuals, Ottoline Morrell. It is bright and cheerful with two floors and a private dining room, but I'm not stopping yet! (Incidentally, I like the large windows but the staff all assure me that they hate looking through them at the huge 'street art' quotation on the wall opposite, and I promised I'd report that they find it tacky.)

Turn left into John Street, continuing as it becomes Doughty Street where you will find…*Oh no, not him again!!!*…the **CHARLES DICKENS MUSEUM** (36).

Actually, this is pretty cool. Dickens and his wife moved here in 1837, and it's where he wrote *Oliver Twist* and *The Pickwick Papers*. You can see all his furniture, writing materials and other belongings. I particularly like the writing desk. I jest about him, but he really was special.

After leaving the museum turn left back the way we came, before turning right into Roger Street. Here you'll find the **DUKE** 🍺, where we shall sink a quick one.

The Duke, a cute little pub with a locals' feel to it, was established in 1938, only a few years before a bomb landed in the same street. Luckily it survived, with its beautiful Art Deco interior evoking that era. It's unusual and quite unlike any pub I've been to, with its wooden booths by the windows and tall stools with canteen-style tables. It serves good old pie and mash, fish and chips and other pub grub, too. None of this fancy gastro nonsense.

Come on… Chin it down.

Come out of the pub and continue along to the end of Roger Street, where you turn right into Doughty Mews, which is a very pleasant walk.

At the end turn left into Guilford Street and keep going until you reach a cute **FOUNTAIN** ㊲. The fountain stands between what were once the entrances to the public lavatories; these have now been converted into a charcuterie, so you can drink wine and eat cheese surrounded by the same tiles against which people used to pee. Sounds delightful.

PUB

Duke

Now turn left into Lamb's Conduit Street. Just before we finish I recommend nipping left into Long Yard, just to see the origin of the name of Lamb's Conduit Street. In the sixteenth century William Lambe, a wealthy cloth merchant, donated £1,500 (an absolute fortune in those days) to install a conduit here, which brought water from the River Fleet for the local water supply. All that remains today is this white stone from the **HEAD OF THE CONDUIT** ㊳ – indicating that they didn't know how to spell the word 'public' in those days – plus the fountain we saw earlier, which commemorates the conduit.

Okay, let's retire to the **LAMB** 🍺, which we just passed. Score some **points** by spotting the parish boundary markers above the left-hand door. Hmm… Looks like St Pancras Parish and St Andrew Holborn to me.

This is another very cosy pub, with 'snob screens' to avoid us being overlooked by nosey punters or barmen (score yourself even more **points**!!).

A pint of Young's Original for me.

Down the hatch and…oh, okay – here's to you, Charlie. (Dickens, that is.) No hard feelings.

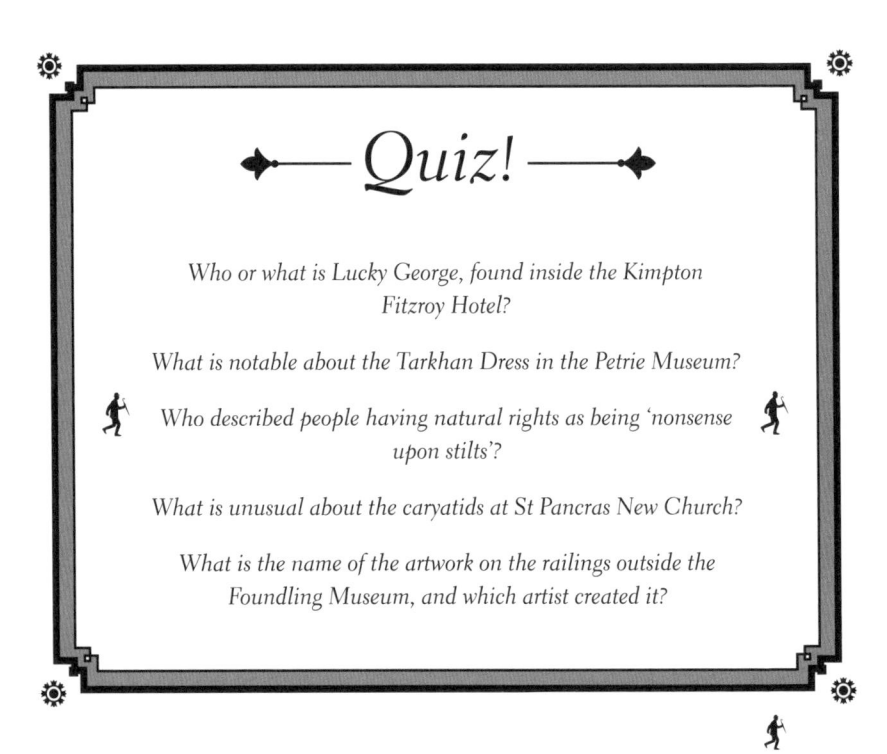

PUB
Lamb

Quiz!

Who or what is Lucky George, found inside the Kimpton Fitzroy Hotel?

What is notable about the Tarkhan Dress in the Petrie Museum?

Who described people having natural rights as being 'nonsense upon stilts'?

What is unusual about the caryatids at St Pancras New Church?

What is the name of the artwork on the railings outside the Foundling Museum, and which artist created it?

Walk 7: Bloomsbury | 135

GRAFTON ARMS

EUSTON ROAD

PORTLAND PLACE

LORE OF THE LAND

8. Number 106

KING & QUEEN

GREAT TITCHFIELD STREET

GOODGE

14. Strand Union Workhouse

OXFORD

11. BT Tower

TOTTENHAM COURT ROAD

GOWER STREET

NEWMAN ARMS

FITZROY TAVERN

21 22 23 24 25

NORDIC BAR

BRICKLAYERS ARMS

BRADLEY'S SPANISH BAR

SHEATSHEAF

8 FITZROVIA

8 A FITZROVIAN FROLIC

DISTANCE
2.6 km (1.6 miles)

TIME
1 hour 20 minutes
with a few pints en route

NEAREST STATION
Warren Street

PUBS
Grafton Arms; Lore of the Land; King & Queen; Nordic Bar; Newman Arms; Fitzroy Tavern; Wheatsheaf; Bricklayers Arms; Bradley's Spanish Bar

What ho! We're meeting in this lovely Victorian pub, the **GRAFTON ARMS**.

It was actually established in 1792 but the current incarnation was rebuilt at the end of the nineteenth century. Fans of political history might be interested to know that the Social Democratic Club used to meet here in the 1870s; one of its key personalities, the anarchist Frank Kitz, went on to become closely associated with William Morris and the Socialist League. I like to think that on sunny days they sat out on the roof terrace.

You'll find an unusually large number of good pubs all close together along this walk, so you might want to stick to halves or slip in the occasional orange juice. The Grafton Arms actually has 'luxurious boutique' bedrooms available upstairs, which I like, because it's how taverns used to be in the old days.

No time for sleeping now, though! Let's chin these down and get started on our walk.

Exit the pub onto Grafton Way and turn

PUB

Grafton Arms

right. Head west and have a trundle around Fitzroy Square at the end.

All these road names like Grafton Way, Fitzroy Square and Euston Road are references to Henry FitzRoy, the bastard son of King Charles II who became the first Duke of Grafton and Earl of Euston, in Suffolk. (In French *fils* means son and *roi* means king, hence 'FitzRoy', meaning son of the king.) A lot of the land around here belonged to the FitzRoy family, although in those days this whole area was mostly fields.

From the late eighteenth century one of FitzRoy's descendants, Baron Southampton, started developing the area. This square was the last part to be finished, making it the edge of London in the 1800s.

The splendid statue in the south-east corner is of **FRANCISCO DE MIRANDA** ❶, a Venezuelan pioneer of Latin American independence who led a rebellion against the Spanish in 1811. Sadly for him, he was captured and died in captivity, although no one ever discovered if his hands were indeed as large or veiny as they seem to be in this statue. He had previously lived here in Grafton Way.

I've always thought that Francisco de Miranda must get very hungry, because he's perpetually staring across at the **INDIAN YMCA** ❷, where you can pick up a pretty good and cheap takeaway curry. Yum!

If you head clockwise round the square you'll notice a plaque for **ROBERT ADAM** ❸, the famous Scottish architect, who designed the southern terrace. Also look out also for plaques for George Bernard Shaw and Virginia Woolf, who both lived at **NUMBER 29** ❹, though not at the same time!

Leave the square at the north-east corner, via Fitzroy Street, stopping briefly to feel sorry for **CAPTAIN FLINDERS** ❺, whose blue plaque is at the corner with Warren Street. He was one of the greatest explorers of the eighteenth century. Although Captain Cook charted the east coast of Australia, it was Flinders who charted the rest of it and first used the name 'Australia' for the continent. Flinders also identified the fact that Tasmania was an island. Unfortunately, on his way back to England he was captured by the French and didn't get home until 1810, by which time everyone was a bit sick of explorers, and he died of kidney failure at the age of forty (on the site of today's BT Tower, of which more later). In the centuries after his death the location of his grave was forgotten, until 2019, when archaeologists working on behalf of the seemingly ill-fated HS2 train line discovered his remains, and his coffin plate, at Euston station. At least he has a mountain range named after him, I suppose, the poor fellow.

Turn left into Warren Street (named after Sir Peter Warren, Lord Southampton's father-in-law) and you'll pass the Smugglers Tavern, where it is suggested that the Great Train Robbery was planned – although I thought that happened at the Star Tavern in Belgravia (see **Walk 5**)! I guess you can plan a robbery in more than one place. It's too soon to stop for a second drink, so let's keep going.

At the corner of Warren Street and Conway Street you'll see an original dairy sign above the café, which has retained some of its beautiful features. **J. EVANS** ❻ was one of numerous Welsh dairy farmers in London who operated from the many little mews streets. Good place for a dairy farmer to work, a 'moooooos'.

Carry on and turn left into Cleveland Street, one of my favourite streets in the area. Somehow it just feels like a little village in itself, with all the shops you need. There's a launderette, a tailor, a fish and chip shop… All it needs is a butcher, a baker and candlestick-maker to be complete!

In 1750 Cleveland Street was just an elm-lined avenue called Green Lane but by 1887 it had all been developed.

This used to be the boundary between the parish of St Marylebone and the parish of St Pancras, before they got rejigged in 1965, but it's still a boundary. If you look at the street signs on the east side of the road you will see 'Camden' and on the opposite side you will see 'Westminster'. (You might still spot some pre-1965 signs reading 'St Pancras', for which I will award **points**!)

Some of the buildings still survive from the 1790s, including **NUMBER 141** ❼, which was home to Samuel Morse, the inventor of Morse Code. I particularly like the doggie sculptures outside **NUMBER 106** ❽, originally a shop dating from the 1830s, with a twentieth-century wrought-iron dragon which would have been the shop sign.

Continue along Cleveland Street and notice the sad sight of the closed-down **BROMLEY ARMS** ❾, with the nice old Charrington's sign, on the corner of Grafton Way.

Carrying on, you'll see another sad closed-down pub, called the **TOWER TAVERN** ❿, named after the **BT TOWER** ⓫, which looms above you.

I knew the BT Tower as the Post Office Tower when I was young (in the intervening years it was also known as Telecom Tower and British Telecom

Tower). It looked so thin from a distance that I thought I could put my arms around it. It opened in 1965 as a telecommunications facility, and Billy Butlin held the lease for a rotating restaurant at the top until 1980. A bomb exploded in the toilets in 1971, leading to the tower being generally closed to the public. However, it still has a rotating platform, and there are currently plans to turn the tower into a hotel – so hopefully it will once again be accessible to bums like me. Weirdly, because of its importance to the nation's telecommunications infrastructure, information about the building was declared an official secret, only being referred to as 'Tower 23', even though everyone could clearly see it! This was so ridiculous that in 1993 Kate Hoey MP stood up in Parliament to say: 'I hope that I am covered by parliamentary privilege when I reveal that the British Telecom tower does exist and that its address is 60 Cleveland Street, London.'

Turn left into Maple Street and left again into Conway Street, where you'll see a curious pointy old **BOLLARD** ⑫ from 1855, which marked the limits of the parish of St Pancras.

Ah, time for a proper drink.

The **LORE OF THE LAND** 🍺 is owned by Guy Ritchie (you know, once married to Madonna, directed *Lock, Stock* and *Sherlock Holmes*, etc.). The main bar downstairs serves beer from Guy's own brewery in Wiltshire, called Gritchie,

PUB

Lore of the Land

and upstairs is the restaurant, where they specialise in seasonal English food and pride themselves on their Sunday roasts. If you can get a seat at the copper kitchen bar you can see the chef cooking over a flame. I don't usually approve of pubs which have turned themselves into restaurants, but it's perfectly acceptable if they leave enough space for people who just want to drink, so this one is okay.

Pip pip. Down the hatch.

Next to the pub is **CONWAY MEWS** ⑬, where William Clayard used to run a cab firm. These mews streets were where horses were kept for milk rounds, hansom cabs and the like. It sounds like Clayard was a strict boss, because in 1863 one of his employees arrived late for work, having drunk too much in the pub the previous night, and Clayard was so annoyed that he smashed him over the head, killing him! The judge seems to have thought

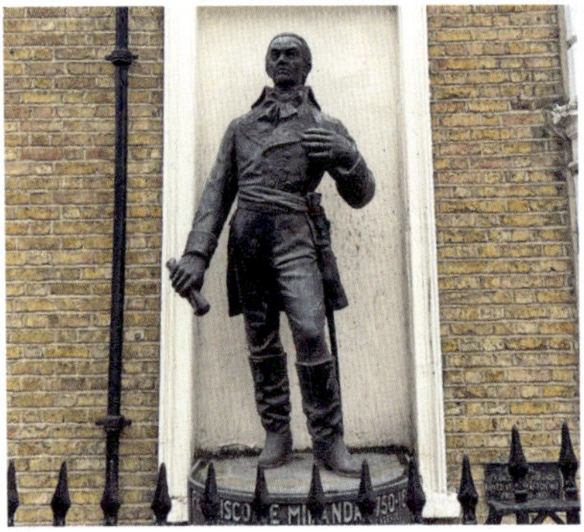

1

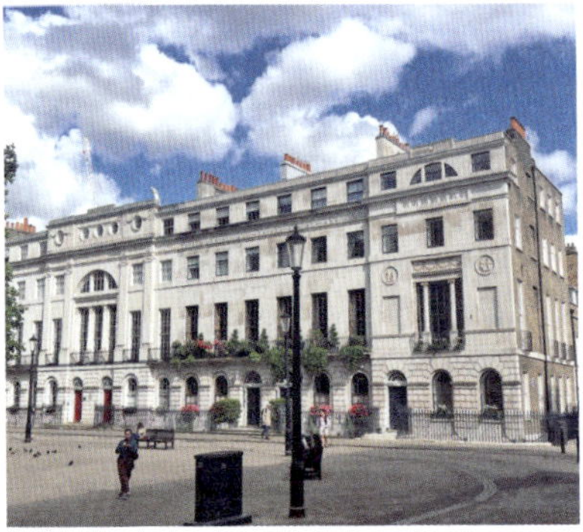

3

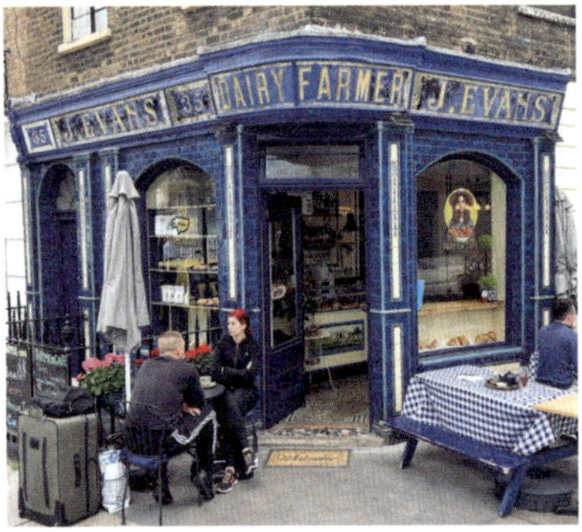

6

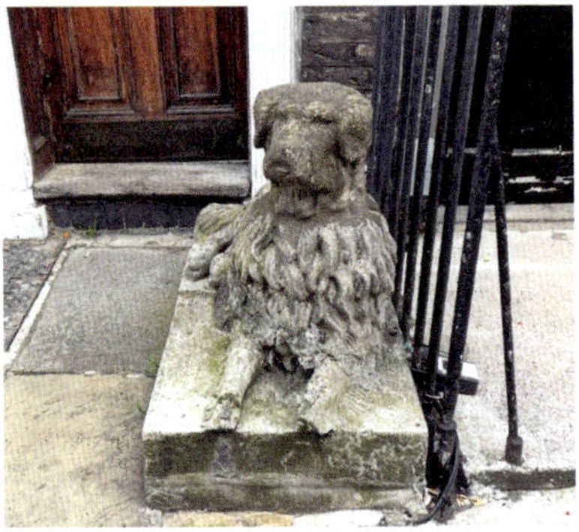

8

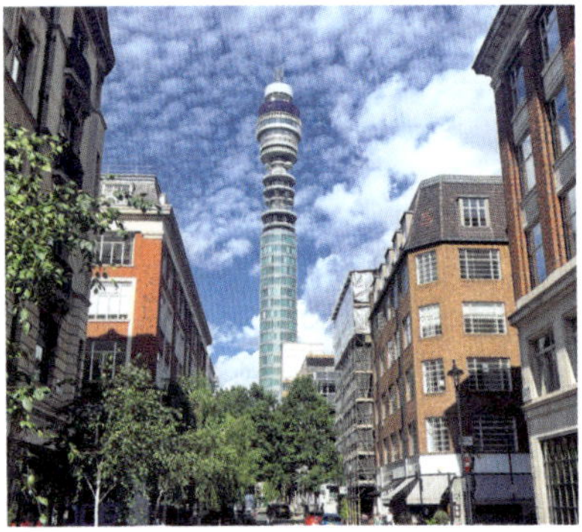

11

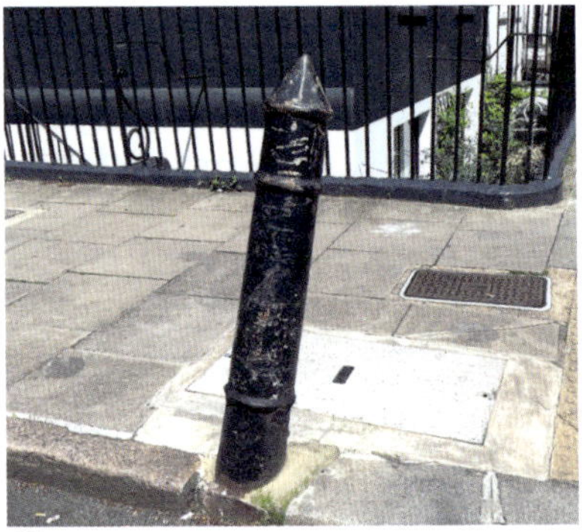

12

it was a fairly reasonable reaction – but maybe a teensy bit over-zealous – so he sentenced him to a measly one month in prison! (You got longer than that for stealing a loaf of bread!)

Return back along Maple Street to Cleveland Street, turning left, and earn **points** for spotting the bollard on the corner of Howland Street reading 'St Marylebone 1828'.

When you reach the King & Queen pub look at the building opposite, originally built in 1775 on a paupers' graveyard. It has been hugely renovated now but originally it was the Cleveland Street Workhouse, or **STRAND UNION WORKHOUSE** ⑭, where conditions were so scandalous by 1855 that 90 per cent of the 500 inmates were horribly sick.

Entering the workhouse was really the last resort for impoverished families; above the door was a sign reading: 'Avoid Idleness and Intemperance'. It is hardly surprising, therefore, that having passed this building every day from yet another one of his childhood homes up the street, Charles Dickens is believed to have had this workhouse in mind when writing *Oliver Twist*.

Now, let's pop into the **KING & QUEEN** 🍺, as they're friends of Joolz Guides! I actually did the signing for my first book in their sister pub, the Red Lion in St James's, and they were very helpful. If you go upstairs you'll see pictures of

PUB
King & Queen

Bob Dylan on the wall, because this was the first place he played a gig outside America. It's also claimed that in the song 'American Pie' by Don McLean, the lines 'When the jester sang for the king and queen, in a coat he borrowed from James Dean' refer to Bob Dylan playing at this pub. Well, it's good enough for me, although I've also heard that this refers to Bob – the court jester and revolutionary leader of the 1960s – stealing the crown from Elvis, who was simply known as 'the King'. Maybe you can argue about it whilst you have a pint. Mine's almost finished, though… Please, sir, I want some more!

Continue along Cleveland Street and glance to your right as you pass the end of Riding House Street to spot the lovely old **GHOST SIGN** ⑮ for 'BUCKNELLS HIGH-CLASS SECOND-HAND FURNITURE, ANTIQUE & MODERN'. Then just after Tottenham Street, on the left, is one of London's quirkiest shops – I'm delighted it's still here. It's based in the same building where Dickens lived, but is now a button shop called **TAYLOR'S** (16), run by Mrs Rose, whose husband bought it from the original Mr Taylor. Taylor's Buttons have been in the West End for over 100 years, and Mrs Rose has made buttons for Queen Elizabeth II, among many others. It's pretty chaotic inside but she knows every button and exactly where everything is.

Roughly opposite Taylor's, at what used to be number 19, is where in 1889 police discovered a gay brothel staffed by Post Office telegraph boys. One night Lord Somerset (equerry to the Prince of Wales) was spotted coming here and a warrant was put out for his arrest! However, the Prince of Wales's son, Prince Albert Victor (the Duke of Clarence and Avondale, and second in line to the throne), became implicated when it transpired that he and the Prime Minister had helped Lord Somerset escape to Paris, and the affair became known as the Cleveland Street Scandal.

Some people think that Prince Albert Victor was actually Jack the Ripper… Weirdly, next door to Taylor's is where Annie Elizabeth Crook worked in a tobacconist, a few doors down from artist Walter Sickert's studio. (Yes, some people also think Sickert was the Ripper!) Anyway, Sickert's son claimed that Annie Elizabeth Crook had a secret love child with Prince Albert Victor, whom she secretly married; and that after she was committed to a lunatic asylum her baby was given to her friend Mary Jane Kelly for safekeeping. Mary Jane Kelly was murdered by Jack the Ripper, leaving behind the baby of Prince Albert Victor! Anyway, the baby was eventually returned to Annie Elizabeth Crook…and whilst no one can confirm this story, it's good enough for Joolz Guides!

Continue and turn right into Goodge Street, before turning right again into Pearson Square. Here you'll see the lovely little hidden **FITZROVIA CHAPEL** (17), formerly part of Middlesex Hospital, which was otherwise demolished. Developers wanted to knock the chapel down, too (idiots), and call this Noho Square. Frankly, that makes no sense because NoHo in New York stands for 'North of Houston' (as opposed to 'South of Houston', i.e. SoHo)… But Soho in London doesn't mean 'South of Houston', so the local residents complained, saying that Fitzroy Place was a perfectly good name. It seems to be known as Pearson Square, too.

The chapel itself is glorious, with a beautiful gold ceiling. The building was designed in 1891 by John Loughborough Pearson, who was also the architect of Two Temple Place near Victoria Embankment, and it's usually open to visitors on Mondays, Tuesdays and Wednesdays (plus one Sunday a month). Rudyard Kipling lay in state here after dying at Middlesex Hospital; but I will remember it as the place where I was showing a nice couple around London when one of them got down on one knee and proposed to his girlfriend.

She said yes… and Joolz Guides was on hand to witness it!

Exit the square via the north-east corner and you'll find yourself back by Taylor's Buttons. This time head straight ahead, into Tottenham Street.

In the basement of number 49, between 1878 and 1902, you'd have found the **COMMUNIST WORKING MEN'S CLUB** **(18)**, where the Bloomsbury Socialist Society met. Karl Marx, Friedrich (Frederick) Engels and William Morris used to meet here frequently – until they were prosecuted for not having an alcohol licence.

Further along, at number 37, is a blue plaque marking where **OLAUDAH EQUIANO** **(19)** lived. Born in Nigeria, he was sold into slavery aged eleven but eventually managed to buy his freedom. His memoir, *The Interesting Narrative of the Life of Olaudah Equiano*, sold so well that it ran to nine editions! He was a Christian, could write English better than most people, was a successful merchant, played the French horn, and eventually became a leading figure in the abolitionist movement. Equiano was buried somewhere behind what is now the American International Church by Goodge Street station. It's a pity the exact location isn't known, so there's no grave stone.

Retrace your steps briefly and then head around the corner into Goodge Place. Here you might find a **MURAL** **(20)** depicting some of the famous people who've lived in the area, including Equiano. I say 'might' because the mural is often vandalised, and has been painted over and repainted a number of times – so whether there's a mural there when you visit is down to pot luck.

Walk along Goodge Place past all the buildings which were famous in the 1840s for housing pimps and prostitutes.

At the end you can either take the short cut down the passage opposite (Charlotte Place) and continue ahead to the Newman Arms on Rathbone Street – or, if you're particularly thirsty, follow me for a Nordic drink first.

From Goodge Place we're turning right into Goodge Street and then left into Newman Street.

Just after Newman Passage on the left, down the stairs in the basement you'll find **NORDIC BAR** 🍺, popular with those younger and hipper than me. Actually, I think I can still swing it with these guys and I've always liked it here. Ultimately it's just a bar, but it does seem to have a jovial atmosphere and the Scandi touches all add to the ambience. Swedish meatballs, a triptych of Max von Sydow on the wall teaching you how to 'Skoal' (or should that be 'Skol' or 'Skål'…?) and saucy pictures on the toilet walls all give it a party-like, almost studenty, feel. Oh, and did I mention it's open until 2.00 a.m. Thursdays to Saturdays? This is a rarity in London, and often spares my blushes when hunting for a place I can simply go to for a beer after 11.00 p.m. (It's so embarrassing when foreign friends come to London and there's nowhere to take them after hours!)

I'll have a pint of Thor's Piss House Lager. (Can't be worse than the usual piss you get served in England!)

Skål!

Now head down Newman Passage (which we passed just before Nordic Bar) and when it bends round to the right you might recognise the location where Terry and Arthur are **HOLDING UP A LAMPPOST** ㉑ in the end credits of the TV show *Minder* (although there's no lamppost there today!).

PUB
Newman Arms

Rather than following the cobblestones to the right, keep straight ahead down the narrow walkway. At the end is the **NEWMAN ARMS**. It's a bit tiny but it's been here since 1730 and, in true Joolz Guides style, it was once a brothel.

Goodness, there are so many pubs in this area you could throw a blanket over them, so I'm just taking a half in this one. The pubs round here were particularly popular with famous literary characters down the years, as we shall see; this one was frequented by Dylan Thomas and George Orwell. In fact, this is the pub on which Orwell based the Proles pub in *Nineteen Eighty-Four*. There's a selection of over ten draught beers, plus a whole bunch of guest beers from around the UK. It's now run by Big Penny, which for a few years had the rights to the Truman's Brewery name (the original Truman's Brewery was founded in the seventeenth century).

By the way, in case you think the bar staff are pouring your pint a bit slowly, it could be because of a joke the landlady made when in mediation with Westminster Council, after receiving

PUB
Nordic Bar

Walk 8: Fitzrovia | 147

Lore of the Land

14

16

17

22

Bradley's Spanish Bar

complaints about drinkers causing congestion outside: she suggested serving drinks more slowly and the council took her seriously, making it a condition of renewing their licence! (How serving customers more slowly could create less, rather than more, congestion is not clear to me – but who am I to question Westminster Council?)

Since it's a bright cold day in April and the clocks are striking thirteen, I'd better have half a pint of Big Penny Lager!

Chin chin.

Opposite the Newman Arms, walk down Percy Passage and turn left into Charlotte Street, which is named after the queen consort of King George III.

On the right is Windmill Street, named after the windmill which stood on the site of the present-day **CHARLOTTE STREET HOTEL** ㉒. (Prior to being a hotel, this building was once used by a false-teeth manufacturer, who purchased the two beautiful listed gas lamps outside.)

Back in 1890, 6 Windmill Street was the headquarters of **CLUB AUTONOMIE** ㉓, a refuge for all Continental anarchists arriving in London. Anarchism was all the rage at the time; they would sit in here and plot their dastardly schemes. In 1894 one member, Martial Bourdin, managed to blow himself up whilst attempting to bomb the Royal Observatory in Greenwich. He survived long enough to be questioned, but didn't give anything away before he died. However, his membership card was found in his pocket… D'oh!

Another pub which attracted the 'Fitzrovia Bohemians', as they became known, was the **FITZROY TAVERN** 🍺, which is now a Sam Smith's pub. This group included George Bernard Shaw, Dylan Thomas and Virgina Woolf, who all drank here, along with the talented Welsh artist and writer Nina Hamnett, who became known as the Queen of Bohemia. The Fitzrovia Bohemians, according to Dorothy Parker, 'lived in squares, painted in circles and loved in triangles.' (Or was that the Bloomsbury Group? Same difference…) Hamnett was friends with Amedeo Modigliani, Ezra Pound and Pablo Picasso, whom she had met in France. She developed a reputation for her bisexual promiscuity and her alcoholism, once dancing naked on a café table 'just for the hell of it'.

PUB

Fitzroy Tavern

Her book, *Laughing Torso*, about her bohemian life became a bestseller, but sadly things deteriorated in later years. She could often be seen at the bar in the Fitzroy Tavern getting free drinks in exchange for lurid tales. In 1956 she died after falling out of a window and impaling herself on the railings below; a rather sad end to a colourful life.

In deference to Nina Hamnett I shall prop up the bar and regale you with steamy tales of seduction from my youth.

Hand me a pint of cider.

Cheers!

Gosh, this is going to be a bit of a fast pub dash now. Come out of the pub and turn left into Charlotte Street.

To your left is Percy Street where, at **NUMBER 4** ㉔, it is claimed that Alois Hitler lived! He was the half-brother of Adolf (of Nazi fame) and rumour has it that Adolf once visited the property in 1912. This is most likely bollocks, but Joolz Guides likes to report rumour and folklore as well as facts!

To the right is the Marquis of Granby, where Dylan Thomas and T. S. Eliot used to mix with arty types as well as rough gangster types. You'd need a strong constitution to visit all of these pubs, so I'll just be visiting a couple of favourites.

Let's head into Rathbone Place, opposite the Marquis of Granby. Just on the right, above the modern-day street sign, is a **BOUNDARY MARKER** ㉕ for St Pancras Parish, dated 1880.

After a while Dylan Thomas got fed up with all the artists at the Fitzroy Tavern and started drinking at the **WHEATSHEAF**, which is where he met his wife. I mean, if he wanted to escape the other artists he didn't try very hard: it's only around the corner and a bunch of others followed him, including George Orwell. Anyway, it's just as well for Thomas that he came to the Wheatsheaf, because in 1936 Caitlin Macnamara, a 22-year-old dancer who had come to London to seek her fortune aged eighteen, was introduced to him here; he drunkenly proposed to her with his head in her lap. (I'm not sure if that's how she intended to make it big… Fnarr, fnarr. What? Come on, there is a comedy club upstairs, after all…)

PUB
Wheatsheaf

They were subsequently married, although it was a rather fractious relationship and he boasted for years about how they were in bed ten minutes after they met.

I'll have half a London Pride.

Now, if you can still see, you may want to drop into former anarchist hotbed the **BRICKLAYERS ARMS** 🍺, just around the corner on Gresse Street. It's another Sam Smith's pub and has the usual Sam Smith's interior. Nice sofas upstairs? Check. Cosy fireplace? Check.

It's sometimes referred to as the Burglars' Rest after a gang, probably from the anarchists' association around the corner, broke in at night and drank the bar dry. Rather foolishly, they fell asleep in the bar and were discovered the next morning with sore heads. I'm surprised it doesn't happen more often, frankly!

Head back to Rathbone Place and continue south until Oxford Street. Turn left here and then left again into Hanway Street.

I don't know why I like this street so much. I suppose it's because it's so close to Oxford Street yet feels a bit hidden. By the 1740s Hanway Street was fully developed; it had been one of the first streets around here, dating back to the sixteenth century. It's named after the eccentric eighteenth-century philanthropist Jonas Hanway, who was the first man in London to carry an umbrella. The umbrella had previously been regarded as 'for ladies', and he was often ridiculed for carrying one! He had the last laugh, though, since they soon caught on…unlike his attempts to use stilts as a way of avoiding the muck and grime on London's pavements!

I recommend finishing in **BRADLEY'S SPANISH BAR** 🍺 – which doesn't seem to be Spanish and isn't owned by Bradley! It's certainly very characterful, with an old-fashioned jukebox adding extra charm.

The premises started life in the 1860s as a sewing-machine manufacturer, but by the 1950s the building had been taken over by a sherry company, which is possibly where it got its Spanish connection. Bradley, on the other hand, was just a regular drinker, so they named it after him.

Weird, because my local hasn't been renamed Joolz's yet!

Anyway, it gets pretty full owing to the small amount of space on offer – so if you can't get in or it's very late you might want to try the options at 22 Hanway Street: Sevilla Mia occupies the basement, with live flamenco music in a wonderfully intimate atmosphere. If you want something more mainstream you can just head upstairs to the Troy Bar, which is another very small bar but open very late, playing disco classics that a man of my age has actually heard of.

Anyway, I've managed to squeeze myself into Bradley's, so I'll have a San Miguel. Salud!

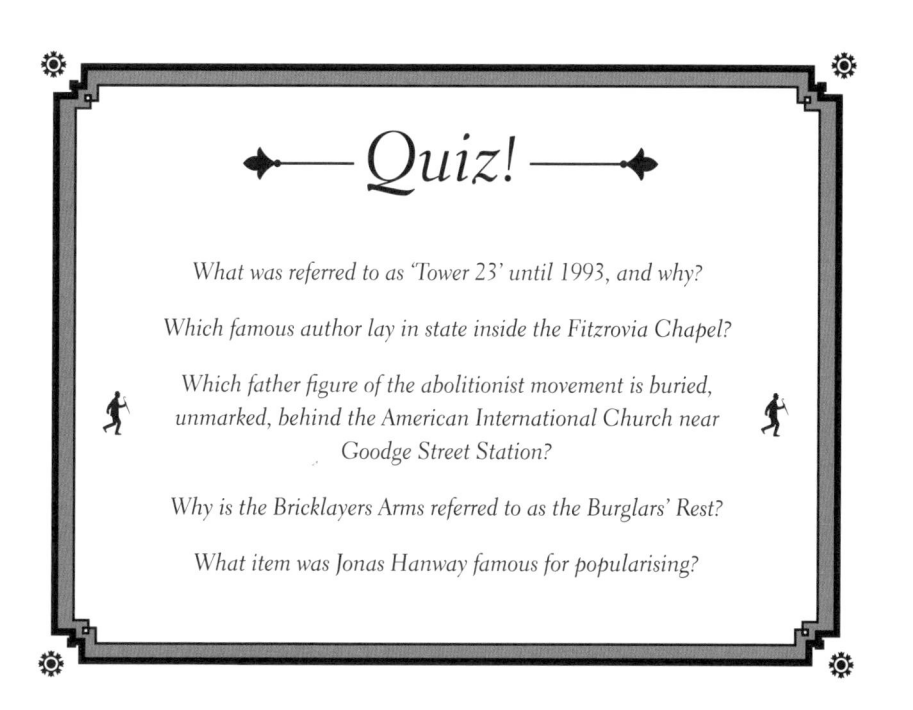

PUB

Bradley's Spanish Bar

Quiz!

What was referred to as 'Tower 23' until 1993, and why?

Which famous author lay in state inside the Fitzrovia Chapel?

Which father figure of the abolitionist movement is buried, unmarked, behind the American International Church near Goodge Street Station?

Why is the Bricklayers Arms referred to as the Burglars' Rest?

What item was Jonas Hanway famous for popularising?

3. Stink Pipes

22. Bell Tower

WOODMAN

BOOGALOO

MUSWELL HILL
MUSWELL HILL ROAD
WOOD LANE
AVENUE R
HORNSEY

GREAT NORTHERN RAILWAY TAVERN

9 CROUCH END

7. Spriggan

9 A CIRCUITOUS CRAWL AROUND CROUCH END

DISTANCE
5.1 km (3.2 miles)

TIME
2 hours 20 minutes
with a few pints en route

NEAREST STATION
Highgate

PUBS
Woodman; Boogaloo; King's Head; Queens; Great Northern Railway Tavern

Pip pip! We're meeting up at the dog-friendly **WOODMAN**. It's conveniently situated next to Highgate tube station and, more to the point, it was the venue where I watched England agonisingly lose a penalty shoot-out against West Germany in the 1990 World Cup semi-final. If it's a nice day you can sit in the beer garden, which is a good size even if it sits on a pretty busy road.

The Woodman dates from 1810, when Archway Road was opened as a bypass for the mail coaches which couldn't make it up Highgate Hill. These days it has a strong focus on food – they talk up their shepherd's pies and their seafood shack.

PUB
Woodman

Come on then. Chop, chop! Let's finish these pints and get on with it.

Turn right outside the pub, and then right again into Wood Lane at the King George V post box (**points** to me for spotting it!), before taking the steep path on your right down towards the tube station.

There should be enough gaps in the trees on your right to just make out the abandoned **HIGHGATE ABOVE-GROUND TRAIN STATION** ❶, which is one of the most beautifully preserved in London – but annoyingly, you can't get to it! Depending on the season, you might get a better view of it from the car park near the Archway Road exit to the tube.

From the 1860s the railway station served the trains which travelled from Finsbury Park to Edgware, but with the tube's Northern Line opening it was no longer needed, and closed to passengers in 1954. Freight trains did continue to run until 1970 but since then it has sat there as a creepy ghost station, which always fascinated me as a child.

At the bottom of the path you'll find yourself in Priory Gardens, outside the exit where you might have arrived by tube at 'Highget', as the lady pronounces it on the tannoy. She is so posh that she is unable to pronounce it 'High–gate'. 'This station is Highget,' she says, as you pull into the station.

Did you know…? American talk show host Jerry Springer was born on the platform of Highgate tube station during a bombing raid in the Second World War!!! Many tube stations doubled up as bomb shelters during the Blitz, so this was by no means unusual.

Je-rry, Je-rry, Je-rry!!

Walk down Priory Gardens as far as **NUMBER 26** ❷, where Bridget Hitler (Adolf's half-sister-in-law) once lived. Remember Alois Hitler from **Walk 8**, Adolf's half-brother? Well, he was a petty criminal who left home at fourteen, moved to Ireland, met Bridget and then eloped with her to England. He later ran away to Austria, faked his own death and was prosecuted for bigamy, leaving Bridget penniless – so she had to take lodgers here, turning it into a hotel.

In a newspaper interview she said: 'Nowadays it's a bit embarrassing being Mrs Hitler. Mind you, I have nothing to say against the Nazis as I've found them.' She even took the credit for persuading Adolf Hitler to trim his moustache into the famous Charlie Chaplin style! I don't know if this increases or decreases the value of the property!

As the road curves round to the right at the end look out for the **DOUBLE STINK PIPES** ❸. Yay! **Double points**!!! You rarely see two together. I like to joke that it's because the people of Crouch End have particularly smelly poo.

156 | Rather Splendid London Pub Walks

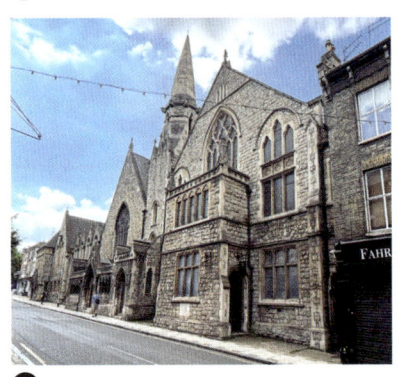

PUB
Boogaloo

Turn right at the end and follow Shepherds Hill back up to Archway Road.

After turning left into Archway Road let's nip into the **BOOGALOO** 🍺. Originally this was an old man's pub, the Shepherd, but in 2002 the landlord, Gerry O'Boyle, opened it up as the Boogaloo and attracted live acts such as Pete Doherty, Suggs and Chrissie Hynde. Celebs like Kate Moss would come and hang out here, too. I once saw a documentary about Shane MacGowan where he was in here with Johnny Depp, which might explain why there are photos of him on the wall. (Gerry O'Boyle was previously the landlord of another favourite Shane MacGowan haunt, Filthy McNasty's, which I mention in my first book.) On Saturday nights it can get quite busy as they usually have a DJ playing tunes that I actually quite like, for a change – 60s, 70s and 80s, amongst other favourites – whilst varied pub-goers of all ages get up for a dance, except me! Once a year my friend Ralph will be found in here trying to get me to dance, and I will spend the whole evening stubbornly resisting whilst all our mates tell me what a miserable git I am.

The Boogaloo even has a radio station, which started after they cleared out the garden shed and turned it into a studio. They were recently voted London's best online radio station!

I'll have a pint, but I'm not dancing! Cheers.

Turn left down Holmesdale Road and enter the **PARKLAND WALK** ❹ on your left. Where the railway tracks used to be is now a lovely nature reserve. On your left you can see the tunnels leading to the old Highgate station, but it has now been turned into a bat sanctuary. A bat cave! But it smells too much of marijuana so we're walking right, following the old railway route. As you proceed you will see remnants of the track and brackets that used to carry cables.

The Parkland Walk leads all the way to Finsbury Park – but we're not going to the end.

If you're a Pink Floyd fan, briefly leave the walk by the first exit on the right, at Northwood Road. Come back under the bridge and turn left onto Claremont Road, following it round as it becomes Stanhope Gardens. **NUMBER 39** ❺ was where Syd Barrett, Roger Waters, Nick Mason and Rick Wright lived in the 1960s. Their landlord was their college tutor, Mike Leonard; one of the early names for the band that became Pink Floyd was Leonard's Lodgers!

Back on the Parkland Walk, keep going straight until you reach another abandoned station, **CROUCH END** ❻, which served the area from 1867 to 1954. I like to stand on the platform singing 'Waiting for the train that never comes' from the Madness song 'Ghost Train'.

Just beyond the station you'll see some graffiti and a man jumping out of the wall! He is actually a **SPRIGGAN** ❼, from Cornish folklore. Kids used to dare each other to walk between the bridges along the track and beware of the scary goat man who used to roam here, haunting the area. He was probably just a flasher, if you ask me! I wonder if that's what inspired Stephen King to write his supernatural story 'Crouch End', after he got lost here on the way to his friend's house.

Take the sloped path leading to the footbridge above (the path is behind you when you're facing the spriggan). Loop around and back over the Parkland Walk using the bridge (the spriggan will now be on your right). Turn left at the end of the bridge, and then follow Vicarage Path.

As you emerge onto Haslemere Road you'll be just behind **COLERIDGE PRIMARY SCHOOL** ❽, over to your left, which you can have a quick look at if you like. This used to be Hornsey College of Art, attended by such famous people as Anish Kapoor, Ray Davies and Adam Ant. Gillian Anderson used to be a pupil at Coleridge Primary School... That's Scully from *The X-Files*!

However, we're turning right at the end of Vicarage Path, to head along Haslemere Road past **FRANK MATCHAM'S HOUSE** ❾. He was the bloke who designed many famous London theatres around the start of the twentieth century, including the Hippodrome and the Hackney Empire. Turn left onto Crouch Hill, where you will get a lovely view of Alexandra Palace in the distance.

NUMBER 135 ❿ was the residence of the famous Mr Trebus, whose story was documented in the BBC's *Life of Grime*. After his wife and kids moved out in 1981 he became one of the world's biggest hoarders. It got so bad that the council started putting up scaffolding to make the place safer, but he kept removing it. He dug trenches, built ponds and collected so much junk that he had to climb in and out using ladders, right up to the sprightly age of eighty!

Eventually, the council managed to move him out to a care home and he died not long after. Poor fellow. He was fine in his mess!

Further down the hill you'll see a church, which is actually **THE CHURCH STUDIOS** ⓫, started by Bob Bura and John Hardwick, who more or less invented stop motion animation, having worked on children's TV shows such as *Captain Pugwash* and *Trumpton*.

Later the studios were taken over by Dave Stewart of Eurythmics, who used them to record 'Sweet Dreams' and many other hits. In 2004 the studios were bought by singer-songwriter David Gray, who in turn sold them in 2013 to record producer Paul Epworth. Musicians who have recorded here include Adele, Madonna, Coldplay, Depeche Mode, Beyoncé and Jay-Z.

There's a lovely story about Bob Dylan when he was recording here (although I don't know if it's true). Dave Stewart said, 'Come to my house first,' so the taxi driver dropped Bob Dylan off at what he thought was the right address and a lady answered the door.

'Is Dave in?' asked Bob.

'No, he's at the shops. You can wait if you like – he'll be back in twenty minutes.'

Later, a bloke called Dave, who was a plumber, came home and said, 'Hi, darling! Any messages for me?'

To which his wife replied, 'No, but Bob Dylan's in the kitchen having a cup of tea!'

Do you think it's true? The answer, my friend, is blowin' in the wind.

By the way, if you're peckish, **DUNNS BAKERY** ⓬ (coming up on the right) is one of my favourites. I'm so jealous of people in Crouch End having a proper bakery here. I like their doughnuts and Bath buns, bread, cakes, sausage rolls… everything! And if it was good enough for Bob Dylan to buy a cheese sandwich here, it's good enough for me!!!!

Across the road, on Crouch End Hill, is the **KING'S HEAD** 🍺. There's been a pub here since 1662, but it only became known as the King's Head in 1812. We shall rest our feet here for a moment whilst I reminisce.

Back in 1997 it was here that I performed my first ever stand-up comedy, in which I wasn't entirely terrible. The pub is famous for its 'try-out' nights, for comedians doing new material or just starting out. It's one of the oldest in Britain, having opened after the success of the Comedy Store in Leicester Square. Founded by Huw Thomas and Peter Grahame it has played host to many of my favourite comedians down the years, including Eddie Izzard, Jack Dee, Robbie Coltrane, Rowan Atkinson, Alexei Sayle, Paul Merton… and Joolz!

Turn left out of the pub and walk towards the clock tower.

On your right is the old **HORNSEY TOWN HALL** 13, built in 1935, which has featured in *The Crown*, *Killing Eve* and also *Bohemian Rhapsody*. Freddie Mercury even played one of his first gigs here.

You'll be amazed to hear that it's been sold to some faceless conglomerate who is turning it into luxury 'aparthotel' units now. That's even worse than luxury flats!

Look out also for the **RELIEFS** 14 by Arthur Ayres, under the windows at Barclays Bank, depicting various uses of gas. This used to be the Hornsey Gas Company, intended to compete with the Electric Company, which was opposite. Fans of TV's *Peep Show*, starring David Mitchell and Robert Webb, might also recognise this location from the programme's opening sequence.

Continue to the **CLOCK TOWER** 15, which was erected in 1895 on the site of the original cross which stood here. The Middle English name 'Crouch End' actually means 'Cross End'; the cross marked the boundary of the parishes of Hornsey and Topsfield. On 11 November 1918 a fiddler played at the foot of the tower to mark the end of the war – but these days it's just a convenient place to meet, what with Crouch End having no tube station. This is rather an inconvenience when you have to meet someone here, but it's probably what contributes to its villagey feel. Lots of parents, pilates and decaf lattes.

In 1936 public toilets were opened beneath the tower, causing uproar by having signs reading 'Men' and 'Women' rather than 'Ladies' and 'Gentlemen'! They closed in the 1990s, along with many others, meaning nowadays you either have to pee your pants or sneak into a pub. (There's always the option of a McPiss with Lies, I suppose.)

Take the right fork and head up Topsfield Parade.

On the left you'll pass what is now a Virgin Active Gym. This building originally opened in 1897 as the **QUEEN'S OPERA HOUSE** 16, later becoming the Crouch End Hippodrome, where it is said that Laurel and Hardy once performed, amongst others. Alas, following bomb damage during the Second World War it never returned to its former glories.

Continue a little further and, for Heaven's sake, let us repair to the **QUEENS** for a Harold or two. (Harold Pinter = Pint.)

I must say, this is my favourite pub in the area, just for the interior, described by the architectural historian Pevsner as 'one of suburban London's outstanding grand pubs'.

Walk 9: Crouch End | 161

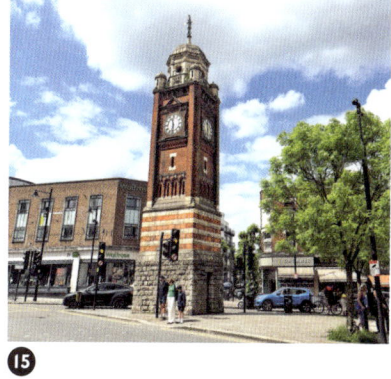

⓮

⓯

Queens

㉑

㉒

Great Northern Railway Tavern

PUB

Queens

It was built in 1899 as the Queen's Hotel, for the diamond jubilee of Queen Victoria, to cater for visitors to the nearby Alexandra Park racecourse, and to go with the Queen's Opera House. Neither of those exist any more – but for once it's the pub that has survived and avoided being turned into flats! Historic England describes it as 'a pinnacle of late-Victorian pub design' with 'exceptional joinery and glass'. There are four spacious sections around the central bar, and everywhere you look there's a mahogany fitting or ornate ironwork, making it one of London's grandest gin palaces.

A pint of Brunning & Price Traditional, please. I might grab some food here, too – it's pretty decent pub grub.

Your very good health!

Turn right out of the Queens, and as Topsfield Parade becomes Tottenham Lane we're actually now heading into Hornsey. You'll pass the **ARTHOUSE CINEMA** **17**, which used to be the Salvation Army Citadel; I rather like the sign indicating that the stone outside was laid by Silas Kitto Hocking in 1912. He was one of the first authors to sell a million books in his lifetime and I am rather ashamed to admit I have never heard of him!

Now, many of you might be *Shaun of the Dead* fans, and it is indeed a fine film. It's a little out of the way, but if you like, you could turn right at Nelson Road and walk up to **NUMBER 83** **18**, on the junction with Weston Park. This is the house from which Simon Pegg's character emerges when he is a bit hungover. Surrounded by zombies, he wanders to the newsagent round the corner without even registering the mayhem surrounding him.

However, we're carrying on straight up Tottenham Lane.

If you're getting thirsty already you could drop into McCafferty's Bar now for a pint of Guinness; otherwise carry on until you reach the **LANE CAFE** **19**

TOTTENHAM LANE

on the right, which you might recognise from the cover of the album *Working Man's Café*, by Kinks frontman Ray Davies. It's not an especially well-known album, but it makes sense because just a little further along, at 84 Tottenham Lane, is **KONK STUDIOS** (20). Owned by Ray Davies, Konk was originally established as the Kinks' private studio, but many other bands have also recorded here, including the Bay City Rollers and the Bee Gees. I once saw the great Lil' Lost Lou perform here, too! (She's my sister.)

Carry on following the curve of the road and you'll come to a building which, at the time of writing, is an empty brick-edged showroom. Petrolheads will be fascinated to learn that in the 1950s this was **THE ORIGINAL LOTUS SHOWROOM** (21) – there's a small plaque on the side of the building next to the entrance to a complex of warehouses and self-storage facilities. Colin Chapman, born in 1928, was the founder of Lotus and his dad used to run the Railway Hotel next to Hornsey Station, while Colin and his mates used to muck around building cars in the stables behind the pub. He was a pioneer of building lighter-weight cars that were less clunky and Team Lotus went on to win seven Formula One championships in the 1960s and 1970s.

Turn left into Ribblesdale Road, cross Church Lane, and walk up the little path to the right until you reach St Mary's Churchyard – and behold the beautiful fifteenth-century **BELL TOWER** (22), the oldest building in N8! There has actually been a church here since the thirteenth century, but a bell tower wasn't added until around 1500, after someone left some money in their will for the purpose.

In the 1830s it was decided to knock down the old church and build a new one, but they left the tower standing. However, owing to the expanding Hornsey population, the new church became too small and got taken out of use in the 1880s, eventually being demolished twenty years later…but they still kept the tower! Every now and again the tower is open and you can go up inside, but you'd have to check with them when that is, as it's only a few times a year.

One rather unusual sight in the churchyard is the **GRAVE OF HARRIET LONG AND JACOB WALKER** (23), both lying interred together. The inscription reads:

> JACOB WALKER
> A NATIVE OF VIRGINIA
> IN AMERICA THE
> FAITHFUL SLAVE
> IN ENGLAND THE
> FAITHFUL SERVANT
> OF
> HARRIET AND GEORGE LONG
> AND AN HONEST MAN
> DIED AT HIGHGATE
> ON THE 12TH OF AUGUST 1841
> IN THE 40TH YEAR OF HIS AGE

It's most unusual to see a mistress buried with her servant like this, but it's thought that Jacob Walker was an enslaved member of the household of Harriet Long's previous husband in Virginia. When she married George Long they moved to London (Jackson's Lane, to be precise), bringing Jacob with them. Slavery was by this time illegal in England so he was described on the 1841 census as a 'male servant'.

It was suggested that Jacob was so upset about Harriet's death that he was found dead on her grave two days later, so they decided it would be convenient just to open it up again and pop him inside! A bit harsh! This was tinged with untruth, though…

Jacob did in fact die two months later than Harriet, after he had received a smallpox vaccination. Before I start any conspiracy theories: he died of smallpox, so it might have been that which killed him, if he contracted it before he was vaccinated. Who knows? Anyway, George Long, Harriet's husband, obviously saw fit to bury Jacob with his wife, so he must have been a much respected and loved member of the household, since George obviously footed the bill to pay for the headstone.

Now leave the churchyard by the north entrance and cross over the High Street to the **GREAT NORTHERN RAILWAY TAVERN**, outside which you'll get **points** for spotting a Metropolitan Drinking Fountain and Cattle Trough Association horse trough, next to a drinking fountain for humans – neither of which work, naturally!

PUB
Great Northern Railway Tavern

We want to get inside this pub, don't we? It was built in 1897 by the same person who designed the Queens. John Cathles Hill was a Scottish architect who became a prolific developer of north London. Another one of his pubs, which is a real beauty, is the Salisbury Hotel on Green Lanes, but it isn't on this walk. The sheer amount of development in suburban London at the end of the nineteenth century made him a rich man, but he ended up borrowing a bit too much and became bankrupt by 1912. Ain't that just the way it is…

Since it's a Fuller's pub, I'll have a pint of Seafarers.

Tally ho!

— Quiz! —

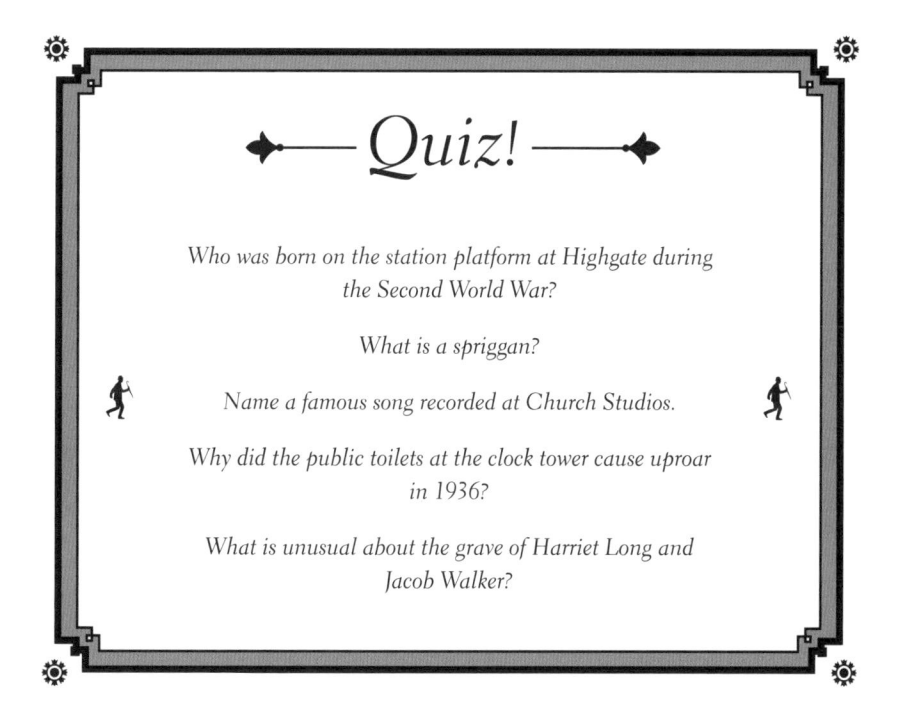

Who was born on the station platform at Highgate during the Second World War?

What is a spriggan?

Name a famous song recorded at Church Studios.

Why did the public toilets at the clock tower cause uproar in 1936?

What is unusual about the grave of Harriet Long and Jacob Walker?

✦ PUB RULES ✦

As you might expect in a city with nine million people, everybody will have their own ideas about what constitutes a good pub environment and how one should behave. Opinion is divided on everything from whether dogs should be allowed to how much attention should be paid to the soft furnishings.

Therefore I have consulted with various friends of Joolz Guides, all of whom have contributed to my videos over the years, to compile a list of rules which you might wish to consider – but might not necessarily agree with! What struck me on asking everyone was how aggressive they suddenly became in their answers! I have tempered down their opinions here, but just imagine a few swear words thrown in and dishes being chucked. At least you will be prepared, in case you end up drinking with someone similar!

THE RULE OF TED

This rule will be familiar to readers of my first book. If you are wandering around looking for a pub to go to but are in an unfamiliar area where you do not know the pubs, just go to the first one you come to. Don't take one look at it and think: 'I know, I might be able to find a nicer one.' This usually results in traipsing around aimlessly for ages, when you could have been happily settled in the first one.

THE RULE OF RALPH

Ralph's rule states that if you arrive at the pub to meet someone and they are already there, the person who is already in the pub must offer to buy a drink for the newcomer. (I'm not sure I like this rule, as it can backfire heavily. Ralph came a cropper recently when I arrived with a couple of friends and they both wanted complicated, expensive cocktails. He was off the alcohol, too. Gutted!)

THE RULE OF JOANNA

If you are sending someone to the bar to get you a drink, make sure you are specific with your order. Tell them exactly what type of gin you want. As Joanna puts it: 'Don't leave me having to answer questions from the bartender about whether you want dark or light rum. How should I know!?'

THE RULE OF DAVE

This rule is inspired by the comedian Dave Gorman. If it's really busy and you're trying to get served (even if you are three rows back), try to get your hand on the bar and communicate your need for a drink by displaying a crisp twenty-pound note provocatively in your fingertips, while nonchalantly maintaining conversation with your companion. (But never fold it length-ways!) This will increase your chances of getting served next. It doesn't work as well with a card – that's why pubs should always accept cash!

THE RULE OF LIL' LOST LOU

If you want to avoid hordes of kids, make sure you choose a pub that doesn't serve food. A secondary rule is that in order to be an authentic boozer, a pub must have tall stools at the bar. If it doesn't then it's a restaurant and not a pub. Preferably it should have a pool table and dartboard too. (Lou likes a salt-of-the-earth pub. She'd probably favour sawdust on the floor, too!)

THE RULE OF HARRY

What ho, barkeep! In this land of tea and crumpets, tipping at the bar is optional, not a blinkin' obligation! This ain't America, you know. Here's a tip: truly exceptional pint-pulling may earn rewards. Standing over us with the card machine, eyeing the gratuity button, doesn't.

THE RULE OF JOOLZ

If a pub is serving apple or rhubarb crumble for dessert they must also (on pain of death) offer custard, not just ice-cream!! I get it, it's easier to serve ice cream and some people want that… but frankly, I don't care if it's just instant custard that they bought from the supermarket, I want custard with my crumble, dammit! (Stamps foot…)

BULL & LAST

23. Sun Fire Plaque

GORDON

AGINCOURT RD

21. Fire Station

HAVERSTOCK HILL

GK

MALDEN ROAD

4. Public Baths

PRINCE OF WALES

10 KENTISH TOWN

- BOSTON ARMS
- SOUTHAMPTON ARMS
- JUNCTION TAVERN
- PINEAPPLE
- BULL & GATE
- ASSEMBLY HOUSE
- THE ADMIRAL (TAPPING)

10 A KENTISH TOWN CONSTITUTIONAL

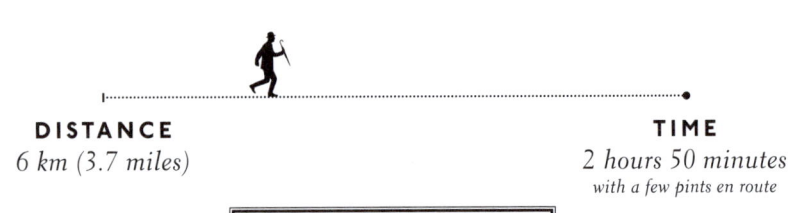

DISTANCE
6 km (3.7 miles)

TIME
2 hours 50 minutes
with a few pints en route

NEAREST STATION
Kentish Town West

PUBS
Tapping the Admiral; Assembly House; Bull & Gate; Southampton Arms; Bull & Last; Boston Arms; Junction Tavern; Pineapple

---

Well now, goodness me. I have to warn you there are a good many pubs on this walk and you may have to take your pick. I shall include a few that I particularly like, but there's nothing wrong with the ones I leave out!!

So let's start by meeting at a lovely locals' pub: **TAPPING THE ADMIRAL** (see **Walk 7** for the origins of its name) has been voted CAMRA North London Pub of the Year four times in the last ten years. It has board games and a pub cat (**points**!) with the appropriate name of Nelson, and it feels to me like the kind of place Withnail (of *Withnail and I* fame) might enjoy. With its cosy roaring fire and atmospheric lighting it could also be the perfect place to *finish* a walk; but we're getting started here today. The ales change regularly and the pies are great, so it will provide good sustenance to see us through.

The pub was erected in the 1850s, near the site of the old Castle Inn – where Admiral Nelson's uncle used to drink, bringing a young Horatio with him sometimes. We shall hear more about Nelson on this walk, so let me

PUB

Tapping The Admiral

down this Adnams Southwold and we'll get going.

Head across Castle Road and up Hadley Street, where you'll see Kentish Town West station to your left at the end. Around the other side of the station, beneath the arches on the right, is **CAMDEN TOWN BREWERY** ❶. Camden Hells Lager is a pretty decent brew, which we're quite proud of in Camden, and if you like you can do a brewery tour or have a drink in their tap room.

But since it isn't strictly a pub, and I've only just got going, from Hadley Street I'm turning right instead, to head east along Prince of Wales Road.

The old stone building on the left with a lovely weathervane on top used to be the **ASYLUM FOR AGED GOVERNESSES** ❷, built in 1849. Governesses were a bit like private tutors or nannies, who usually served rich households where the parents were absent (like in *The Secret Garden*). When they got old and fell on hard times the idea was to retire here in relaxation; except a few years later the railway opened up and ruined their garden and their view, so by 1872 they had to move to Chislehurst in Kent.

It's worth doing a quick detour up Ryland Road (immediately after the old asylum), just to take a look at **BRINSMEAD** ❸, the gated block of flats behind the station (it's visible from the platforms). This used to be a piano factory and I must say it does make a marvellous place to live or work. Spacious and bright. Many of the warehouses around Kentish Town were piano factories and in Victorian times all the best households would aspire to have a piano, since there was no TV or Joolz Guides back then. Kentish Town became the main hub of piano manufacturing in England and John Brinsmead and Sons provided pianos for Queen Victoria and King Edward VII. If you're able to gain access you'll see they still have some of the trolley tracks (like tram tracks) leading to the front of the building for unloading pianos.

Back on Prince of Wales Road, continue until you reach the large terracotta building on the left, built in 1901, which used to be the **PUBLIC BATHS** ❹. The two statues are of St Pancras (he's the one trampling a Roman beneath his feet) and St George; Kentish Town was in the borough of St Pancras. In those days many homes didn't have bathrooms, let alone running water, so families would come here to take a bath every now and again, but not as often as I do. I have one on Saturday night, whether I need it or not!! Of course, they'd have to enter by the correct doors, which are still marked with 'First Class' and 'Second Class' for men, on Prince of Wales Road, and 'Ladies' around the corner in Grafton Road. I rather like the fact that these days part of the building is still used as a swimming pool.

At this point I should mention the Grafton, a popular family and dog-friendly pub, named after the Duke of Grafton (Henry FitzRoy from **Walk 8**) – the Grafton family owned much of the land around here. I'm not stopping, though, so let's carry on.

Turn right into Castlehaven Road, passing a somewhat uncommon sight these days: a minicab office! I feel duty bound to mention **BEE GEE CARS** ❺, not only because it's such a rarity (since taxi apps seem to have taken over) but also there's something charming about the exterior, which looks like it's been lifted straight out of the 1970s. If I ever shoot a feature film, I'm setting it here!

After that slight delve into the past, continue along Castlehaven Road briefly and then turn left, following Kelly Street around to the end.

Kelly Street is very cute, lined with what were once workers' cottages, built by John Kelly (a local builder) around the 1850s. Like the pub we started in, much of Kentish Town was redeveloped around that time, but by the end of the nineteenth century a couple of brothels were thought to exist in Kelly Street; a police inspector who toured the area with a researcher working on behalf of Charles Booth, the social reformer who compiled his 'poverty maps' of London, described this as 'the worst street for immorality' in Kentish Town. We assume it has changed these days, since the houses look very quaint and beautifully painted in different colours; but who am I to comment on the immorality that might be taking place behind any of these doors!

As you emerge onto Kentish Town Road, turn right. The building on the next corner, opposite Leverton & Sons on the right, used to be a pub called the **CASTLE** ❻, built in 1849. This replaced the much older Castle Inn, which had pleasure gardens stretching down to the River Fleet.

The Fleet runs underground now, having been incorporated into Joseph Bazalgette's Victorian sewers, but it started in Hampstead Heath and ran past here all the way to the Thames. The area towards Camden Town used to flood regularly, and in fact the name 'Kentish' is believed to come from the Old English *ken-ditch*, meaning 'bed of a waterway'; though some people say it might be related to the Celtic word *ken*, meaning both 'green' and 'river'.

The Castle Inn was near where the uncle of Admiral Nelson, William

Suckling, resided. It is joked that Nelson would come to the pleasure gardens 'to keep an eye on the Fleet'. Hilarious.

The red-tiled building adjacent to the old Castle is the abandoned **SOUTH KENTISH TOWN TUBE STATION** ❼. This opened in 1907 but closed down in 1924, after they had one of their famous power cuts and decided not to open it up again as not many people were using it – trains only stopped there occasionally, anyway. In the 1950s John Betjeman, who lived nearby, famously wrote a story about a passenger who alighted here and got stuck in the disused station.

Naturally, the station is haunted – a fact to which I can testify, since I visited with the paranormal investigators in the Kentish Town video which accompanies this walk. It's certainly a creepy place, and if you want to get locked in with the ghosties you can do one of the escape room challenges here run by Mission: Breakout.

Now go back the way you came, up Kentish Town Road.

On the right, immediately before **ST ANDREW'S GREEK ORTHODOX CATHEDRAL** ❽, is Rochester Road, with two trees at the start. These replaced two chestnut trees planted by Lady Hamilton, Admiral Nelson's mistress!

After Nelson died she moved to the house roughly opposite the cathedral, where Stanley James Jewellers is now. It's rather sad because despite Nelson's last wish being that the government look after her and their daughter, Horatia, Lady Hamilton had to flee to France, where she died in poverty. That's how to honour your national heroes!

You can probably see for yourself that we are passing another pub, the Abbey Tavern, but time waits for no man so we're carrying on. The pub sits at the end of a terrace of houses along Kentish Town Road where Mary Shelley, author of *Frankenstein*, lived and she recalled watching Lord Byron's funeral procession from her window here. She didn't enjoy living in Kentish Town, describing it as 'an odious swamp', even though the street would have been much wider back then: look at where the houses actually would have had their front doors, before they all had these shops tacked onto the front.

Carrying on you'll see a charming coffee house on the corner of Church Avenue. This used to be a **POST OFFICE** ❾ (before they stuck post offices in the backs of newsagents), and to the right of Church Avenue is the original gatepost of the congregational church from 1848, standing there rather isolated and not matching anything else. I hope it's still there by the time you visit.

① ② ④ ⑤ ⑦ ⑨

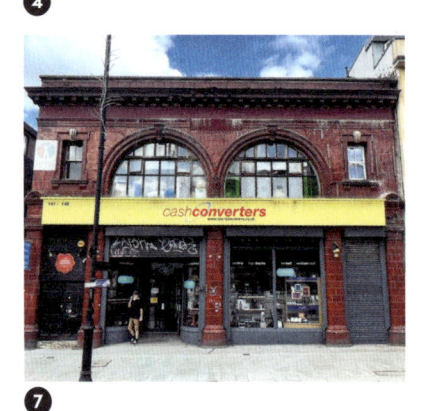

ANGLERS LANE

Turn left into Prince of Wales Road and just before you reach the public baths we saw earlier, turn right into Anglers Lane.

Points for spotting the pointy listed bollard reading 'SPPM' (St Pancras Parish Middlesex)!!!

For many years this was a popular spot for fishing in the River Fleet. In Gillian Tindall's book about Kentish Town, *The Fields Beneath*, a 1909 interview with an elderly gentleman gives a sense of what it was like in the nineteenth century:

> *When I knew it as a boy it was one of the loveliest spots imaginable – so deserted in the early hours of the morning that, when the anglers were not there, some of the youngsters from the cottages around, and some who were not youngsters, used to bathe in the river.*
>
> *I passed through Angler's Lane some time ago, an aged man in a bathchair, and I found it hard to realise that my wheels were rolling their way over the Fleet river!*

How times have changed.

The large building on the right, opposite Alma Street, was once Europe's biggest **FALSE TEETH FACTORY** ❿, opened by Claudius Ash. He came up with an innovative way to make them out of porcelain, mounted on gold plates, when others were still using hippo or walrus ivory! Rather weirdly, the women who worked here had to be unmarried (slightly creepy); but they all said it was a great place to work until it closed in the 1960s.

We'll be coming back shortly, but we're going to nip up to the end of Anglers Lane first. You'll emerge next to Nando's, which was once a pub called the **JOLLY ANGLER** ⓫, dating from 1725. Just round to the left you'll find **RIO'S HEALTH SPA** ⓬. I don't know, maybe it's your bag?

Now, look: I have never been in! However, I know people who have, and let's just say it's seen as London's leading naturist spa. Goodness only knows what goes on in here, but if you find bathing with other naked strangers relaxing then this is the place for you. I've heard stories…

Well, we all have stories.

Now return down Anglers Lane, keeping an eye out for the plaque commemorating **BORIS THE CAT** ⓭. He was a much-loved stray who was rescued and could be seen loafing here for ten years, before being squished on the main road.

Now turn right into Alma Street.

Some of these cottages would have been used by workers at the false teeth factory, but now they're very desirable and expensive homes. They were built around the time of the Crimean War, which is why these streets are named after battles (Alma and Inkerman) and commanders (Raglan and Willes). In fact, at the end of Alma Road is what used to be the **CRIMEA** ⑭, which has now become flats, but at least they've kept the pub sign. Charles Booth's research found that three prostitutes lived in this street; but there were no brothels, so maybe they worked from home, like many people do these days…

Turn left at Inkerman Road and then immediately right into Cathcart Street. You should pass a **GRATE** ⑮ in the ground, roughly outside Better Sound, where you might be able to hear the flow of the River Fleet. We're approximately following the route of the river; it last flooded in 2002 but you should be safe, I reckon.

At the end of Cathcart Street turn right into Holmes Road and keep going until you get to the **POLICE STATION** ⑯, which moved here in 1896. I like the archway with the gate to the right of the entrance, which was once used for the horse-and-cart police wagons known as 'Black Marias'.

Continue and turn left into Kentish Town Road by the Lady Hamilton, a pub which shut down in 2023; here's hoping someone can get it opened up again.

Goodness, how it's changed here – but I love the fact that some of the shops still have gloriously 1980s signs, especially **ABBA ELECTRONICS** ⑰ at number 236, with their old Grundig logo and offer of 'T.V. VIDEO ETC. REPAIR'. (I mean, who still gets their TVs repaired?)

Coming up on the left is the site of a sports shop where I famously featured in a TV commercial for egg.com bank, in which I had a sock on my hand yelling at me. Alas, both the sports shop and the egg.com brand have disappeared, like my acting career.

Turn right into Islip Street.

On your left you'll come to **KENTISH TOWN CHURCH OF ENGLAND PRIMARY SCHOOL** ⑱ where Madness recorded the video for 'Baggy Trousers', in which the saxophone player flies up in the air. Other parts of the video, featuring kids running around, were filmed on the estate on Peckwater Street a little further along; but let's turn back the way we came and turn right to continue up Kentish Town Road.

Just opposite the station is a conveniently positioned pub!

There's been a pub on the site of the **ASSEMBLY HOUSE** 🍺 since 1721, when visitors on days out from London

> **PUB**
> *Assembly House*

would come to their pleasure gardens to play skittles and indulge in other leisure activities.

On the far side of the exterior on Leighton Road there's a statue of a boy (who was decapitated about ten years ago) holding up the year '1898', which is when the pub was rebuilt. The present building was described by the art historian Nikolaus Pevsner as one of the best examples of pubs from this period.

You might recognise it from the 1971 film *Villain*, starring Ian McShane and Richard Burton. Speaking of villains, back in 1784 the landlord, Thomas Wood, was tried at the Old Bailey for highway robbery! He was acquitted but his accuser wouldn't let it lie and continued accusing him, until poor Thomas Wood went totally bonkers and died in 1787.

I love a boozer with large windows on a corner, allowing me to stare at the passers-by as I wait for my friend who is always late. It's very spacious, too, with beautiful Victorian etched mirrors, which I have a thing for.

If it hasn't been scrubbed off, you might be able to see an old sign on the brick building across the railway, reading 'Trellis and Joinery Works'. I guess no one has seen the need to go up there and remove it. Maybe they like it, as I do. (Not sure about the big 'Welcome to Kentish Town' graffiti, though.)

I'll have a Greene King IPA.

When I was making my video for this walk I decided to split it into two videos, finishing the first one here. So you can stop here if you like, but we're carrying on.

Cross the road and head up Highgate Road.

On the left is the **BULL & GATE** 🍺, where I used to go to a lot of gigs, so even though we've just left the Assembly House, I can't resist a quick half.

The back room where the stage used to be seems to have been converted

> **PUB**
> *Bull & Gate*

into a dining area now, as with many of the Kentish Town pubs. Many famous bands played here before going on to bigger things, including Blur and Oasis. In terms of personal highlights, I remember seeing the Senseless Things here, and Perfect Daze. (What ever happened to them?)

There's been a pub here since 1715; the current incarnation dates from 1871. I suppose I have to grudgingly accept that they've made a good job of the recent refurbishment. I'm always a fan of pubs which display pictures on the walls of the local area in bygone days, as this one does upstairs.

Round the back of the pub, up the cobbled path, was the site of the stables for the London General Omnibus Company.

Continuing on up Highgate Road you'll pass the **FORUM** (19). This was built in 1934 as a cinema, with Art Deco features which are still very much in evidence, though by the time of my youth it had become a music venue, known as the Town and Country Club. They brought back the Forum name in the 1990s. (A nearly identical Forum cinema, also from 1934, was built on New Broadway in Ealing; they knocked most of that one down during recent redevelopment, but retained its façade.)

Rumour has it that the frieze inside was donated by Mussolini, who wanted the place to be suitable for Oswald Mosley's fascist Blackshirt rallies of the 1930s! I don't know how true that is, but you'll see it if you go to a gig here.

On the other side of Greenwood Place is **CHRIST APOSTOLIC CHURCH** (20) – the scene of Damien's christening in *Only Fools and Horses*. Damien was the son of Raquel and Del Boy; every time the camera fell on him, Rodney would hear the music from *The Omen* playing in his head!

The church is also mentioned in John Betjeman's poem 'Parliament Hill Fields':

> *Launched aboard the shopping basket, sat precipitately down,*
>
> *Rocked past Zwanziger the baker's, and the terrace blackish brown,*
>
> *And the curious Anglo-Norman parish church of Kentish Town.*

Opposite the church is the new **FIRE STATION** (21). You should be able to see the isolated tower which the fire fighters use for practice. The only part of the old fire station that survives is the red gatepost on Fortess Walk around the side, opposite which is **TALLY HO APARTMENTS** (22). Pip pip!!

The development is actually named after the Tally Ho pub, which was here from 1838 until 2006. In the 1970s the pub was credited with being the birthplace of pub rock, a sort of forerunner to punk rock, with regular performers here including Ian Dury and Dr Feelgood. I like the fact that the 134 bus still runs past here with its destination on the front reading 'Tally Ho'! (It's actually heading to Tally Ho Corner in North Finchley.)

Return to Highgate Road and continue up past various carpet shops.

The area to the left (down Sanderson Close) was occupied by sheds used for servicing locomotives until 1914, as well as more former piano factories. It had all been abandoned by the 1980s, when I used to come here and play with my friend Michael, who lived in Leighton Road – couple of scallywags that we were. They've ruined it now by making it respectable!

Now, I'm not going in, but if you're hungry and like good gastropubs you could pop into the Vine. It was originally called the White Horse, dating from 1730, and despite recent modernisation there's still a surviving mosaic as you enter. It was from here in 1778 that one of the earliest daily coach services to London started up, with two per day… not unlike some bus routes I've travelled on recently!

Carrying on up Highgate Road, earn yourself **points** for spotting the **SUN FIRE INSURANCE PLAQUE** ㉓ outside number 102. Then head right into Little Green Street, which is where The Kinks filmed their promotional video for 'Dead End Street', all dressed as undertakers and Victorian pallbearers. Apparently the BBC thought it was in bad taste and banned it, but it's now regarded as one of the earliest pop videos. If you want a quick detour, you can take the next right into the charming College Lane, full of beautiful eighteenth-century houses. But we're returning to carry on up Highgate Road.

After the railway bridge is **SOUTHAMPTON HOUSE ACADEMY** ㉔. This was a boys' school, built in 1820 to teach boys 'the fear of God and bodily health'! However, the railway came along in the 1860s and cut straight through their playground. It's been turned into flats, but not to worry, next door is the **SOUTHAMPTON ARMS** 🍺, where we are definitely stopping!

(They had me at 'ALE | CIDER | MEAT' on their sign.)

PUB

Southampton Arms

ALE | CIDER | MEAT

This is a most charming and unusual-looking pub, with an array of excellent beers and ciders, eighteen of which are hand-pulled. Widely regarded as one of the best craft beer pubs in London, it feels a bit like you are in someone's house due to its laid-back atmosphere.

They have a small garden out the back, with an outdoor toilet – much more civilised than those horrible indoor ones with carpets!!

Two large gins, two pints of cider. Ice in the cider.

Cheers!

Further up Highgate Road, on the right after the crossroads, is Grove End, which becomes Grove Terrace, with its grand houses dating from 1780 set back from the main road.

Up until 1980 a regular sight at number 23 was one Polly Rogers, who used to bring her horse in every day through the front door! I imagine she must have had a stable in the garden, but had no access around the side.

In the eighteenth century these houses would have had a lovely view across the fields towards Hampstead, but these days they overlook what John Betjeman described as 'the Red Cliffs': **PARLIAMENT HILL MANSIONS** ㉕, where he grew up. It's worth a trundle through the mansions to peruse some of the blue plaques. It's rather peaceful.

PUB
Bull & Last

Now, if your legs are giving out, you could finish your walk a little further up Highgate Road at the **BULL & LAST** (which has been in existence since 1721), if only because the great guitar hero Gary Moore lived next to the pub, at 2 Woodsome Road. (Cue 'Parisienne Walkways' playing in my head.)

Back in 1763 a patrol left here every evening for Great Ormond Street Hospital, accompanying pedestrians for fear of banditry and highwaymen! (Cue 'Stand and Deliver' by Adam and the Ants playing in my head.) It's another gastropub with decent grub. Kentish Town really has gone up in the world since I were a lad.

Okay, it would be rude not to.

A pair of pints. Cheers.

There's some life in this old dog yet, so I'm going back the way we came, down Highgate Road, and turning left into Chetwynd Road, which leads down into the valley of the River Fleet.

When you reach York Rise you'll see

Walk 10: Kentish Town | **181**

10

12

16

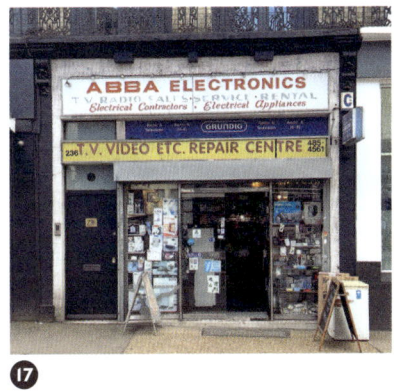

17

19

28

it's a charming parade of shops with a local villagey feel. Nip up to the left, and when you reach the Dartmouth Arms turn around and look back across Bellgate Mews to the building opposite. This used to be **LARN'S DRAPERY** ㉖, where the ghost sign tells us what was available, including haberdashery, flannels, underclothing and maids' dresses! There's also a nicely kept (for a change) King George V post box.

Return to the junction with Chetwynd Road. Since this is a pub walk it would be remiss of me not to mention that if you were to head to the end of Chetwynd Road to your left you would reach the Lord Palmerston, named after the third Viscount Palmerston, who was twice Prime Minister and died in office in 1865. I have been known to enjoy their excellent Sunday roasts, but today I'm going to continue straight ahead, following York Rise south.

On the right you'll come to **YORK RISE ESTATE** ㉗, which was built in 1937.

They did estates nicely in those days, with spacious balconies and washing lines in the gardens. You can still see the columns from which the washing lines were strung, once adorned with beautiful sculptures of dragons designed by Gilbert Bayes and produced by Royal Doulton. He did these finials for a number of local estates and based them on animals from nursery rhymes. No wonder they got removed, though – they can fetch over £10,000 in auctions!

PUB

Boston Arms

Follow York Rise round to the left as it becomes Churchill Road, and then take the little alleyway to your right which leads to the steps over the railway. If you're tall enough you can get a good view of the big pipe to the right of the bridge. This is actually a **STORM DRAIN** ㉘ which encases the River Fleet! I guess it crossed the route of the railway, so they said: 'I know, we'll take the whole river and divert it through a tube!'

After crossing the railway continue straight and then turn left into Burghley Road, which was named after Queen Elizabeth I's Lord High Treasurer William Cecil (who was made Lord Burghley).

Walk to the end, past **ACLAND BURGHLEY SCHOOL** ㉙. The school's unusual name was formed when Burghley Road School amalgamated with Acland School, itself named after Sir Arthur Acland, an MP who worked to improve the education system in the nineteenth century. Famous former pupils have included Mercury Music Prize winner Ms. Dynamite, Eddy 'Electric Avenue' Grant and Lee Thompson – the saxophone player for Madness who flies up in the air!

When you reach Dartmouth Park Hill look up at the old street sign above front of the **BOSTON ARMS** 🍺. It shows just 'NW' rather than 'NW5', which means it most probably pre-dates 1917.

The Boston Arms, with the Dome round the back, is a great place for live music as well as a drink. I saw some wonderful bands here in my time, but the best one I remember was Snuff. Whatever happened to them? They were superb.

Oh, go on, then. Just a quick half, for old times' sake.

In the days of omnibuses this was as far as the horses would come, because they got a bit tired going straight up the hill to Highgate. So Junction Road was created for them to go around instead. However, we're going the other way, into Fortress Road.

I say, here's a splendid-looking pub on the right: the **JUNCTION TAVERN** 🍺 at number 101, with a Courage cock above the door. It first opened in 1874 and by the late 1990s this had become what you might call an 'old man's pub'. I sometimes wonder where all the old men go after they modernise these pubs. Thankfully, the owners who took over in 2002 retained some of the nice Victorian mahogany features around the bar and fireplace. What's now the conservatory was once the pool room, where naughty kids from Acland Burghley school used to come and smoke fags whilst drinking their first ever pints.

People often lament the loss of these old-school boozers, with sawdust on the floor and an old bloke with a glass eye and wooden tooth propping up the bar. But it got to the point where all three doors were frequently left open and rubbish would blow down the street and gather next to the bar – so it's probably just as well they fixed it up, on reflection. These days it's another swanky Kentish Town gastropub with a garden.

I'll have a pint of Moretti (unless you want a latte, yah).

> **PUB**
> *Junction Tavern*

Come on, almost there! At least it's downhill from here.

On the left, look for the plaque at number 56, for **FORD MADOX BROWN** ㉚. Earlier I was mentioning the view across to Hampstead. Well, in 1857 he did a painting from his house here, called *Hampstead: A Sketch from Nature* (sometimes known as *Hampstead from*

My Window). All I can say is, I don't think he would have bothered if he were living here today!

Regular viewers of my YouTube channel will probably be familiar with the Black Watch green trousers that I often wear. Well, coming up on the right is **CHRIS RUOCCO TAILORS 31**, who made them for me. It's a real throwback going in here. You just don't get many traditional old shops like this any more. It looks like the window display hasn't changed since the 1960s!

Opposite his shop, at numbers 28 and 30, is where the first ever anti-vaxxer lived! Well, okay, I'm trying to be sensational, but Dr William Rowley, who lived in what seems to have turned into another piano factory, objected strongly to Edward Jenner's novel cowpox vaccination – claiming that it was turning people into cows, and creating ox-faced boys and cow-mange girls! Anyway, I don't think he was an anti-vaxxer in the modern sense, so don't write in, but this is the origin of the word 'vaccination', because *vacca* is Latin for 'cow'.

Lordy, lordy… I'm tired.

FALKLAND ROAD

PUB
Pineapple

Turn left into Falkland Road, past the multi-coloured houses, and left again into Leverton Street.

Coming up on the left is Railey Mews, next to the Pineapple (whither we shall shortly bend our steps and retire). It's worth a quick look in the mews, actually, as it's another very charming street. A house towards the top end has a hoist from bygone years, presumably for lifting things onto carts. In the 1890s, whilst the Giraffe House was being built at London Zoo, a giraffe called Zara had to be housed in a stable just behind the Pineapple. I used to get called 'Mr Giraffe' by my housemaster at school, on account of my height; so I shall drink to Zara now and imagine her looking down on the drinkers in the pub garden.

The **PINEAPPLE**, which was built around 1868, exudes charm. It would have suffered an all-too-usual fate in 2002, when developers (idiots… maniacs!) wanted to tear it down – had it not been for the Powell family, who took it over, and a group of locals, including journalist Jon Snow and actor Rufus Sewell, who all fought to save it.

The bar has a lovely Victorian back piece, while pineapples adorn every corner – they're said to have represented hospitality, since they were so expensive to get hold of in the old days.

Who cares?

I'll take a pint of Pineapple Amber Ale, please.

Here's looking at you, Zara.

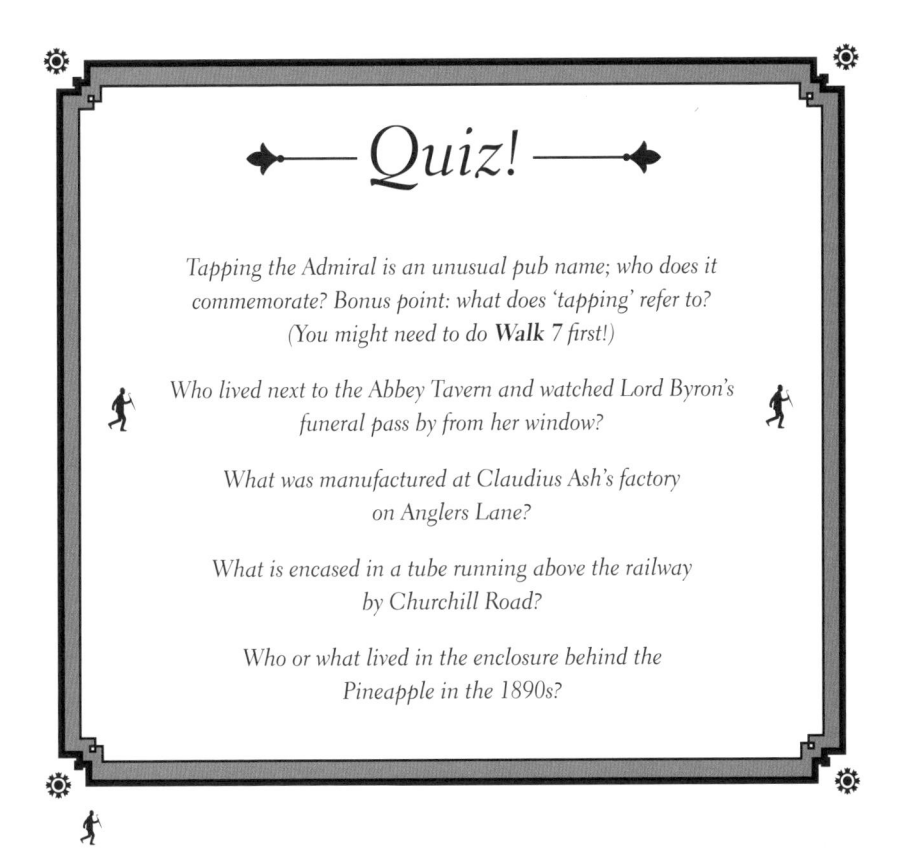

Quiz!

*Tapping the Admiral is an unusual pub name; who does it commemorate? Bonus point: what does 'tapping' refer to? (You might need to do **Walk 7** first!)*

Who lived next to the Abbey Tavern and watched Lord Byron's funeral pass by from her window?

What was manufactured at Claudius Ash's factory on Anglers Lane?

What is encased in a tube running above the railway by Churchill Road?

Who or what lived in the enclosure behind the Pineapple in the 1890s?

21. Civic Centre

2. L. Manze

YE OLDE ROSE & CROWN

CHEQUERS

TRUE CRAFT

13. God's Own Junkyard

11 WALTHAMSTOW

11 A WONDERFUL WANDER AROUND WALTHAMSTOW

DISTANCE
5.3 km (3.3 miles)

TIME
2 hours 40 minutes
with a few pints en route

NEAREST STATION
St James Street

PUBS
True Craft; Chequers; Queen's Arms; Village; Nags Head; Wild Card Brewery Barrel Store; Ye Olde Rose & Crown

We're starting here in **TRUE CRAFT** – even though it isn't, strictly speaking, a pub. It's nicely located near St James Street station, with a handsome selection of craft beers, which are all the rage these days, especially with young trendy people. I'm more of a proper pub man myself, but I'm an old fogey. The cool kids these days are hanging out in these smart, bright, clean and cheerful tap rooms specialising in beers from the many local breweries and also from around the UK. Installing a pizza oven is a popular move in Walthamstow, too.

That sourdough pizza does smell mighty fine – I must say, maybe these millennials are onto something.

Let's not go too far, though. I'll play safe with a pint of Tottenham Lager.

Down the hatch!

Coming out of True Craft, turn left. On your right you'll see Indiano Pizza, where you can buy some pizzas with remarkable toppings. Whilst making my video about Walthamstow I bought their Mighty Meaty Pizza with tandoori

PUB

True Craft

chicken, spicy beef and Chinese chicken, and alas, it was the last pizza my mother ever saw me eat. I often wonder what she, as an Italian, thought – but in deference to Oscar Wilde, she refrained from saying 'One of us had to go.'

They seem to like pizza (of all varieties) in Walthamstow and, to be fair, it was quite nice (but not very Italian).

Turn right at Oxfam onto the High Street.

One of the things Walthamstow is most famous for is supposedly having the longest market in Europe – although I don't think Istanbul and Palermo are quite quaking in their boots! The market used to stretch a mile and a quarter, all the way down to here from the other end of the street and further, but that was in 'the good old days'. As you walk up you'll notice more stalls appearing.

OXFAM ❶ used to be a Burton's Menswear store. The Burton chain was started by Sir Montague Burton, who arrived in the UK in 1900, aged fifteen, as Meshe Osinsky, fleeing the Russian pogroms in what is today Lithuania. He changed his name to Burton and started making suits manufactured for measurement, and soon became known as 'the tailor of taste'. By 1931 there were 400 of these stores and most towns had one, with their distinctive art deco exteriors and often a billiard hall upstairs! (He knew how to look after his staff.) It is thought that the expressions 'going for a Burton' and 'the full Monty' derive from Montague Burton!!

Continue past the buildings on the left dating from 1900, adorned by rather cute little dragons, and soon, on the right, you'll see the sushi bar Taro with its green canopy. If the canopy is not down you'll be able to see the original façade of the shop, reading **L. MANZE** ❷ – from the days when it was a good old East End pie and mash shop.

The Manze family arrived in England from Italy in 1878, founding fourteen pie and mash shops, this one dating from 1929. It's still lovely inside, retaining the tiled walls, and there are still a few of them serving pie around London in places like Peckham and Hoxton. I prefer sushi myself… I'm not a proper Cockney! I must say, it doesn't seem like a very Italian dish.

Walthamstow was recorded in the eleventh century as *Wilcumestowe* ('the Place of Welcome'), with the spelling *Wilcumestou* listed in 1086's Domesday Book. It was a pleasant village where the landed gentry could come and escape the dust of the city. It wasn't until the late nineteenth century that it became what they call 'Cocknified'. What's strange is, as you'll see, it's now reverting back to being more gentrified.

Keep going and you should now start seeing more of the market, which has been here since the 1880s, and you can definitely pick up some good bargains as well as nice doughnuts and other food of all ethnicities.

I say, shall we pop into the **CHEQUERS** for a swift half? I feel contractually obliged to drop into buildings of a certain age. The Chequers has been trading for over 300 years; the present building dates from around the 1790s after a maid accidentally set fire to the linen cupboard and burnt the old one down. Whoopsadaisy! Don't worry, it's been redecorated since then.

I've been told that this is one of the best pubs in Walthamstow, although no one has ever explained to me what criteria are required for a pub to be 'good'. Me? I like historical places, so I'm intrigued by the local legend that the Kray twins came here to change their bloody clothes after murdering Jack 'the Hat' McVitie in the 1960s. It's rather more well-to-do these days, with its table football, wacky wildlife wallpaper and cocktail menu, and is big enough to have a bit of everything, from big-screen sports to a cosy snug room and an outside drinking area.

PUB
Chequers

I'll have half a cider...

Tally ho.

Now continue up the High Street and eventually you'll come to the **CENTRAL LIBRARY** on your right, with a bust of Andrew Carnegie, of Carnegie Hall fame! He was actually a Scotsman but became one of the richest men in American history, having made his fortune from steel, and was a great philanthropist, financing a good many libraries and other public buildings which you can see all over London.

Walk around to the right, behind the library, and through the garden. Then turn left (past the bus station) into Selborne Road and then turn right into Hoe Street, over the railway.

Eventually you will reach Third Avenue on your left. Just beyond this, look above the parade of shops and you'll see a rather nice relief of a **BEEHIVE**, along with the dates '1911' and '1915'. This was a branch of the Stratford

MORE PUB RULES

THE RULE OF TOM
You should always be able to recognise at least one beer. Alongside craft beers, pubs should serve at least one celebrated Continental lager, for those who don't like the newfangled stuff. Otherwise it's not a proper pub – it's a tap room.

THE RULE OF ROBERT
Don't trust the friend who holds the door open for you as you enter the pub. It might seem like they're being polite… but actually, they're ensuring you get to the bar first and have to pay!

THE RULE OF LAURA
If you can't see it, they are unlikely to have it – so don't ask for stupid drinks. Everything they have, including the peanuts, is clearly displayed. Pork scratchings? They will be stapled to the wall and clearly visible. They don't hide them in a special place.

THE RULE OF PAULS
If you're involved in buying rounds and you're drinking expensive cocktails, make sure you buy a round early on. Don't wait until ten rounds in, when the evening is coming to an end, thus benefitting from all the free drinks and never buying one yourself! The more expensive your drink, the earlier you should buy a round. (By the way, the enforcer of this rule really is called Pauls. At least, that's what I call him…)

THE RULE OF SIMON
Dogs must be permitted in pubs.

THE RULE OF DAN
If you are a man in the gents' toilets, do not attempt to strike up a conversation with the man in the next urinal. Whilst the ladies' can sometimes be a place for socialising (or so Dan and I have been told), Dan feels that the urinal should be preserved as his sacred space, where he can quietly contemplate what to drink next.

Cooperative & Industrial Society, in which members owned the stores and shared the profits. There is a similar one in Mile End, which has the same beehive motif with its worker bees representing the hard-working shop owners. Sorry, I just like these little details.

Now go back again and turn right into Third Avenue (by the second-hand furniture shop which makes you feel like you're in an episode of *Minder* from the 1970s).

Lots of the houses along here have names like Heathfield, Cleveland and Lansdowne. Try as I might, I cannot establish why they were given names other than to make them feel a bit upmarket and important. Charmingly, many of the houses in this part of Walthamstow have imitation blue plaques placed in the windows, to commemorate some of the lesser-known people of the area who weren't famous enough for a proper blue plaque on the wall. They remind us about the everyday goings-on in people's lives. (There's one I rather like in Exmouth Road, near Queen's Road station back on the other side of Hoe Street, for Richard Dore, a house painter whose first wife died in 1897 after their daughter was born; he then married widow Clara, who was eighteen years his senior. Who cares? Well, it's nice to be remembered.)

Soon you'll reach **ORFORD HOUSE** ❺ on your right-hand side, dating from the early nineteenth century and named after Orford in Suffolk, whence came one of its later occupants. It's now a social club with a pleasant bar area, snooker tables and a large bowling green in the garden. If I lived in Walthamstow I would certainly join, as it's a rather splendid place to relax.

PUB
Queen's Arms

I mean, we're now really entering the gentrified swanky part of Walthamstow: Walthamstow Village. I ain't got no homies here, bro', so it won't surprise you to hear that some of the cafés and pubs around here are really quite upmarket. By the way, I don't *only* drink in places with sawdust on the floor and dartboards; I do also like gastropubs, especially if one of my friends has had the presence of mind to book a table for lunch. The **QUEEN'S ARMS** has changed a lot since it opened in Victorian times, but I guess it reflects the changing nature of the area, and on a nice day you can sit outside and almost feel like you are on a mediterranean

PUB
Village

piazza. The food is jolly nice, although I did require a translation of at least two items on the menu – usually a sign that I might require open-wallet surgery soon – but this isn't too bad for London. There are plenty of tables and bar stools for us just to neck a quick pint; but let's take these outside and gaze at the beautiful old **HOVIS SIGN** ❻ opposite, above the Village Bakery (and all the people staring at their phones).

Two pints of lager and a packet of (posh) crisps, please (and a dandelion juice latte for my friend).

Cheers!

Let's now take a quick stroll along this quiet road and back again.

Some time ago Walthamstow was given plenty of moolah to create a low-traffic neighbourhood, which made areas like this much safer – although many local motorists weren't happy about it because it means you have to drive much further to reach your destination. This led some residents to put signs up saying 'Walthamstow – twinned with North Korea', which seems a bit extreme! It does, however, mean that this road is pleasant to walk along. Look out for the quaint Victorian shop signs on your right, and the community hub on your left, which was once the schoolhouse dating from 1866 and which looks a bit like a church.

Maybe just walk as far as the **OLD TOWN HALL** ❼, dating from 1876, which is opposite the Walthamstow Labour Party office, and then turn back.

It's probably asking a bit much that you drink in all these pubs, so you can really take your pick. The **VILLAGE** 🍺 on your left is a more modern place, having only opened within the last forty years or so; but as you'd expect from pubs in this charming little enclave, it does have a good selection of beers, as it's not affiliated to any one brewery. It's a rather smart place with wooden flooring, a nice 'courtesy distance' between tables and a newly refurbished garden.

I think I'll take a pint of Gamma Ray Pale Ale and watch a bit of the footy…

Come on, Ref! That was never off-side!

Chin chin.

Now return to the Queen's Arms and turn right into East Avenue, then right again up Vestry Road.

The red-brick building you'll pass on the right is the **OLD POST SORTING OFFICE** ❽, from 1903. If you look up you'll see 'E' and 'R' either side of the coat of arms, standing for Edward Rex (King Edward VII). It's remarkable, the pride that was taken in their work in those days. Even a sorting office was pretty grand. Not like today.

A bit further along on the left you'll come to the **VESTRY HOUSE MUSEUM** ❾, with a rather isolated column sitting outside. This column originally formed part of another grand post office building, in St Martin's Le Grand (near St Paul's Cathedral), dating from 1829. When it was demolished (why?) it was bought by a local stonemason, Frank Mortimer, and presented to the Borough of Walthamstow (again, why?), who presumably said, 'Err… thanks, Frank… Let's just put it here…'

The museum started life in 1730 as a workhouse, and as a reminder of its grim past the slogan above the door still remains:

> *If any would not work, neither should he eat*

Later it was a police station, but in 1931 became a museum where you can still see the old cells inside, along with all sorts of other exhibits relating to Waltham Forest. My favourite is the first English motorcar, which was built by Frederick Bremer in 1892 outside his house in Connaught Road, Walthamstow. They have the actual car here! You might have to wait a bit, though, as the museum is closed for a 'revitalisation' project, with its reopening scheduled for 2026.

Continue up Vestry Road and on the right, as it curves round and becomes Church Lane, you'll see what looks like a green garage door. This used to be a **FIRE STATION** ❿, where a man would pull his cart by hand with water on it. It wasn't until 1863 that they added a horse to it!

Opposite are the **ALMSHOUSES** ⓫ erected in 1795 for the flatteringly named 'decayed tradesmen's widows of this parish'. Charming.

When you reach the Penfold post box dating from Queen Victoria's time (you get **points** for spotting this) turn right into Orford Road, passing on your left the **ANCIENT HOUSE** ⓬.

ORFORD ROAD

Now that London has expanded this far it can be claimed that this is the oldest house in London – built around 1435, during the reign of Henry VI! It was restored in the 1930s, but look out for the intentional wonkiness of the brickwork on Orford Road, presumably a requirement by the local planning authorities to keep it authentic.

Walk 11: Walthamstow | **195**

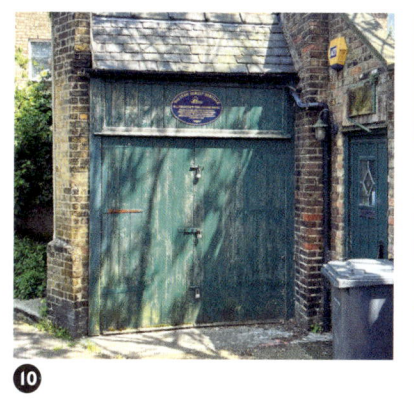

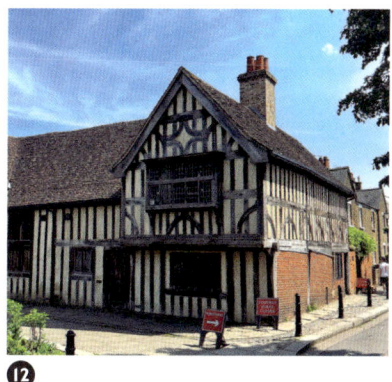

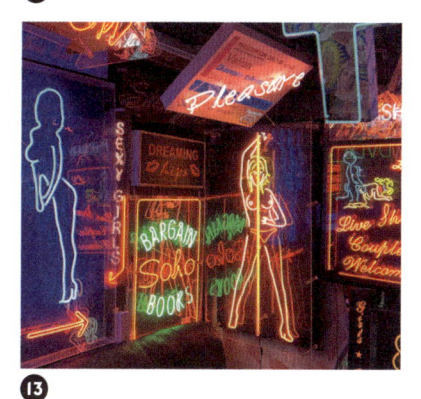

The Joolz Guide...

BARTENDER INTERVIEW

This is the result of my highly scientific process of researching the answers to some of the big pub questions of our day, by interviewing one random barman.

Q: How long should a ¾ pint of Guinness be left to rest before filling it up to the top?
A: Sixty to eighty seconds.

Q: What is a lager top?
A: A pint of lager filled almost to the top, with a dash of lemonade to finish.

Q: What is a lager and light, and in what sort of glass should it be served?
A: A bottle of light ale and a half pint of lager, in a standard pint glass.

Q: What is a lime soda and bitters?
A: A half pint glass containing soda water plus either a dash of lime cordial or a fresh lime slice, and then a few drops of Angostura bitters – which is a strange herbal concoction in a small bottle that could be mistaken for Worcester sauce but is definitely not! (Worcester sauce should, of course, be used for a Bloody Mary…)

Q: How should a Newcastle Brown Ale be served?
A: In a half pint glass; an initial pour with a head, and then topped up regularly, keeping a head. Never call it 'nookie brown'! Colloquially, it's 'a bottle of dog'!

PUB

Nags Head

Continue along and on the left you'll come to the **NAGS HEAD** 🍺, which was built by Francis Wragg in 1857 at the same time as the coach house next door. Wragg decided it would be a good idea to run a coach service from here to Lea Bridge Station eight times a day, so that people could then hop on a train to London. (Walthamstow didn't get its own station until thirty years later.) I don't know if he intended the coach house to be turned into flats, but that seems to be what's happened. At least the pub is still here – and a rather eccentric place it is, too, with its eclectic furniture and bright colours. A quick glance at the events programme reveals that one can show up for pilates, live jazz or an art class. (I did check for aboriginal finger-painting classes for the over-fifties, but I was out of luck.) Anywhere that encourages you to light a candle for David Bowie gets my vote.

The Nags Head is a friendly local with loads of pictures of local cats all over the walls. Resident cats seem to come and go, but they had one last time I was here. (Possible **points**? See page 11.)

There's a pretty good selection of local beers, too, and a lovely spacious beer garden with – you guessed it – pizza! But other food is available, as I recently found out when a man next to me enquired about the burgers. He took exception to burgers served in brioche baps or buns, rather than traditional baps or buns, but luckily they had both. (I've always like baps and buns myself.)

I'll have a pint of ale.

Here's looking at you.

Turn left out of the pub and left again into Summit Road and through the gate at the end.

Check their website for opening hours, but **GOD'S OWN JUNKYARD** ⑬ is a truly wonderful experience, inside a warehouse. It's Chris Bracey's collection of neon signs, including Soho sex shop signs from the 1960s, and neon from other famous TV and film productions you'll recognise, such as *Top of the Pops* and *Captain America*. It's a real treasure trove and great for your Instagram (or TikTok, if that's what the kids are doing these days). There are cafés inside, too, so you can pretend you're sitting in a sleazy cinema in the red-light district, or in some dystopian film scene watching an erotic nude bed show for 50p. (Seems quite reasonable, that!)

I expect the owner has a coronary every time his electricity bill arrives.

PUB
Wild Card Brewery Barrel Store

Now, you'll have already clocked the **WILD CARD BREWERY BARREL STORE** 🍺 on your way in. Strictly speaking, it isn't a pub, but these microbreweries are all the rage, as I mentioned, especially if you have a beard and like pizza. (Yes, they also have a pizza oven.) Despite it being in what seems to be a garage in a carpark, it's actually quite pleasant to sit here and try their excellent selection of New England-style IPA.

Please note they're currently only open Wednesday to Sunday…and on that bombshell, I'll have a Wild Card Main Hustle.

Cheers!

Now go all the way back to the Ancient House and then straight ahead through the churchyard of **ST MARY'S** ⓮, which has been here since the twelfth century – although all that remains of the original church is some pillars inside.

On the other side follow Church Hill around to the left and keep going all the way past an example of what postal sorting offices look like these days.

Then turn right into Hoe Street at the **CLOCK TOWER** ⓯, which was built in the 1950s after a bomb dropped here in the Second World War, killing twenty-two people.

I like all the shields on the side of the building relating to important families with a connection to the area. A small chart on the left tells you their names.

This is also the location where Anthony Shields was riding his unicycle in 2015, when he got run over by a bus. This could have turned into a tragic story – but before you could say 'What on earth was he doing riding a unicycle down a busy road?' his life was saved by all the passers-by who got together and actually managed to lift up the bus with their bare hands, thereby freeing him! That's true community spirit, folks.

Carry on up Hoe Street and you'll pass Victoria Hall on the left, built in 1887, which in 1930 became the **GRANADA CINEMA** ⓰. As well as being a cinema it was used for several years as a concert hall. Many famous musicians performed here, including the Beatles, the Rolling Stones, Little Richard and Johnny Cash.

More recently it was almost turned into a church, but thanks to the efforts of Paul McGann (of *Withnail and I*) and Griff Rhys Jones, amongst others, it was saved, with plans to become a theatre and cultural venue. Yay!

Keep going and you might want to nip into Hatherley Mews on the left. This used to be tram sheds until the 1950s, but now the buildings contain restaurants, which still retain their character with old hoists and other details on the outside.

Continuing down Hoe Street you'll pass **ARBAT CONVENIENCE STORE** (17), which is where Small Wonder Records was situated. They worked with many bands, including Bauhaus, Cockney Rejects and, most importantly, the Cure; but Pete Stennett, the owner, closed the label in 1982.

In fact, many bands hail from Walthamstow. Ian Dury first met members of the Blockheads here – and who can forget the great East 17, who named themselves after the local postcode? (And their lead singer, Brian Harvey, who somehow managed to run himself over with his own car, because 'I had just been stuffing my face with a load of jacket potatoes and I felt sick.')

Next turn left into Jewel Road and walk to the end. Cross over Forest Road and continue into Winns Terrace, where you'll find some of the **WARNER ESTATE HOUSES** (18) on your left.

FOREST ROAD

Sir Thomas Courtenay Warner, who became an MP and was later Mayor of the Borough of Walthamstow, received a large inheritance in 1875 and used it to provide social housing intended to last at least 100 years. These were very sought after by a 'higher class of tenant' at a time when the area had somewhat lost its appeal.

On the right is **LLOYD PARK** (19), named after Edward Lloyd, who lived in the big house here. He started a newspaper called *Lloyd's Weekly*, which was the first to feature stories like *Sweeney Todd, the Demon Barber of Fleet Street*. In fact, it was after *Lloyd's Weekly* that the famous music hall artiste Marie Lloyd, who sang 'My Old Man (Said Follow the Van)', named herself.

A later occupant of the big house here was Walthamstow's favourite son, William Morris. He was not only one of the most important designers of the Arts and Crafts period, but also a key member of Britain's first socialist party.

The house is now a museum, the **WILLIAM MORRIS GALLERY** (20), where you can see many of his designs, including my mum's favourite, 'The Strawberry Thieves'.

Exit the museum into Forest Road and turn left and walk a little further.

Hmm… Now, at this stage you could pop into the Bell, which is perfectly nice, but I'm not stopping yet as I've got a different pub in mind for our last drink. But I will quickly tell you about how in 1890 when a rival nearby pub, Ye Olde Rose & Crown, applied for a full licence, a local MP objected on behalf of the Bell's landlady, Mrs McDaniell, claiming it would be harmful to her trade. Rather amusingly, at the hearing a death certificate was produced, stating that Mrs McDaniell had died one year before – so she couldn't possibly have any objection! Lucky for us, since we're heading to that rival pub imminently.

If you're tired you can just turn right here, but I think it's worth carrying on a little up Forest Road briefly, where you'll find the **CIVIC CENTRE** ㉑ on your left.

I just happen to rather like these grand buildings from the 1930s, even if they do almost look like they belong in the former Soviet Union. They have some interesting designs on the side, inspired by William Morris, representing creation, motherhood and work, while the Assembly Hall building on the right carries the cheerful slogan 'Fellowship is life and lack of fellowship is death'. It's worth a look inside, since it retains its beautiful Art Deco interior and makes me feel like I'm in an episode of *Poirot*.

PUB

Ye Olde Rose & Crown

Okay, now go back the way we just came along Forest Road and then turn left up Hoe Street.

And so let us decamp to **YE OLDE ROSE & CROWN** 🍺, which is a pub I rather like because it's more what I'm used to. It just feels to me like an old-school Victorian pub with beer mats decorating the wall and where all types of clientele, old and young, get on just fine; no fancy clap-trap. There's a theatre upstairs and space in the downstairs bar for live music and a discotheque… although the fact that I'm using the word 'discotheque' probably tells you something about me.

I'll have a pint of New River London Tap. I might ensconce myself here for a while, actually.

Cheers – and let the marsh breezes blow, all over Walthamstow.

— Quiz! —

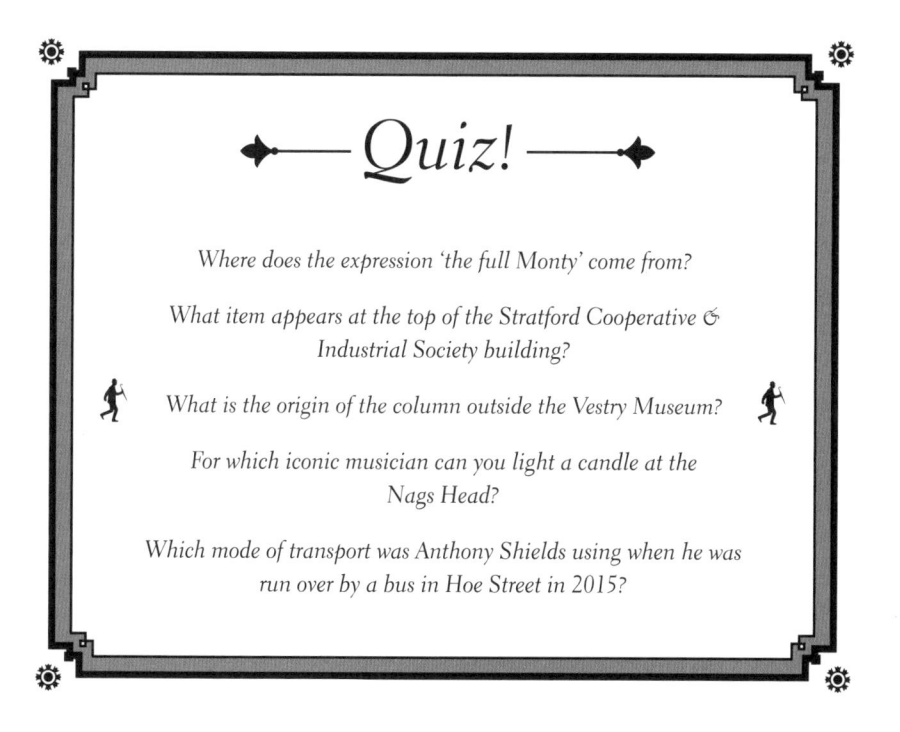

Where does the expression 'the full Monty' come from?

What item appears at the top of the Stratford Cooperative & Industrial Society building?

What is the origin of the column outside the Vestry Museum?

For which iconic musician can you light a candle at the Nags Head?

Which mode of transport was Anthony Shields using when he was run over by a bus in Hoe Street in 2015?

24. Oak of Honor

18. Horniman Museum

NORWOOD ROAD

ELDER ROAD

S CIRCU

5. Fountain

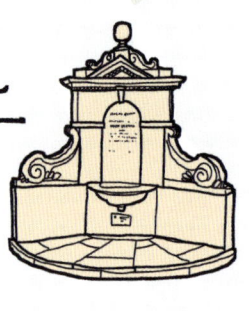

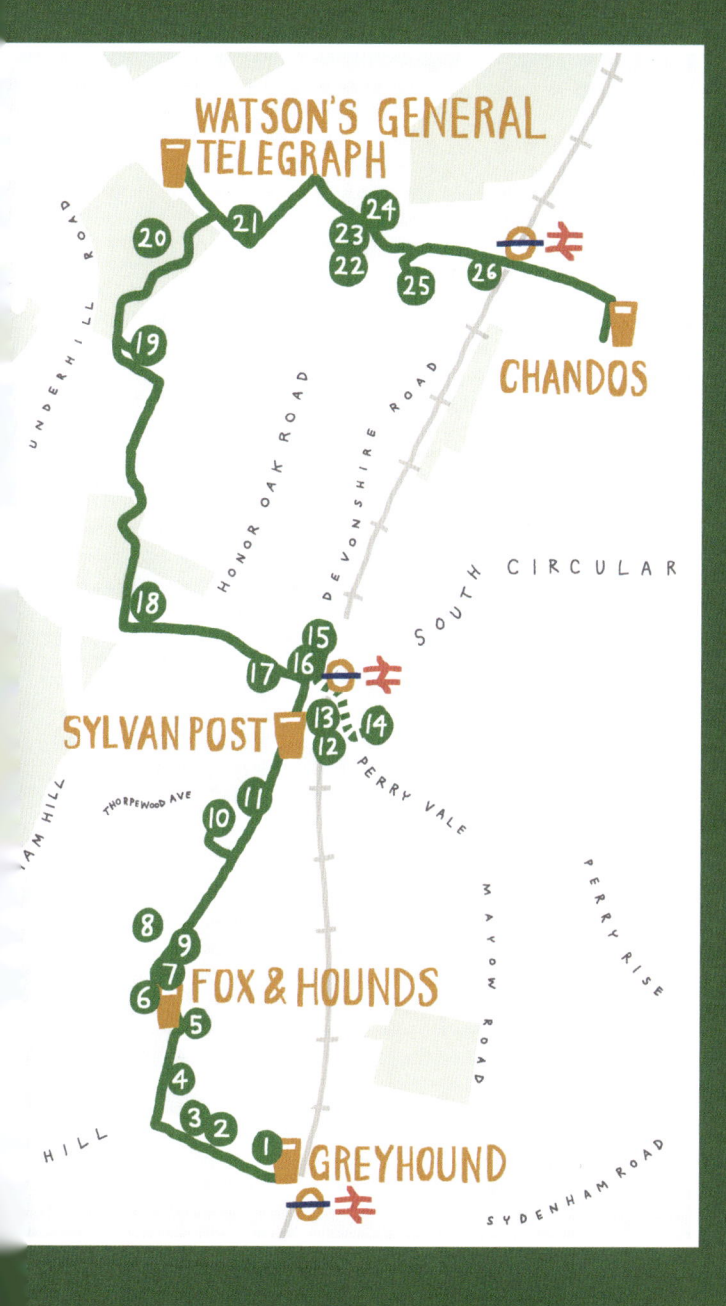

WATSON'S GENERAL TELEGRAPH

CHANDOS

SYLVAN POST

FOX & HOUNDS

GREYHOUND

12 SYDENHAM

12 THE SUN ALWAYS SHINES ON SYDENHAM

DISTANCE
6.6 km (4.1 miles)

TIME
3 hours 20 minutes
with a few pints en route

NEAREST STATION
Sydenham

PUBS
Greyhound; Fox & Hounds; Sylvan Post; Watson's General Telegraph; Chandos

What's that? My nose is bleeding again? Tish tosh, nonsense! It's true, though, that I don't make it to south London as often as I should…

We're starting in Sydenham and walking through Forest Hill towards Honor Oak, so let's start at the **GREYHOUND** (which, I should point out, is a cashless pub).

It might not look it since its refurbishment, but this is actually Sydenham's oldest pub, first mentioned in 1727, when this was just a little hamlet surrounded by the Great North Wood. Sydenham was originally named Sippenham, meaning 'Cippa's village' (no

PUB
Greyhound

one is quite sure who Cippa was). Having said that, a bloke down the pub told me that it was called Sippenham because of all the people sipping the waters around here! In the seventeenth century medicinal wells were discovered in the area, attracting people to 'take the waters'. It was all the rage to visit wells in those days, and they'd pop up all over England. The Greyhound would offer accommodation for people visiting the ones here, in what today is the nearby Wells Park.

Daniel Defoe was a bit sniffy about the local wells, though, remarking:

> *Whereas the nobility and gentry go to Tunbridge, the merchants and rich citizens go to Epsome, so the common people go chiefly to Dulwich and Streatham.*

Nevertheless, King George III visited, though that was some time later.

Let me finish my pint of Gipsy Hill Hepcat and we can get going.

Cheers.

Turn right out of the pub and head up Westwood Hill (the left fork at the roundabout).

The building to the right of the roundabout with a dome on top was added to the parade of shops in 1902. Walter Cobb had opened a little shop here in 1860 and eventually he did so

WESTWOOD HILL

well that it grew to become a large department store. **COBB'S CORNER** ❶, as it became known, even expanded onto the other side of the road and the department store was still trading up until 1981.

Along Westwood Hill you'll come to **ST BARTHOLOMEW'S CHURCH** ❷, opened in 1832. If you walk a short way down Lawrie Park Avenue (to the left off Westwood Hill) and turn around to look at the church, you'll get the same view that Camille Pissarro depicted in his 1871 painting *The Avenue, Sydenham*, which hangs in the National Gallery. Lovely.

If you enter St Bartholomew's churchyard you'll find a rather moving grave on your right, for ten builders who fell to their deaths whilst reconstructing the famous Crystal Palace in 1853, after it was moved from Hyde Park to Sydenham. (The site of Crystal Palace is a little way south of here, and jolly nice it is, too; but our walk is taking us the other way.)

Next door to the church along Westwood Hill is the former house of **ERNEST SHACKLETON** ❸, the great explorer. It's extraordinary to think that the houses along this side of the road were mostly squatted during the 1960s. They all seem so well-to-do these days.

Many of the houses along here have wonderful details. I usually award **points** for spotting gargoyles! These are not to be mistaken for plain old grotesques, which are just characterful, often ugly, faces. Gargoyles, specifically, have water coming out of them, from the French *gargouille*, meaning 'throat'.

Carry on and turn right into Jews Walk. There are a number of theories about this name, seemingly the most likely being that it relates to David Ximenes, whose Jewish family fled the Spanish Inquisition (which they really weren't expecting). He lived in a house just on the other side of Westwood Hill where the Sheenwood Estate now stands. Around the 1760s he is said to have planted elm trees all along this road, which would have constituted a sort of driveway leading to his house, with just fields on either side. Those trees have since been replaced with the ones you see today. The 1850s saw the appearance of some rather splendid Gothic houses, which you can imagine Dracula living in.

Speaking of horror stories… Coming up on the right is **NUMBER 7** ❹, where Karl Marx's daughter, Eleanor, committed suicide in 1898. The doctor who attended the scene was none other than Ernest Shackleton's father!

At the end of Jews Walks you'll come to the **FOUNTAIN** ❺ which commemorates the diamond jubilee of Queen Victoria. Turn left and start walking up Kirkdale.

It's wonderful looking at old paintings of these areas from the early nineteenth century because you can see all the fields, hills and dales to which the place names refer. The **FOX & HOUNDS** 🍺 on the left, first licensed in 1826, recalls the times when fox hunts would regularly pass by this spot.

Let's nip inside for a drink, since it's on our way.

It's lovely and bright, as it's on a corner with large windows on both sides, and has been newly refurbished. There are even rooms available to stay in upstairs, like in the olden days of taverns. The pub is definitely modern, though, offering art classes, quizzes and open mic nights, whilst serving a selection of craft beers and flavoured ciders.

As we're in south London I'll have half a Brixton Lager.

Cheers.

PUB

Fox & Hounds

Come out and continue up Kirkdale, to your left.

Pass the amusingly named **HIGH STREET BUILDINGS** ❻ on the left. These date from around 1900, when this was still Sydenham High Street. Since the 1820s this had been the main place people came to do their shopping – until Walter Cobb opened Cobb's Corner.

(Shoppers could probably see that these were buildings which stood on the high street…but it's always good to remind people with a nice sign.)

Soon, on the right, you'll get **points** for spotting a post box with King George V's cypher on it (this one reads simply 'G R'). It's situated just outside a convenience store, which is the most important stop on this walk – and not just because I fancy a choc-ice!

In 1983 John Ratcliff ran a recording studio here, at 107B, called **RENDEZVOUS** ❼. He took pity on a group of penniless musicians from Norway, who were staying in a flat in Shepherd's Bush, by letting them use his studio (especially since they liked his *Space Invaders* machine so much), and they recorded a bunch of demos here. Ratcliff particularly liked one of their songs, called 'Lesson One', so he hooked them up with one of his contacts at Warner Bros. – resulting in them renaming the song 'Take On Me' and releasing one of the greatest singles of all time! Of course, the band was

a-ha (who don't like capital letters!)… and I actually used to think I was Morten Harket, the lead singer. I even ripped my jeans.

If you want to get a flavour of how this area might have looked in the early nineteenth century, continue up Kirkdale for a bit, past the roundabout, and look at the two **TIMBER HOUSES** ❽ on your right, which have survived since 1820.

I've been hunting high and low for something like this. (Oh, did I mention you get **points** for gratuitously squeezing in a-ha lyrics?!)

Now go back to the roundabout and turn left down Dartmouth Road.

DARTMOUTH ROAD

NUMBER 221 ❾ on your right, next to a pizza shop, became the humble dwellings of a-ha, rented for them by John Ratcliff. Morten, Mags and Paul would take a short cut to Rendezvous by climbing out of the back window and clambering across the roofs into the back of the studio.

Continue along Dartmouth Road, past Sydenham School, and then take a steep left up Round Hill.

Up ahead of you at the top you'll see a green stink pipe in the distance, but we're not going all the way up to that. Keep an eye out on your right for an opening, guarded by a large tree, leading to a **CHURCH SPIRE** ❿.

As you approach the spire you will see that it is, rather strangely, lacking a church! In fact, it looks as though the church is underground and the spire is poking up through the paving.

This was actually designed by Sir Christopher Wren in the 1680s, for the church of St Antholin, which used to stand in Budge Row in the City. The spire is made of stone, rather than the usual tiles which adorn roofs, so it became too heavy for its church – especially after it was struck by lightning in 1829 and had to be replaced.

One of the church wardens, Robert Harrild, decided to buy it for £5 (thanks to his new-found wealth from a printing invention), and had it placed here. This means it has stayed erect for nearly 200 years! There's hope for us all. (How in*spir*ing.)

The original church was demolished in 1875. Initially the spire would have looked like a nice feature in the grounds of Round Hill House, Harrild's manor house which stood here at the time; but ever since that was also demolished, and turned into a housing estate, the spire looks rather more out of place.

Let's head back down the hill, admiring the view, and then turn left to continue along Dartmouth Road, past the splendid red-brick **FOREST HILL LIBRARY** ⓫, built in 1901. Along this stretch it's worth keeping an eye out for the various ghost signs and other remnants of past businesses which have occupied these properties. Some are present on the brickwork above the shops opposite the swimming pool, as well as further along down alleyways and above your head.

We're now arriving in the area of Forest Hill, with the 'forest' bit referring to the Great North Wood, which encompassed a large part of south London.

Keeping going until you reach the Bird in Hand. Glance to your right down Bird-in-Hand Passage, where you should be able to see the railway running behind the houses.

This was once the route of the **CROYDON CANAL** ⓬, opened in 1809, which connected Croydon with the Surrey Canal, and ultimately the Thames. Some of the buildings along Dartmouth Road were businesses where you could rent a boat and go for a jolly up the canal. However, within just thirty years the canal had been filled in and replaced with the railway, following a similar route, after which the area started to become more popular.

There are some nice cafés and shops in this area, a couple of which – the cafés

Walk 12: Sydenham, Forest Hill and Honor Oak | **209**

⓻

⓼

⓽

⓾

⓯

⓰

PUB

Sylvan Post

at **NUMBERS 25 AND 27** (13) – have rather pleasing mosaics on the floor as you enter, preserving the names of the previous occupants, Dewhurst Butchers and FH&W.

The Rule of Ted (see page 166) would suggest that we enter the first of the various pubs along here, the Hill, which we just passed; but take your pick. The Hill is the sort of no-nonsense place that my sister likes, with cheap beer and a pool table with the winner-stays-on rule; the Bird In Hand also has pool tables, but no kitchen (although you can bring your own food). Personally, I rather like the look of the **SYLVAN POST** across the road, simply because it used to be the Post Office. Naturally, they boast a first-class service!

It's rather modern but with eclectic retro furniture, and they do decent grub. I think I might stop here for a Sunday roast and a pint of Notting Helles while reminiscing about my childhood, when I would frequently visit post offices that looked like this (before they moved them all to the backs of newsagents). Here they have retained the post boxes marked 'London', 'Abroad' and 'Country' and you can even sit inside one of the money vaults, which still have their heavy security doors!

Amazingly, you could still get a pint for under a fiver here when I last visited! (Albeit before 7 p.m. on weekdays…) I'll drink to that!

Now let's continue along Dartmouth Road and past the Dartmouth Arms, which had frequent custom from owners of canal barges before being rebuilt in 1866.

When you reach Forest Hill station you have a choice.

If you're a snooker fan, follow me on a quick detour – but if not, you can skip this bit, as we're coming back in a minute.

Snooker fans: follow me through the subway next to the station, under the railway, and then turn right into Perry Vale. Then turn left into Church Vale.

Situated in a modest-looking building on the right is **PARRIS CUES** (14). John Parris is the guy who makes snooker cues for all the famous snooker players. He was the one who sawed Steve Davis's cue in half (the cue he won the world championship with) in order to make it easier to carry around as a two-piece cue. If you're lucky you might be able to see all his elves working away making cues by hand. (Or you can just watch them in the Joolz Guides video!) You can design your own cue using his fancy software, and he'll even measure you to make sure you get the right cue. It's a bit like going to Savile Row for a suit!

Now head back to Forest Hill station and rejoin the non-snooker lovers (heathens).

From the station, cross over and turn right past yet another pub, the Signal, and you'll see a raised section of pavement leading round to David's Road, with some lovely-looking cafés.

This is the former route of the canal, so the upper section would have been the **TOWPATH** ⓯. If you go down to the lower part, where the canal would have been, you'll see a rather splendid frieze depicting various locations relating to the area, including the canal itself and the Honor Oak, where we're heading on this walk.

As you face these cafés turn to your left and follow the road round (back past the Signal) into London Road. You'll pass a charity shop on your right (British Red Cross at the time of writing). Unless the shutter is down, take a look at the floor in front of their door and you'll see that it used to be a **J. SAINSBURY GROCER'S** ⓰ many years ago, before they became a huge supermarket chain. The supermarkets don't tend to have these lovely mosaics outside their entrances these days!

The next turning on your right is Havelock Walk, a charming cobbled street full of warehouses dating from the mid-to-late 1800s. These days many of the buildings are occupied by artists, as you can probably tell from some of the funky murals.

Cross to the other side of London Road, where you will find the **CAPITOL** ⓱. This started out in 1929 as an Art Deco cinema and then became a bingo hall, before eventually turning into a J. D. Wetherspoons pub. I suppose the final part of that cycle is still in progress, since the pub has recently shut down, but it has yet to become luxury flats. Give it time…but you never know – it might actually become a cinema again!

Although it's now closed, I find it interesting the way Wetherspoons have a habit of buying up these huge buildings with lots of space inside, and they generally seem to have very reasonable prices. Did you know that 'J. D.' isn't the founder's initials, but a reference to Jefferson Davis Hogg (Boss Hogg) in *The Dukes of Hazzard*? And that Wetherspoon was the name of the founder's teacher, who disparagingly said he'd never make much of his life?

Okay… Well, I hope your boots were made for walking, because we've got a bit of a hike coming up.

Walk up the hill until you come to the **HORNIMAN MUSEUM** ⓲ on your right.

Now, we spoke about Frederick Horniman in **Walk 4**, so I've already cracked my hilarious 'horny man' joke. He was a very successful tea trader who travelled the world collecting amazing artefacts, which he kept in his house and wanted to show to the public, because he was a genuine philanthropist. After his wife (understandably) got fed up with his finds cluttering up the place he decided to display his collection here – and it's truly one of my favourite museums.

In the days when people didn't have TV or the internet they couldn't see all these amazing curiosities, so it was a real treat to come and see one of the best collections of taxidermy in the world – they boast over a quarter of a million objects in their natural history collection alone. Whilst there are hordes of musical instruments, Egyptian mummies, an aquarium and even a supposed merman (a male mermaid), the most famous exhibit is the overstuffed walrus. Apparently, the taxidermist had never seen a walrus before and ended up stretching his skin too much, so he lost all his wrinkles and flab (the walrus, not the taxidermist). He was probably basing his measurements on a seal, but this didn't prevent Queen Victoria referring to him as a 'magnificent specimen' (the walrus, not the taxidermist). The natural history gallery, which includes the walrus, is currently closed for refurbishment and is due to reopen in 2026; but don't let that put you off – there is still plenty to see in the meantime!

After looking around, head into the gardens and enjoy the wonderful view of London, which I think is one of the best.

You might wish to finish your walk here, or back at one of the pubs I mentioned near Forest Hill station, but if you're a glutton for more then strap those walking boots on again.

Take the little path behind the bandstand in the gardens overlooking London and follow it round to the right. From here we're following the signposted route marked Green Chain Walk. This will take you out of the park to the right, down a passageway leading to Westwood Park, where you turn left.

Follow Westwood Park as it curves round to the right, and turn left once you reach Langton Rise.

Ahead you will see a cemetery – but before entering, just turn right briefly and pop into **K & J LIBRETTO & DAUGHTERS** ⓳. I can't resist this lovely characterful butcher's shop, because of all the clutter and paraphernalia they have accrued. The current owner has been here for forty-two years, but it's been a butcher's for over ninety. Whilst you get plenty of businesses called '… & Sons', it's rare to see '… & Daughters'. In fact, this is just the owner having a little joke: he had plenty of sons, none of whom wanted to get involved, so he called it '...& Daughters' – but when finally a daughter did come along, she wasn't interested either! I love the vintage charity box for the blind where you send a coin spinning round and round, which takes me back. No use these days, with the cashless society... The owner also laments the drop in poppy sales in the lead-up to Armistice Day, the records of which he keeps and posts on the wall every year. It has gone down and down. As you can see from the New York taxi and vintage car outside, he is obviously a collector of interesting things.

PUB

Watson's General Telegraph

Five rashers of bacon, please!

Now enter **CAMBERWELL OLD CEMETERY** 20 opposite, which isn't one of the 'Magnificent Seven' but was nevertheless opened for the same reason in 1855 – to alleviate the problem of overcrowded cemeteries in central London. The lodge and chapels were designed by Sir George Gilbert Scott's architectural firm and can be seen in the 1970 film adaptation of Joe Orton's *Entertaining Mr Sloane*.

Now for a Joolz Guides challenge!! See if you can find the grave of Frederick John Horniman! If you were coming from the Forest Hill Road entrance it'd be just after the paths split...somewhere to the right of the left path. (Well, it's hard to describe – and it's supposed to be a challenge!)

Unless you stopped for refreshments at the Horniman Museum, I expect you're rather thirsty, so exit the cemetery into Forest Hill Road and turn left to head into **WATSON'S GENERAL TELEGRAPH** for a restorative pint. They have a beer garden, with heated wooden huts for the winter, and – if it's not booked up for a private function – a games room with darts and (a definite pub rarity) table tennis. They also serve an interesting selection of 'smokehouse food', which makes a change from the usual pub staples of fish 'n' chips, burgers and pizza.

If you're wondering about the pub's odd name, the telegraph in question was situated on the nearby One Tree Hill (which we'll be coming to shortly), set up in the nineteenth century as a relay station enabling communication between London and ships in the English Channel.

They do lots of craft beer here, but I'm having a pint of Guinness to keep my strength up.

Cheers!

After leaving the pub, head back along Forest Hill Road the way we just came, past the cemetery. On the corner of Wood Vale is a newish-looking housing development, which is where the original Honor Oak railway station used to be. This served the old route to Crystal Palace, passing behind the houses in Marmora Road and along **BRENCHLEY GARDENS** (21), which is now a lovely nature trail.

Enter Brenchley Gardens through the gate and follow what would have been the railway, with the road on your right. It's hard to describe, but keep your eye out for an exit onto the road on your right, with another entrance on the other side of the road leading up some large steps into another nature reserve.

Take these steps and at the top you'll find another terrific view of London, where you might want a little rest if, like me, you're a bit tired!

This is One Tree Hill. You should be able to see a **BEACON** (22) nearby, which was lit for the jubilees of King George VI and Queen Elizabeth II, as well as to warn of invasions by the French and Spanish in times gone by!

In more recent times a large **GUN** (23) was placed here to fend off Zeppelins during the First World War; but the gun has gone and all that remains is a large round pedestal. You really do get glorious views from One Tree Hill, which is why the East India Company constructed a semaphore station here, to signal the arrival of boats on the Thames, but the inclines do make it a bit tiring, I'll admit. Nearly finished!

Following the path around to the left you'll find the famous **OAK OF HONOR** (24), although it's not the original tree that grew here in 1602, under which Queen Elizabeth I is said to have picnicked with Sir Richard Bulkeley. That was struck by lightning in the 1880s.

Elizabeth is said to have knighted the tree!

'I dub thee Sir Oak Tree!' I suppose that's why it's the Oak of Honor. (Couldn't they spell? Or were they American?)

Now head down by taking the path to the right, crossing the little road by St Augustin's Church, and you'll emerge onto Honor Oak Park.

Turn right and then have a peek down **WALTERS WAY** (25), on the left.

In 1984 Lewisham Council didn't know what to do with this land because it was unsuitable for building on. However, Walter Segal, an enterprising architect, persuaded them to offer it to people waiting on the housing list, as long

Walk 12: Sydenham, Forest Hill and Honor Oak | **215**

⓱

⓲

⓳

⓴

㉓

㉕

as they built their own homes. Using the special technique he'd developed, thirteen lucky people were able to build lightweight but robust homes which were more suitable for this location. There are some very interesting and creative designs, despite the fact that the people who constructed them had little or no building experience. Some of the structures even look like treehouses. It's a magical little community.

Walter Segal was no relation to Steven Seagal, but he must have had similar skills (although he didn't also cook). Apparently, in the 1960s Walter Segal rebuilt his whole house in his garden in Highgate, for £800!

Now head back along Honor Oak Park, past the path you came out of, and walk down the hill.

There's a terrific **POST BOX** 26 on the corner of Devonshire Road, with the cypher of King George VI, plus one of those boxes attached which the postmen used for storing letters. More **points** for me!

Okay… Well, we came this way because I thought it might be nice to finish near a train station – but I don't see a pub, so we'll have to invoke the Rule of Ted (see page 166) and just go to the nearest one.

Keep going, past Honor Oak Park station, until you reach Stondon Park, and turn right.

PUB
Chandos

At the roundabout you'll find the **CHANDOS**, where we'll finish up.

It's a friendly place, with board games, craft beer and pizza. (There isn't much else on the menu, but who doesn't like pizza?) They also have plenty of outdoor space for when it's warm, in the form of a roof terrace and a beer garden.

I'm assured that all the kids are gone by 7.00 p.m. They don't take cash, so you'll either have to pay with a card or just do the washing up!

Oh, it's Sunday, so I'm sticking around to try the pub quiz.

In the meantime, a pint of Brewdog Punk IPA for me.

Cheers!

— Quiz! —

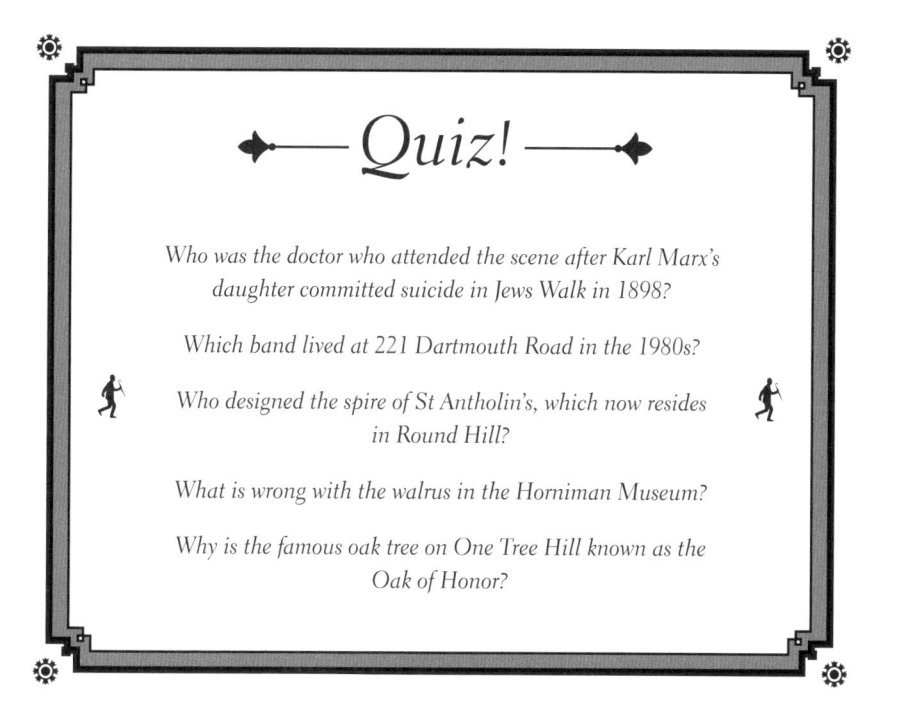

Who was the doctor who attended the scene after Karl Marx's daughter committed suicide in Jews Walk in 1898?

Which band lived at 221 Dartmouth Road in the 1980s?

Who designed the spire of St Antholin's, which now resides in Round Hill?

What is wrong with the walrus in the Horniman Museum?

Why is the famous oak tree on One Tree Hill known as the Oak of Honor?

OXFORD STREET

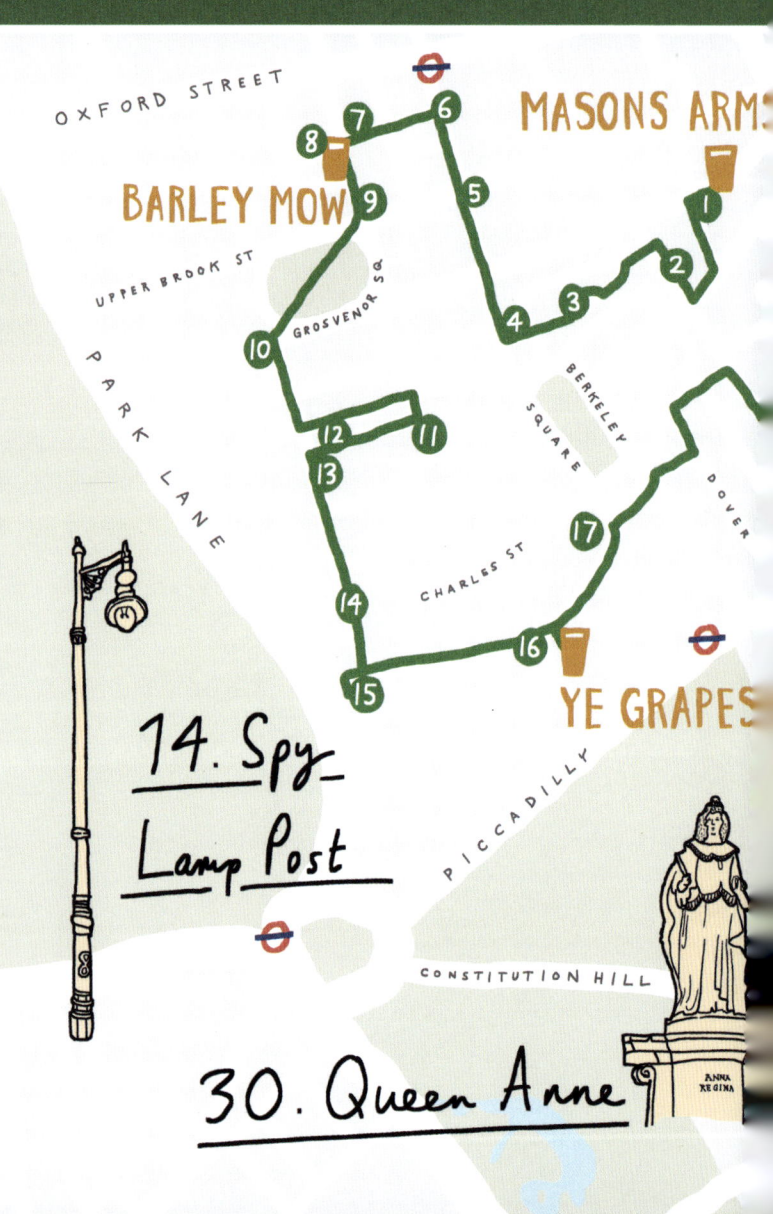

MASONS ARMS

BARLEY MOW

UPPER BROOK ST

PARK LANE

GROSVENOR SQ

BERKELEY SQUARE

DOVER

CHARLES ST

YE GRAPES

PICCADILLY

CONSTITUTION HILL

14. Spy Lamp Post

30. Queen Anne

ANNA REGINA

29. Duck Island

RED LION

COCKSPUR ST

HEQUERS

THE MALL

WHITEHALL

HORSE GUARDS ROAD

29

WESTMINSTER ARMS

TWO CHAIRMEN

13 MAYFAIR TO WESTMINSTER

13 A HISTORICAL STROLL FROM MAYFAIR TO WESTMINSTER

DISTANCE
6.1 km (3.8 miles)

TIME
2 hours 50 minutes
with a few pints en route

NEAREST STATION
Oxford Circus

PUBS
Masons Arms; Barley Mow; Ye Grapes; Red Lion; Chequers; Two Chairmen; Westminster Arms

---

Ah, hello there. You've arrived. Well, I thought we'd meet in the **MASONS ARMS** because I like a pub in a little back street, especially if it first started serving in 1721. It was rebuilt in the 1930s but hey ho, let me chin this down and we can get going.

Outside the pub head right along Maddox Street and you can have a look inside **ST GEORGE'S CHURCH** ❶, built in the 1720s by John James, who was Christopher Wren's apprentice. I think he did a decent job.

I know, I know. Not another bloody church! Actually, this one is quite interesting because St George's was a very cheap and fashionable place to get married in the eighteenth and nineteenth centuries, especially if you were famous.

George Eliot, Grimaldi the clown, Teddy Roosevelt and Percy Shelley all got married (or remarried) here. It also happens to be the church where Eliza Doolittle's father weds in *Pygmalion*... So when Stanley Holloway sings 'Get Me to the Church on Time' in the film

PUB: Masons Arms

adaptation *My Fair Lady*, this is where he's heading!

Come out of the church and turn left, down St George Street.

Turn right into Conduit Street and then right into New Bond Street.

On the right is **SOTHEBY'S ❷**, the largest fine art auctioneer in the world, where you can often see amazing items that they are planning to sell. I saw all of Freddie Mercury's belongings in here before they got sold off!

The Egyptian figure above the door is Sekhmet, the goddess of healing, who supposedly formed the desert with her breath to protect the pharaohs. Yikes! Imagine having to kiss her.

She dates from around 1300 BC and some claim this is the oldest outdoor statue in London. Cleopatra's Needle, on Victoria Embankment, is surely another contender, dating from around 1450 BC – but that is often said to be an 'artefact' rather than a 'statue'... You be the judge! It's said that a bidder paid £40 for Sekhmet in the nineteenth century but failed to collect it, so Sotheby's decided to put it here. The man on the door verified this story... although apparently there's no record of such an auction taking place.

Cross the road and turn left down Bloomfield Place, then left into Bourdon Street, where you'll pass a plaque on your left for fashion photographer Terence Donovan. In the 1960s he did a famous photoshoot with Twiggy in front of a union flag. If you bear to your right along Bourdon Place you'll see a **SCULPTURE ❸** of this event. The sculpture is by Neal French and I rather like it, especially the figure of a pedestrian who has stopped to see what's going on (even though the photoshoot actually took place in Knightsbridge).

Turn left, then right, to continue on Bourdon Street. Turn right at the big house with the Dunhill signs, which is **BOURDON HOUSE ❹**, dating from the 1720s.

Until the 1950s this was the residence of Hugh Grosvenor, the second Duke of Westminster, whose family were granted the Duchy of Westminster in 1874. The Grosvenors own large amounts of land in Park Lane, Belgravia and Mayfair, making them one of the richest families in Britain. They trace their history back to 1066, when Gilbert le Grosveneur (his surname meaning 'the fat hunter') arrived in England with William the Conqueror and was granted land. In 1677 his descendant Sir Thomas Grosvenor married Mary Davies, who had inherited 500 acres of marshland north of the Thames, and bingo, the dynasty really began!

Walk up Davies Street, which was named after Mary; she was only twelve when she married Sir Thomas Grosvenor – it was different times... On your right you'll come to **CLARIDGE'S** ❺, where celebrities like to stay.

Mussolini famously brought a prostitute here in 1922, during an international conference. He arranged for the Blackshirts to congregate outside, singing the fascist anthem 'Giovinezza'. He was also furious that the French delegation to the conference got better rooms than him, and spent most of his time complaining about the London fog, eventually swearing never to return to England. He never did!

In 1945 Crown Prince Alexander of Yugoslavia was born here, in what was suite 212. The Yugoslavian royal family were in exile and Winston Churchill is said to have arranged for some soil from their home country to be placed under the bed, so that Alexander could be born on Yugoslavian soil.

Cross over Brook Street (its name refers to the River Tyburn, which runs beneath the ground here) and further along Davies Street you'll come to **GRAYS ANTIQUES MARKET** ❻, which used to be a toilet manufacturer (look for the original sign of John Bolding and Sons in the brickwork outside).

You used to be able to see a trickle of the River Tyburn downstairs here, but they have now closed that section. It's still worth a look at the treasure trove in here, though. My particular favourite is a pornographic Victorian pocket watch. Most amusing. (Did I just say that out loud?)

Turn left down Weighhouse Street and you'll come to the rather beautiful **UKRAINIAN CATHOLIC CATHEDRAL** ❼, which was designed by Alfred Waterhouse, who was also the architect of the Natural History Museum. If it's open it's worth a peek inside, if you're not tired of churches.

At the end of Weighhouse Street we're going to turn left, into Duke Street, but first take a look at **BROWN HART GARDENS** ❽ in front of you. There used to be a communal garden here enjoyed by the locals, but in 1902 it was turned into an electricity substation. In order to make up for the loss of the garden the Duke of Westminster decided to have it all spruced up, with nice plants and Italian-style paving, so today people can once again enjoy their sandwiches here. Sitting in the middle of it feels a bit like being surrounded by a Victorian red-brick jungle!

If you're desperate for a pint you could try the **BARLEY MOW** 🍺 along Duke

Walk 13: Mayfair to Westminster | **223**

Street. This used to be the Japanese ambassador's residence around the beginning of the twentieth century. I'll be honest, the Barley Mow is lovely – but this is Mayfair, where things aren't that cheap. The restaurant upstairs is very good, but I've gone and mislaid my wallet, so I'm carrying on.

What? Oh, go on, then: a quick half of London Pride. Kanpai!

Continue down Duke Street and you'll come to Grosvenor Square. On the left corner is **NUMBER 9** ❾, occupied in the 1780s by John Adams, who became the second president of the United States.

Head into the garden and walk over diagonally to the far corner. Then nip across to **48 UPPER GROSVENOR STREET** ❿, the former home of the Duchess of Argyll (a Scottish heiress and social butterfly who was known for numerous steamy 'liaisons'). This is the house in which a very British scandal took place! When the suspicious Duke of Argyll bust open her closet and discovered a photo of her 'getting her gums around someone's plums', while wearing nothing but a pearl necklace, he filed for divorce. Unfortunately, the man in question couldn't be identified because the photo cut him off at the neck – so all sorts of rumours abounded about who it could be. Even Lord Denning was enlisted to get to the bottom of it. In the end they narrowed it down to Duncan Sandys (the Minister for Defence) and Douglas Fairbanks, Jr. Sandys offered to resign but ultimately everyone thought it was Fairbanks, the dirty rotter. He denied it, but I suspect he was inwardly rather smug.

Head down South Audley Street, to your left. Turn left at the Audley (unless you already want another drink!) and walk along Mount Street until you see the Connaught Hotel on your left.

Now turn right into the little park and you'll see ABC (another bloody church).

This one is the **CATHOLIC CHURCH OF THE IMMACULATE CONCEPTION** ⓫ – and it's stunning inside, so worth a look for sure.

Continue through the pleasant Mount Street Gardens, emerging by the splendid **LIBRARY** ⓬, built in 1894, and you'll find yourself back on South Audley Street. Turn left past the **GROSVENOR CHAPEL** ⓭ on your left, built in 1730, where Florence Nightingale used to worship.

PUB
Barley Mow

We're whizzing through this because there is so much to cover, but do keep your eyes open for the mixture of beautiful eighteenth-century houses next to Art Deco buildings and typical Victorian carvings inside the red brickwork. You could spend hours wandering these streets.

When you come to Tilney Street look at the building across the road. This is the **UNIVERSITY WOMEN'S CLUB** **14**, which opened in 1883 as a riposte to all the gentlemen's clubs that were opening up. We'll certainly be going past a few of those on this walk.

Note the lamppost just outside the building. Russian spies used to draw a figure '8' on this during the Cold War to indicate that there was a package to be picked up at a 'drop' in Knightsbridge (see **Walk 5**). Sometimes they would even leave things inside the access flap on the back of the lamppost.

Keep going until the end of South Audley Street and you'll arrive at a beautiful row of houses in Curzon Street, with very nicely preserved torch-snuffers outside. You will see quite a few of these on this walk since we're going through a rather wealthy neighbourhood. Rich people could afford to pay 'link boys' to light their way home at night, carrying a torch that would then be snuffed out on arrival to preserve fuel (but the Joolz Guides points-awarding scheme for spotting these didn't exist back then).

Turn right and then left into Curzon Square. Look up at the back of the house you passed on your left, **I CURZON SQUARE** **15**. It was upstairs here in 1974 that 'Mama' Cass Elliot of the Mamas and Papas died from a heart attack (she was said to have choked on a ham sandwich, though in later years it turned out this was a journalist's embellishment, as a way to divert attention away from talk of drink and drugs). The flat was owned by Harry Nilsson – but he must have considered changing his name to Jonah after Keith Moon, the drummer from The Who, also died in the very same bed four years later! To be fair, Nilsson did try to warn Moon that it might be cursed but the drummer told him to stop being so stupid.

Now go back to Curzon Street and turn right.

Walk for a while and then turn right just before the Church of Christ Scientists, into a little archway.

This will lead you to **SHEPHERD MARKET** **16**. This is a very cute little enclave, with lots of shops and cafés, which makes you feel like you've been transported into a village setting from an Agatha Christie novel. By 1746 the area had been developed by Edward Shepherd, but before that the annual May Fair was held here beside the River Tyburn. That's why the greater area came to be called Mayfair.

Ye Grapes

Hmm… There are a few pubs here, so let's use the Rule of Ted (see page 166) and enter **YE GRAPES**, which started life as the Coffee House in 1742. By 1827 they were calling it the Bunch of Grapes and by 1997 my friend was calling it the Arse Grapes (of course). They actually do nice Thai food upstairs; since a friend recently accused my prawn linguine of tasting more like a pad Thai, I'd better go and see what the difference is.

I reckon it will go well with a pint of Madrí Excepcional.

Cheers!

After nosing around the area a bit, head back out to Curzon Street the way you came and turn right.

Soon it will turn sharp left, becoming Fitzmaurice Place.

The building on the left here is the **LANSDOWNE CLUB** ⑰, where Harry Gordon Selfridge used to live. Prior to that it was occupied by Prime Minister William Fitzmaurice, the Marquess of Lansdowne, also known as the Earl of Shelburne. It was in his study here that he helped draft the Treaty of Paris, which ended the American Revolutionary War. There is a copy of it on the wall, but you'd need a member of the club to show you around. These days the private members' club contains an Art Deco swimming pool, a fencing salle and squash courts.

PUB

Ye Grapes

Cross the road here and run the gauntlet of shisha lounges in the alleyway (you might like to hold your breath to prevent asphyxiation).

Once you emerge at the end, cross Berkeley Street and walk up Hay Hill.

Turn left at Dover Street and then follow the corner round to the right, into Grafton Street.

At the end of Grafton Street turn right into New Bond Street, past Ralph Lauren with its posh café and the fancy jewellery stores, and turn left into Burlington Gardens.

Now head right, into **BURLINGTON ARCADE** ⑱. I won't go into the history here since I have a whole section on it in my first book, but you need to observe a few unusual rules… No running, shouting, opening of umbrellas or whistling! (One of the beadles in his top hat and cloak once also reprimanded me for piddling in the shallow end, which is also frowned upon.)

When you emerge onto Piccadilly turn left. Naturally, Piccadilly has a million things one could talk about. I would usually pop into Fortnum & Mason, established in 1707, since it's one of my favourite shops; but not this time.

Have a look up at the building on the other side of the road. At the time of writing this still had excellent lettering on it, with the name of **FRENCH RAILWAYS HOUSE** ⓭. Sadly, by the time you read this it will probably have been flattened, after the council approved a complete redevelopment. I was very fond of this building because I remember how my mum used to bring us down here to book our overland trips to Italy (since we were scared of flying). It would be the same woman working there every year and she'd sit with you for hours, planning the rail journey to Dover and then the ferry to Calais, followed by a train to Paris and then the sleeping car to Rome. While I'm very sad that the council approved the demolition, I'm at least happy to say that you can still see French Railways House in the video which accompanies this walk, dedicated to my mother.

The building on your left houses the Royal Academy and numerous other institutions – but I've brought you here to have a look at a **PHONE BOX** ⓴ under the arch. You'll spot two, but the first one is the original wooden prototype designed in 1924 by Giles Gilbert Scott. Subsequently 1,500 of these K2 boxes were manufactured in cast iron, to be installed around London. However, they became too expensive, so they were replaced with later designs including the K6 which you can find throughout Britain.

Carry on up Piccadilly and cross over towards **HATCHARDS** ㉑, which opened in 1797 and has been on this site since 1801, making it the UK's oldest bookshop. It's a lovely place with creaky stairs and lots of rooms, but my favourite thing is the table they have at the back. It's a perfectly ordinary-looking table in constant use but it's called 'Oscar Wilde's table' because it was where he used to sign copies of his books. (I have also signed copies of mine on that table, so that obviously makes me his equal.)

Now continue along Piccadilly. On your right you'll come to **ST JAMES'S PICCADILLY** ㉒. This church was designed by Sir Christopher Wren (of course) and consecrated in 1684. It's worth popping inside to look at the wonderful altarpiece and marble font carved by Grinling Gibbons, the finest wood carver in England. Both items are over 300 years old.

I rather like the churchyard as a peaceful place to eat my sandwiches. There's also a little caravan where you can seek help or advice if you're feeling in need of some mental support. A bit like the Samaritans, I guess.

You should be able to walk through the

PUB

Red Lion

café beside the church and through to Jermyn Street, where you can turn left and then right into Duke of York Street. (If the café is shut, continue past the church on Piccadilly, take the alleyway to your right, to then turn right into Jermyn Street and left into Duke of York street.)

One really must nip into the **RED LION** here for a swift half. It's been here since 1781 but was rebuilt during the 1880s, with the current building being a perfect example of a Victorian gin palace. It's a bit small but that makes it all the cosier, with an island bar occupying the middle area and original etched mirrors and cut glass with mahogany features. You might end up just staying here for the rest of the day, but I'll take a quick half of Seafarers before moving on. Cheers!

Now walk back towards the church and turn left into Jermyn Street (which was named after Henry Jermyn, Earl of St Albans, who was granted the freehold and started developing the area from the 1660s). The street has developed a reputation for dandyism and smart tailoring, boasting some very fancy shops fit for gentlemen and ladies!

Walk past Paxton and Whitfield (the oldest cheesemonger in England) and then have a quick nose around **FLORIS** ㉓ (the oldest fragrance retailer in England). Juan Floris arrived from Menorca in 1730 and it's still run by his family today, eight generations later.

I love this shop with its mini-museum in the back where you can see the fragrances and invoices of past customers like Marylin Monroe, Ian Fleming, Winston Churchill and Queen Victoria! The counter was bought from the Great Exhibition in 1851 and you can even book yourself in to create your own fragrance – not that I'd need to!

My favourite is Elite, which was favoured by David Bowie.

Now continue and turn left into Duke Street St James's, where there's another pub: the **CHEQUERS**. I know you might be thinking, 'We've only just left the Red Lion!' – but this is a cute little place and I can't resist another quick half when this part of London is so full of nice pubs, and in nice weather it's pleasant to be able to sit outside at the back. The Chequers opened in 1732 and was originally named the Mason's Arms, either because stonemasons used the yard behind for cutting stone to build Westminster Palace, or because two of the houses here were owned by a victualler called Henry Mason.

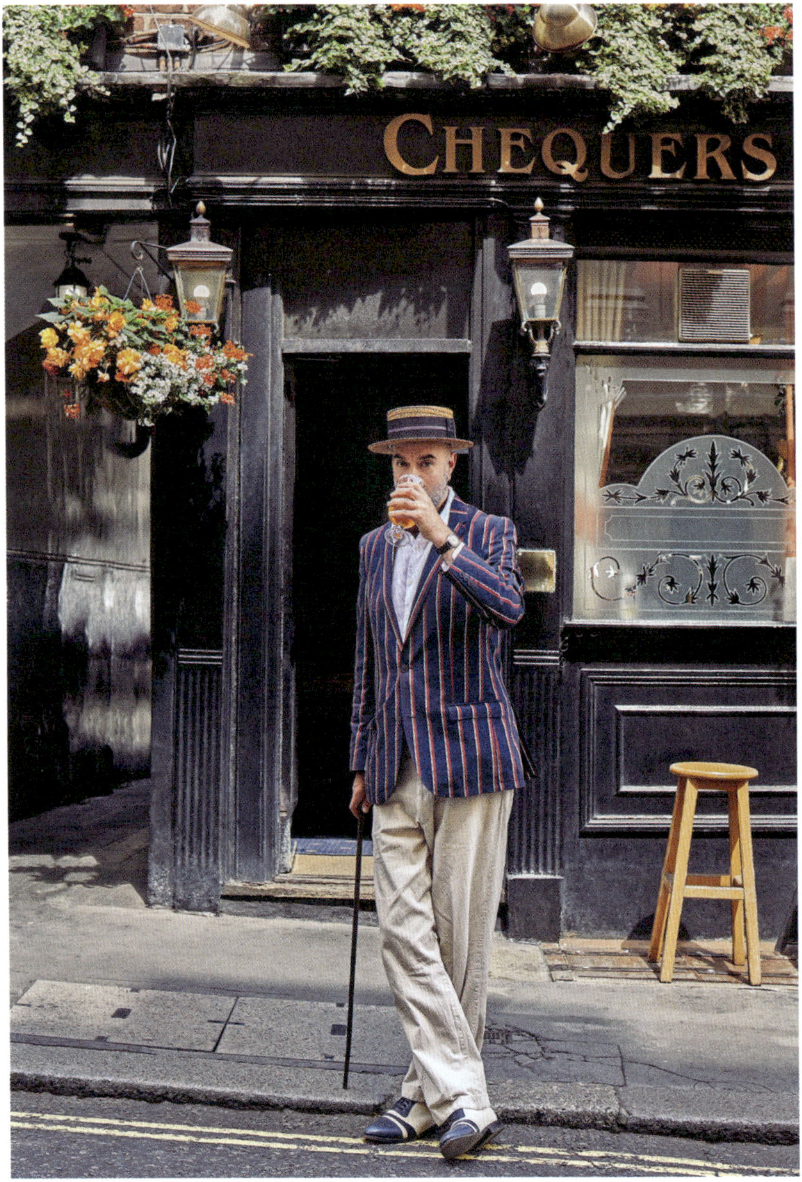
CHEQUERS

PUB: Chequers

Many of the coachmen and grooms for the posh houses around here would while away the hours waiting for their masters by playing chequers on the steps of the pub, so they decided to change the name. If you need fuelling up you can sample their filling pub grub, which includes a satisfying range of toasted sandwiches, and good-value Sunday roasts.

Walk through to Masons Yard and on the far side is the **SCOTCH OF ST JAMES** (24), where all the big names in the 1960s music scene hung out. The Beatles and the Rolling Stones had their own tables and it was here that Jimi Hendrix first performed in 1966 when he arrived from Canada. Apparently Eric Clapton declared that he was giving up the guitar after watching in awe.

The art gallery, **NUMBER 6** (25) on your left, was where John Lennon met Yoko Ono after she held an exhibition here. One of the exhibits was called *Apple*, consisting of an apple on a stand. It cost £200 (a lot in the 1960s) and, quite understandably in my opinion, John Lennon just picked up the apple and took a bite, much to the horror of Yoko, who didn't actually recognise him. Funnily enough, the only one she knew was Ringo – whose name means 'apple' in Japanese! I wonder if that has any connection with them creating the Apple record label!

Leave the yard to the left of the Chequers, past the Yoko Ono mural, and turn left.

Turn left again into King Street, passing the **OLDEST SURVIVING BLUE PLAQUE IN LONDON** (26), dating from 1867. It commemorates Napoleon III, who lived here in exile from 1847 to 1848, and is the only blue plaque to have been installed while the honouree was still alive. In case you were wondering, Napoleon III was the nephew of the 'original' Napoleon. He became the first president of France in 1848, before declaring himself emperor and eventually ending up back in exile in England in 1871, after his defeat and capture in the Franco–Prussian War.

Now, if it's open, walk into the centre of **ST JAMES'S SQUARE** (27), where you'll find a statue of King William III.

I don't know if it's true but I like the story as to why his horse's foot is slightly raised, above what looks like a molehill: it is said that William tripped over a molehill and was taken to Kensington Palace to recover from his injuries – but someone left a window open and he died of pneumonia. (The sucker couldn't catch an even break.)

Okay, let's quickly whizz around the square, but I won't talk about all the gentlemen's clubs because there are too many!

In the north-west corner is the London Library, occupying this site since 1845, which I like because amongst its many famous members was Bram Stoker, and they recently found the books he used to research *Dracula*. Apparently, *The Book of Werewolves* by Reverend Sabine Baring-Gould has his notes scrawled in the margin! You could get done for defacing library books! Just ask Joe Orton!

Walking clockwise you'll come to Chatham House, which was a popular residence for Prime Ministers. William Gladstone, William Pitt the Elder and the Earl of Derby (though not at the same time). **Points** for spotting the torch-snuffers outside the entrance!

Number 5, in the north-east corner, is where the Libyan People's Bureau used to be. I remember watching the news in 1984, when poor PC Yvonne Fletcher was shot from here during an anti-Gaddafi demonstration. An eleven-day siege followed and forty officials were deported for not cooperating with the police. The culprit was never caught and you can see Fletcher's memorial opposite the building.

Continue clockwise, past Charles II Street on your left, and take the next road off the square down to Pall Mall.

The fancy building in front of you to the left is the **REFORM CLUB 28**, from where Phileas Fogg sets off in Jules Verne's *Around the World in Eighty Days*. It's supposed to have the finest club room in all of London, not that the likes of me ever get to see it! Except, that is, in films like *Die Another Day*, where James Bond has a fencing match overseen by Madonna, or (a personal favourite of mine) *The Man Who Haunted Himself*, starring Roger Moore!

Cross the road and walk down Carlton Gardens ahead of you, where you'll be able to peek over into the gardens used by the Reform Club, the Travellers Club and the Athenaeum. Maybe some of the gentlemen in suits, smoking their pipes, might rustle their copies of the *Daily Telegraph* in disapproval at your nosiness.

Turn right into Carlton House Terrace and then turn left at the statue of Charles de Gaulle, taking the steps down to the Mall past King George VI and his wife, whom I knew as Queen Elizabeth the Queen Mother.

Cross the road and enter St James's Park. We're trying to walk diagonally to the right in the direction of a bridge, which you should be able to see (or just ask someone).

Take the bridge across the lake and keep an eye out for the park's famous pelicans – and also for spies! This is supposedly where new recruits to

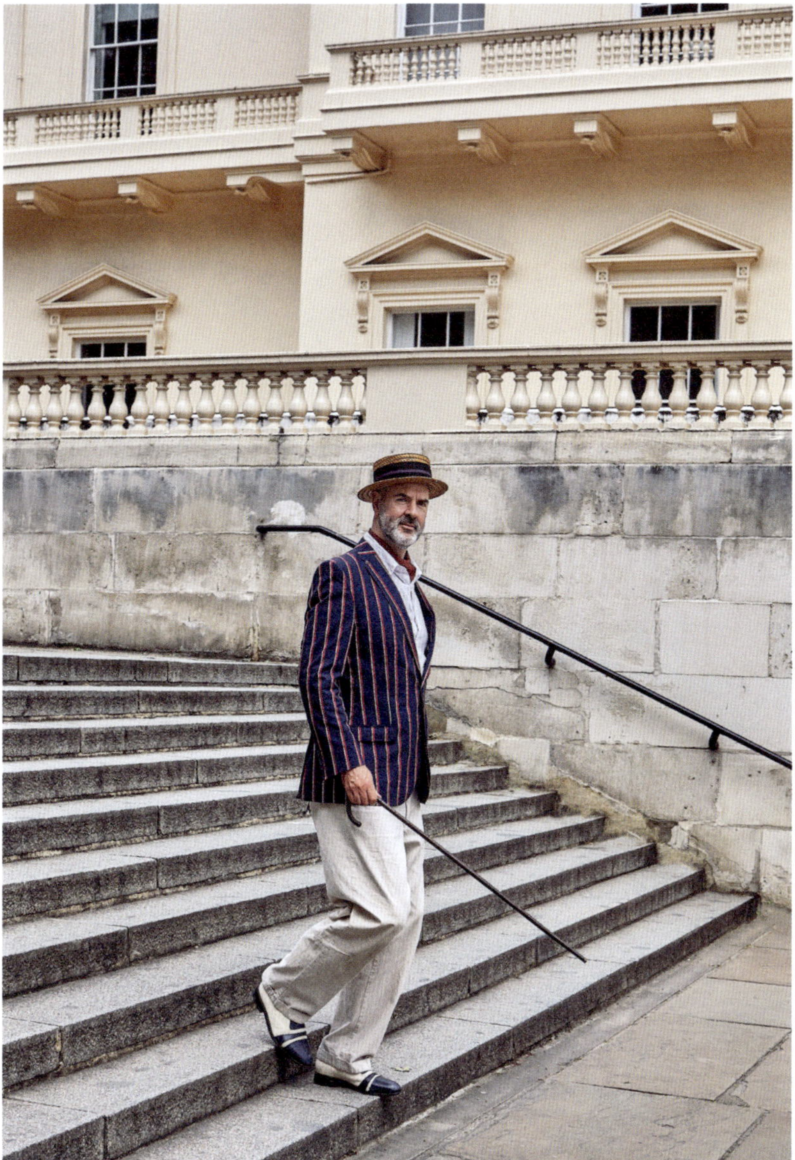

British intelligence are greeted as a sort of initiation, although it doesn't seem very secret if even I know about it!

To your left you can see **DUCK ISLAND** ㉙, with its cottage donated in 1840 by the Ornithological Society of London for the use of a bird-keeper. (The bird-keeper would have looked after the park's famous pelicans, although today the cottage is used by the London Gardens Trust and the pelicans are fed by the Royal Parks' wildlife officer.)

In 1661 poet Charles de Saint-Evremond was forced into exile from France and came to London to suck up to King Charles II. Since he was popular, the king didn't want to offend the French – but he also didn't want to be too generous, so he concocted a new position, that of Governor of Duck Island, which sounded perfectly fine to Saint-Evremond, who had no idea what it was! Meanwhile the French knew that it was just this island, but since they'd exiled him they were fine with it and everyone was happy. Charles II also gave him a pension because he found the fellow rather amusing and was grateful to him for introducing the king to champagne.

Saint-Evremond was eventually invited back to France but Hortense Mancini, the delectable and rather sexy niece of Cardinal Mazarin, had come to London in 1670 and set up a salon for love-making, gambling and erudite conversation, and Saint-Evremond liked it so much that he decided to stay, scrounging off the king!

From the bridge, continue along the path straight ahead. As you go, keep an eye out for all the beautiful original gas lamps, some of which will have the initials of the monarch who was on the throne when they were installed. If you walk through the park at night it feels like you are in *Oliver Twist*!

When you reach Birdcage Walk, you'll see a pelican crossing. (Well, you will definitely see a place to cross the road – but if you see one of the park's pelicans actually crossing here, score yourself lots of **points**!!)

Head over and walk through the gates on the other side. Then turn left into Queen Anne's Gate.

Look at the wonderful keystones above the windows. They're made of a material called Coade Stone, which was specially formulated to withstand the London weather. After the death in 1821 of Eleanor Coade, after whom it is named, she took the formula to her grave; it was only at the end of the twentieth century that the correct composition was successfully recreated!

Soon you'll see a statue of **QUEEN ANNE** ㉚. This was originally intended to be outside St Mary Le Strand – but when she died in 1714 they changed their minds and decided to put her here instead, which seems rather less complimentary, though she does have another one outside St Paul's Cathedral, so it's fair enough.

Above her head is a property marker indicating that the building was owned by Christ's Hospital (an old English public school). You get **points** for spotting this, as well as the old street sign next to it. Fans of the 1960s TV show *The Persuaders* might recognise this house as the one where Roger Moore lives.

Keep going and around to your left you'll see Cockpit Steps, named after an infamous cock-fighting arena which stood on this site. William Hogarth's *The Cockpit*, from 1759, is believed to depict a fight here, so it's assumed that he must have visited. It's worth quickly popping down the steps here to take a look at the pillar on the left, which still has some ancient-looking graffiti on it. It's hard to tell how long it's been here, but certainly some of it dates from the nineteenth century.

I wonder if Hogarth also visited the **TWO CHAIRMEN** opposite.

Look, we've almost finished and there's another pub around the corner, but we'll just have a quick half because this is thought to be the oldest pub in Westminster, dating back to at least 1729. The 'two chairmen' are the sedan chair carriers who would wait in the pub until the posh people came out of the cockpit and then take them home.

PUB

Two Chairmen

Thirsty work, I bet!

For some reason Thursday nights get pretty rammed, possibly because of the employees of *The Spectator* magazine, whose office is on Old Queen Street. Being so close to the Houses of Parliament, they get a lot of politicians and journalists in this pub.

Half a pint of Greene King IPA and make it fast.

Cheers.

Turn right out of the pub, along Old Queen Street. I won't mention all the blue plaques because there are so many, but you can have fun reading who lived where.

I like **NUMBER 26** **31** on the left, with black bricks. This was where the king's falconer lived until the end of the eighteenth century. He was the only man who was allowed to drive his carriage down Birdcage Walk (apart from the king). The bricks of the house are not actually black – they're more likely to be yellow or red underneath. Exactly the same thing happened with 10 Downing Street.

After years of people burning coal to keep warm, many of the houses in London became covered in soot. Once they'd decided to bring in the Clean Air Act in the 1950s they started scrubbing the soot off the Prime Minister's home. They found the bricks to be yellow, but this didn't look very appropriate for such an important building, so they decided to paint the house black again!

The same decision was made for this house on Old Queen Street, which is kept black by some sort of concoction made with coal dust. I don't know why, since the falconer doesn't live there any more!

Keep going and turn right into Storey's Gate, where you'll find the **WESTMINSTER ARMS**, with a huge clock above it. (It's usually closed on Sundays, but there's no shortage of other pubs nearby for Sundays, such as the Sanctuary House on Tothill Street.) All the touristy Parliament stuff will have to wait for another walk. I'm knackered and fancy a pint. As long as you don't mind rubbing shoulders with civil servants and politicians, you'll be fine. They even have an old Division Bell in here – in times gone by, if you'd heard a bell ringing in the afternoon it wouldn't have been last orders! It would just be reminding MPs to go back to the House of Commons to vote! The Division Bell system was finally switched off in the 2010s, so it won't bother the likes of you and me, or Angelina Jolie or Bill Clinton (who have also drunk here).

I'll take a pint of Spitfire. Hear, hear.

Cheers.

PUB

Westminster Arms

— Quiz! —

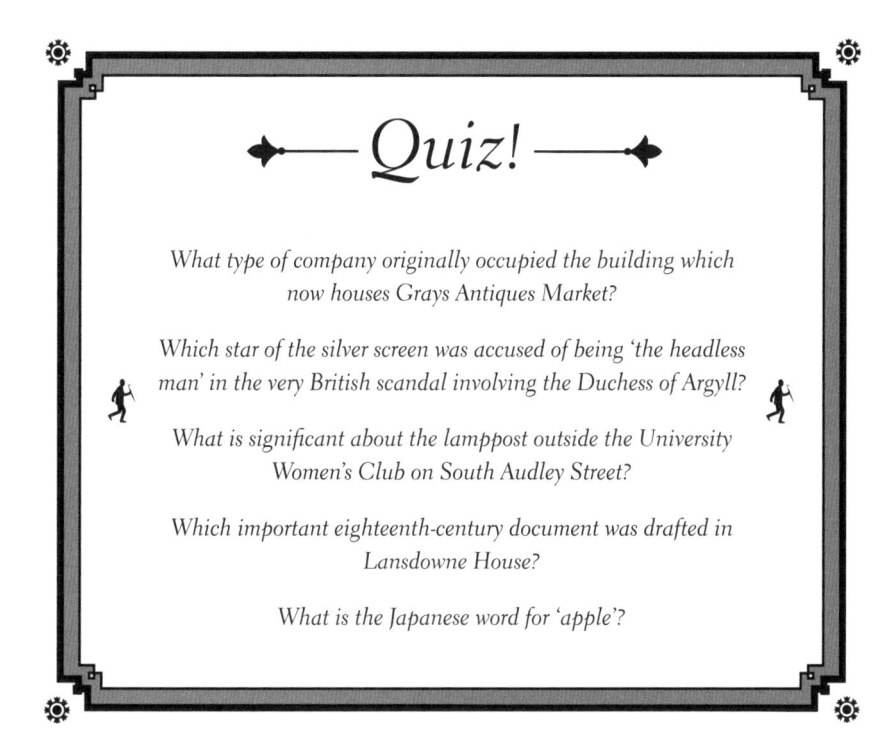

What type of company originally occupied the building which now houses Grays Antiques Market?

Which star of the silver screen was accused of being 'the headless man' in the very British scandal involving the Duchess of Argyll?

What is significant about the lamppost outside the University Women's Club on South Audley Street?

Which important eighteenth-century document was drafted in Lansdowne House?

What is the Japanese word for 'apple'?

7. Electric Street Lamp

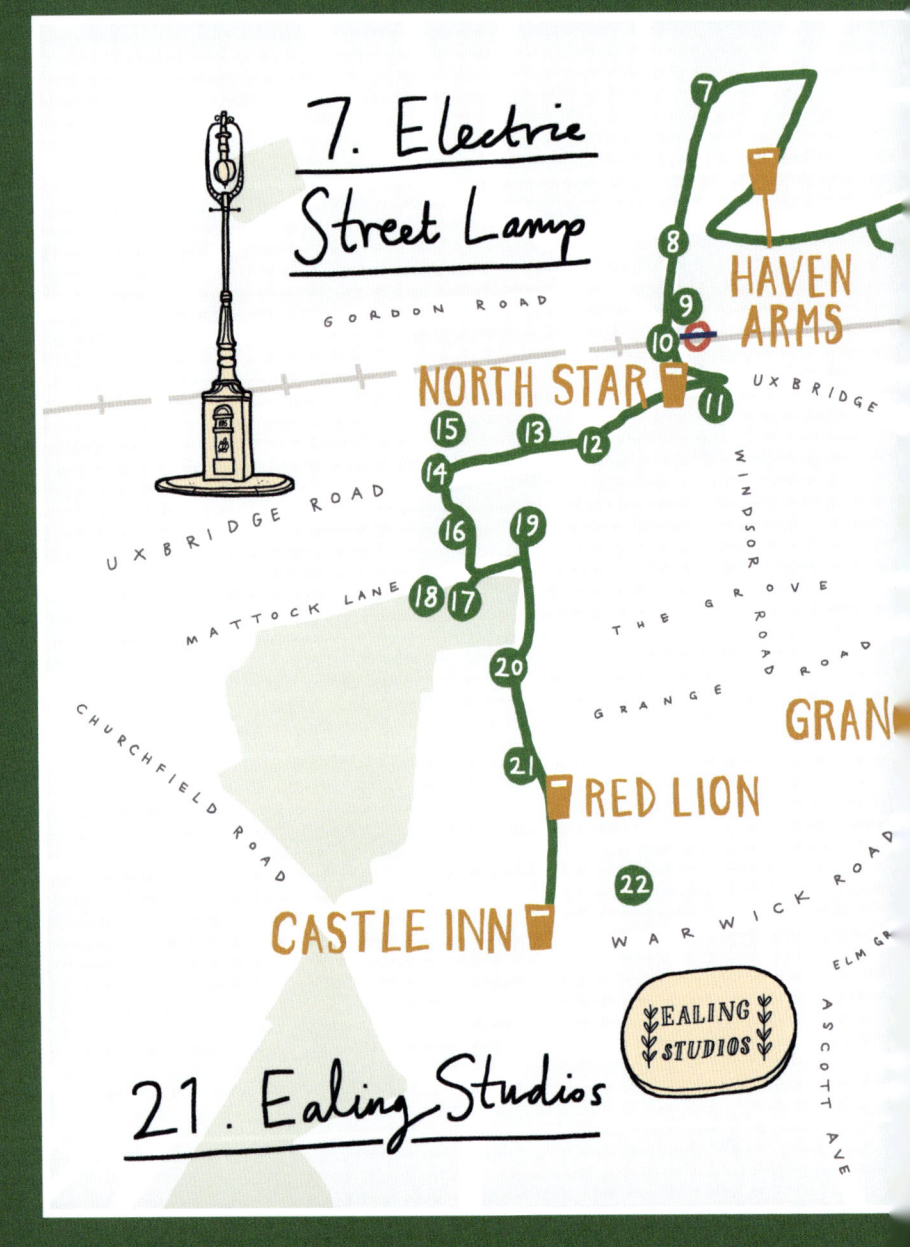

GORDON ROAD

HAVEN ARMS

NORTH STAR

UXBRIDGE

UXBRIDGE ROAD

MATTOCK LANE

WINDSOR ROAD

THE GROVE

GRANGE ROAD

GRAN

CHURCHFIELD ROAD

RED LION

CASTLE INN

WARWICK ROAD

ELM GR

ASCOTT AVE

EALING STUDIOS

21. Ealing Studios

4. Milepost

14 EALING

14 AN APPEALING WHEELING THROUGH EALING

DISTANCE
5.1 km (3.2 miles)

TIME
2 hours 30 minutes
with a few pints en route

NEAREST STATION
Ealing Common

PUBS
Grange; Haven Arms; North Star; Red Lion; Castle Inn

Ah! Well met!

I thought we'd meet in the marvellous **GRANGE**.

I like pubs on corners, especially if there's a large space to look out onto. The Grange has been here since the 1870s. It has clearly had a lot of refurbishment and is now a tolerably comfortable place with plenty of space, healthy-looking young people, and a hearty menu that earns my respect because they serve custard (not ice cream) with their apple crumble.

PUB *Grange*

I know! What are those other places thinking?! Lucky thing too, because it's a bit of a walk to the next pub!

Let me finish my pint of Young's Original and we'll be off. Chin chin.

Come out of the pub and cross Warwick Road towards the post box, scoring **points** for noticing that it's got Queen Victoria's cypher on it.

Walk down Warwick Dene, with the little **GARDEN** ❶ to your left. This was a rest garden for the elderly and the blind, dating from 1905, but these days it's more of a children's play area.

At the end you'll come to **ALL SAINTS CHURCH** ❷, which stands on the site of Elm Grove, the home of Spencer Perceval, the only British Prime Minister to be assassinated while in office. He lived here with his wife and twelve children, who last saw him one day in 1812 when he left to go to work (not all Prime Ministers lived at 10 Downing Street).

The man who shot him in the House of Commons, John Bellingham, was an angry businessman who blamed Perceval for failing to compensate him after he was imprisoned in Russia for unpaid debts. He was apprehended and before you could say 'I'm Bellingham and so is my wife' he was hanged – just seven days later! They didn't hang about in those days. What if it had been some terrible mistake?

Anyway, when Perceval's last daughter died in 1900 she left money for the building of a church, to be called All Saints because her daddy was born on All Saints Day, 1 November.

Now, there are few interesting things around here, but you might not want to visit them as they're a bit of a diversion – but let me tell you about them, anyway, and you can follow the dotted line on the map if you want to see them.

Let's head north-east across Ealing Common, towards the corner of Gunnersbury Avenue and Uxbridge Road.

It would be remiss of me not to mention the **NORTH KOREAN EMBASSY** ❸, which you would come to if you were to turn right down Gunnersbury Avenue to number 73 – a two-storey semi-detached family home. You wouldn't think it was an embassy… but if you lurk around too long taking pictures, you'll soon find out!

There was an amusing incident in 2014 when a nearby hairdresser put a photo of Kim Jong Un in his window with an offer: 'Having a bad hair day? 15 per cent off all gents' haircuts!' Soon afterwards he received a knock on the door from the angry North Korean officials, but he gave them pretty short shrift, saying, 'This is England, pal!' And in a scene befitting of *Dad's Army* the officials said: 'What is your name? Your name shall go into the book!'

No further action was taken.

Anyway, back on Uxbridge Road there are a couple of street furniture beauties. This was the old road to Oxford, and in the days when Ealing was just a small village there were many pubs along this stretch, which meant rich pickings for highwaymen.

A rather splendid metal **MILEPOST** ❹ stands further along to the left – you only get **points** if you walk all the way up to it! These days Ealing is part of London, but when this milepost was installed we would have been six miles from London and nine miles from Uxbridge.

Closer to Gunnersbury Avenue you'll see a lovely old **FOUNTAIN** ❺ dating from 1878, installed by the splendidly-named Metropolitan Drinking Fountain and Cattle Trough Association. Fountains were often erected in memory of people, which I think is a nice touch, a bit like how we sometimes have memorial benches these days. I suppose it got a bit silly having fountains all over the place. If you find one that actually works you get **double points**!

Now walk north up Hanger Lane, which forms part of the North Circular Road. This is more pleasant than it sounds, since you can take the grassy path beside the road (which should also make it safe enough to read this next bit without getting run over).

The name Ealing comes from the Anglo-Saxon *Gillingas*, meaning 'people of Gilla' (Gilla was a local chieftain). By the twelfth century it had become Yllinges or Zealing, before eventually ending up as Ealing in the nineteenth century.

During the Great Plague Londoners would escape the big city to the villages of Ealing and Hanwell (which is nearby), so they started calling them 'Healing' and 'And Well'.

After you cross over the railway tracks you'll come to a housing estate on your left, with green gates carrying the initials 'EV'. This is **EALING VILLAGE** ❻, a beautiful 1930s development intended as a mini-Hollywood to attract film stars who could rent a place near Ealing Film Studios. Unfortunately the location didn't prove popular with the film stars, so it was mostly crew who ended up staying here, and by the 1980s the houses were being sold off. I'm hoping you can get in, because sometimes the gates are locked. If they're open, you might end up having to come back this way afterwards if you can't get out at the other end – so keep your eye out for any residents walking that way to exit with them…

This might all sound like a bit of a hassle, but the estate is stunning and very much worth a look around if you can! There are tennis courts, a swimming pool and a club house, which used to have billiard tables and a grand piano. The windows and other features are still original and it really does feel like you're in an episode of *Poirot* or *Columbo*. When I last visited, residents were having barbecues in the communal garden, in what looked like an idyllic Hollywood scene.

Now, do you want to risk walking to the end and turning right? If you're lucky you can ask someone to use their code for the gate, to let you out onto Madeley Road as a shortcut. Otherwise you have to climb over and might get into trouble… Or simply go back the way you came. (If you need to retrace your steps, or couldn't get in to begin with, turn left back on the North Circular, then left again into Madeley Road.)

There are many detached houses along here, all built around 1888 as you can see from the dates on the buildings. At the time Ealing was known as 'the Queen of the Suburbs', and looking at the splendour of the houses I can see why. Very genteel!

Turn right into Haven Lane, where you'll find a choice of pubs in close proximity. I expect you'll need a drink after that walk.

Today I fancy the **HAVEN ARMS**, with its etched glass windows and unusual tiling on the upper part of the building. The pub dates to the late nineteenth century, though exactly when is anyone's guess, with the signs displaying '1861' and '1872', plus 'Licensed 1893'. It has a courtyard beer garden and last time I was here it still

PUB

Haven Arms

had a pool table – a relative rarity these days. Oh, and look: they have a pub dog, called Bella! **Points**!!

Time for a pint, I think… Make mine a Guinness.

Cheers!

Exit the pub and turn left up Haven Lane. Then take the second left, into Woodville Road, following it round.

On the corner of Aston Road is a stupendous example of an early **ELECTRIC STREET LAMP** ❼ from 1895. The inscription reads 'LEB' – London Electricity Board. It's a pity that every time I walk past it seems to have some sort of electrical tape wrapped around it, ruining its splendour. I mean, it looks like it was repaired by me, not by the electricity board!

At first I thought it must be one of those Pluto lamps, which dispensed

244 | Rather Splendid London Pub Walks

Grange

❸

❹

❻

❽

⓭

hot drinks such as tea and coffee. I've only seen a photograph of one, and the size and shape of the Aston Road installation is very similar to that – but alas, the Pluto lamp wasn't introduced until a couple of years later. If you've got your phone with you, try searching for 'Pluto lamp'. They were pretty cool, although they didn't really catch on.

Continue along Woodville Road and pass the roundabout, keeping the green on your right, as you enter Ealing Broadway.

On your left you'll pass the beautifully preserved chemist **D. L. LEWIS** ❽, which amazingly still operates as a pharmacy over a century after it opened. The exterior retains its 1920s appearance and the inside still has some features from 1902.

We're coming to **EALING BROADWAY STATION** ❾, which is now served by the new Elizabeth Line, but the original old District Line entrance, dating from the 1880s, can still be seen to the left of the modern one. If you go down to the District Line platform you'll see a nice example of how the Underground roundel used to look, like the one we saw in Maida Vale (**Walk 3**). It wasn't until 1913 that Edward Johnston designed the new typeface and roundel with which we are more familiar.

I've always liked the general ambience upon emerging from this station, with the green in front of you…unlike many stations that are less appealing. Continuing along the Broadway, look for the blue plaque on the right, on a building which currently has an estate agent on the ground floor. The basement is the site of the **EALING CLUB** ❿, where some members of the Rolling Stones first met. Mick Jagger and Keith Richards already knew each other, but it is said that in a tiny bar downstairs here the British rhythm and blues scene was created, making it as important as the Cavern Club in Liverpool. Rod Stewart and many others also played here; Keith Richards said that without this club there would have been nothing.

There's still a club in the basement at least, called the Red Room.

As the road splits at the end have a look up at the old signs, including the one above the Metro Bank on your left, for the Feathers Restaurant from 1929, or on the lovely building next to the pub, which used to be Edwards' Furniture Store. Some careless oaf has placed an advertising board over the half of the sign in the alleyway. The full sign told you that they also had branches in Bayswater, Kensington and Acton, but you can still see the date '1902' on the building, as well as some lovely sculptures on top.

I don't know why they decided to replace lovely old signs with these hideous new ones but I can only assume it's due to the invention of plastic.

Did somebody say pub? Okay, let's nip inside the **NORTH STAR** for a quick one.

This dates from the early nineteenth century, although it has had some refurbishment in the last few years. It's still rather splendid inside, with wooden floors and plenty of room for drinkers who don't want to eat. That said, the food is pretty decent, too, and they have a selection of craft beers from various breweries I hadn't heard of (there are so many these days) and they have outdoor heating in the groovy garden area too.

I'll play safe with a pint of Peroni.

Salute!

Come out of the pub and if you want you could turn right to take a quick look at the **POLISH CATHOLIC CHURCH** (11), also known as Parafia Ealing, which was the first Polish church in the UK. I mention it because Ealing has the largest Polish community in Britain, so if you want to buy some Polish *bigos* or *kabanos* you should be able to find them around here.

Anyway, we're turning left out of the pub and following the Broadway over to New Broadway, with the Church of Christ the Saviour on your right.

As you approach the church, look behind you at the branch of Marks and Spencer, which started out in the late nineteenth century as **JOHN SANDERS DEPARTMENT STORE** (12). Sanders was only twenty-three when he opened his first shop in Ealing in the 1860s, but he realised that the area was up and coming because of the arrival of the railways. He did pretty well because it remained trading until 1990.

In fact, Whovians (that's *Doctor Who* fans to you and me) will recognise this building from the episode starring Jon Pertwee where the Autons, who are basically mannequins in the shop window, come to life and start shooting everyone dead. Even though they were clearly just actors wearing masks they still looked creepier than a lot of the CGI rubbish you get these days.

Just after the church on the right is a lovely monument remembering **GEORGE FORMBY** (13), one of the biggest stars who worked at Ealing Studios. It carries the lyrics to one of my favourite songs, 'Count Your Blessings and Smile', which I always felt was a sentiment I could learn from. Formby was famous for playing a banjolele, which makes me think the monument

PUB

North Star

probably represents the strings and frets on that instrument.

Further along on the left you'll come to what used to be a beautiful Art Deco cinema. It opened as the **FORUM** ⑭ in 1934 and looks nearly identical to the Forum in Kentish Town. It was renamed the ABC in the 1960s but eventually closed as a cinema in 2008, remaining rather abandoned for a while, until the redevelopment of the site now known as Filmworks.

Opposite is the wonderful **TOWN HALL** ⑮, built by Charles Jones in 1888. He's the one who developed a lot of Ealing, leading to it being named 'the Queen of the Suburbs'. That's why you see many of the buildings with dates from around that period on the brickwork. Jones was accused of lining his pockets and taking advantage of his position on the council to get rich through property development; nevertheless, he's fondly remembered and it's quite a rarity for these original town halls still to be used as actual town halls. If you can get inside it's worth a look at their lovely events hall and staircase…or you might genuinely need to register a birth, death or marriage.

Cross back towards the old cinema and take the little walkway, Filmworks Walk, to the left. Then turn right when you reach the Ealing Picture House.

Soon you'll see the rather oddly positioned **WALPOLE PICTURE THEATRE** ⑯ on your right, with blue tiles looking like an entrance leading to nothing. Back in 1908 this was the entrance to the Walpole Hall Roller Skating Rink, which was located around the corner in Bond Street. In 1912 they added the blue tiles and it became a cinema. For many years, up until the 1970s, it was an Odeon cinema, but when they eventually demolished it in 1981, to make way for a modern office block, they moved the lovely entrance to here to preserve it. They should have just left it alone and preserved the whole thing, if you ask me.

Another group who tried to demolish Ealing (but failed) consisted of Martians! Chapter 16 of H. G. Wells' *The War of the Worlds* is entitled 'The Exodus from London'.

> *Another bank drove over Ealing, and surrounded a little island of survivors on Castle Hill, alive, but unable to escape.*

Come out onto Mattock Lane and to your left you should be able to see an entrance to the park and gallery.

Inside you'll find **PITZHANGER MANOR** ⑰, which was designed around 1800 by Sir John Soane, after he demolished most of the previous house that stood here. (He is the one whose tomb in St Pancras Cemetery inspired the design of the telephone box!) Soane was a famous architect and, after living here for a while, the house then passed

Red Lion

to the daughters of Spencer Perceval (the assassinated Prime Minister), one of whom married a Walpole, which explains why a few things around here carry the name Walpole.

After the death of Frederika, the last of the Perceval daughters, it became a library in 1902 before later becoming a museum and art gallery, which you can visit if you pay to enter.

The gardens of the house are rather splendid on a nice day, so go round to the right of the house and you should find a memorial for **CHARLES JONES** ⓘ⑱ on the right-hand side.

Now walk left, behind the house and alongside Soane's ornamental lake, and take the exit after the café (Pitzhanger Pantry), to the left past the postal delivery office, and walk to Ealing Green at the end. (If this isn't open you can walk back to the front of Pitzhanger Manor to Ealing Green.)

At this stage you might like to explore some of the shops over to the left on Bond Street and the High Street. One in particular that catches my eye is **CITY RADIO STORES** ⑲ at 39A Bond Street, which has been there since 1929 selling electrical accessories, and still retains its vintage shop front. In the film *Carry on Constable* when PC 'Potty Poos' Potter asks directions from two robbers, the jewellery shop that they had just robbed stood in Bond Street.

Just to the south of Ealing Green College look for the lovely **KING GEORGE V POST BOX** ⑳ recessed into the wall. You get **double points** for this one because it is accompanied by one of the old stamp-dispensing machines. I strongly doubt this one still works, but these were quite common when I were a lad!

Continue south along Ealing Green, past some lovely houses which look very much like the ones you see in old English movies starring Will Hay and George Formby (since many of those were filmed around here) and soon you'll come to a lovely white building with the **EALING STUDIOS** ㉑ sign on it.

Ealing Studios started in 1902. This was the original studio complex (along with some greenhouses out the back), making Ealing the oldest continuously operating film studios in the world – it's where the British film industry began. These studios have produced many, many famous films: *The Lavender Hill Mob*, *The Ladykillers*, *Passport to Pimlico*, *Notting Hill* and *The Theory of Everything*, to name just a few, and they shot some of the first Shakespeare ever to be put on film here. The blue plaque is for Sir Michael Balcon, who from 1938 to 1956 produced many of the famous films here and was a mentor to Alfred Hitchcock.

Later they got rid of the greenhouses and built the huge studios behind the building you're looking at. All the downstairs scenes from *Downton Abbey* were filmed here, as well as *The Singing Detective*, various bits of *Monty Python*, *Spice World*, *Doctor Who*, *The Crown* and so many more. I'm told that when actors come to film here they are overcome by the weight of history in these studios.

Actors like filming here because it's not in the middle of nowhere, as many film studios are. They can pop over the road to buy cigarettes, although when they did just that during the filming of *Shaun of the Dead* it caused many local residents to call the police, reporting sightings of zombies!

Carry on along Ealing Green and when it meets St Mary's Road you will see the **RED LION** on the other side of the road.

Get me a pint of London Pride and I'll tell you about the pub.

At one time the Red Lion was known as 'Stage 6' because many of the actors would come here after filming. Alec Guinness (later known for his *Star Wars* role) was just one of the regulars here, as was Sid James (of *Carry On* fame). The two of them worked together in *The Lavender Hill Mob*.

I certainly had a most excellent Sunday roast in here recently, so I hope they are still as good!

Okay, let's chin this down and pop down the road as I want to take you to one last pub before we finish.

Cheers!

Turn left out of the Red Lion and you'll pass the **UNIVERSITY OF WEST LONDON 22**. This used to be Ealing Art College, which was attended by Ronnie Wood, Pete Townshend and one Farrokh Bulsara, who used to model nude for the art classes here for £5 a go – before going on to become Freddie Mercury!

On the other side of the road you'll come to our final stop, the **CASTLE INN**. It started life as a coaching inn in the early nineteenth century and even retains its arch to the left, where carriages could enter – and the toilets used to be the stables! It can get quite lively, especially on live music nights.

We'll finish our walk here, surrounded by students and tutors from the university and other locals.

PUB
Red Lion

PUB

Castle Inn

To whom shall I propose a toast? I know: Michael Staniforth, the actor who played Mr Claypole from the children's TV show *Rentaghost*, which was also filmed in Ealing. Sadly he died of an AIDS-related illness, aged just forty-four. I never quite understood the show but I definitely remember it featuring prominently in my childhood – and being slightly freaked out by it most of the time. Maybe that was the whole point! It was the 1970s and those were weird times.

Cheers, Mr Claypole.

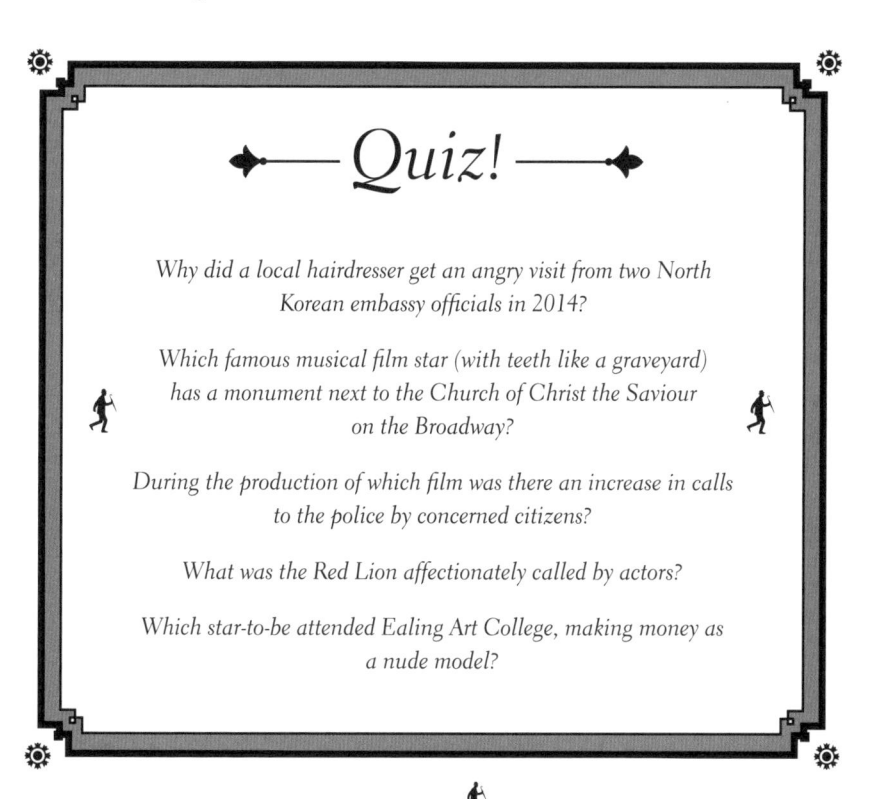

◆— Quiz! —◆

Why did a local hairdresser get an angry visit from two North Korean embassy officials in 2014?

Which famous musical film star (with teeth like a graveyard) has a monument next to the Church of Christ the Saviour on the Broadway?

During the production of which film was there an increase in calls to the police by concerned citizens?

What was the Red Lion affectionately called by actors?

Which star-to-be attended Ealing Art College, making money as a nude model?

CROWN
COCK
CHESHAM ARMS
GUN
KENTO
CAT & MUTTON
ROYAL INN ON THE PARK

7. St. Augustine's Tower

15. Round Chapel

33. Coal Hole Cover

15 HACKNEY

15 AN EAST END ODYSSEY THROUGH HACKNEY

DISTANCE
5 km (3.1 miles)

TIME
2 hours 20 minutes
with a few pints en route

NEAREST STATION
London Fields

PUBS
Cat & Mutton; Cock; Crown; Chesham Arms; Gun; Kenton; Royal Inn on the Park

Alright guv'nor, apples and pears, lovely jubbly, top banana. We're meeting in this rub-a-dub-dub called the **CAT & MUTTON**, which has been here since 1729.

It certainly has an unusual name, and as ever, when it comes to the murky history of pub names, nothing is entirely clear. Over the years the pub has enjoyed a number of animal-related names, including the Leg of Mutton & Cat; the Cat & Shoulder of Mutton; and the Cattle & Shoulder of Mutton. A cat-based explanation could be that coal barges on the Regent's Canal were known as 'cats'; but the cattle reference suggests a pub catering to thirsty drovers on their way to Smithfield cattle market, which seems more likely when combined with mutton. I mean, there's a Sheep Lane just around the corner, so I reckon it's definitely got something to do with cattle.

The pub is sometimes said to have taken its name from the nearby Cat & Mutton Bridge, over the canal – but does that mean the bridge kept changing its name, too?

PUB
Cat & Mutton

Anyway, it's in a fine old building, with some lovely Charrington's signs in the windows, and they do good food, good beers and good cocktails. And the beautiful spiral staircase earns my respect!

On a warm summer's day there's a constant stream of trendy good-looking young people (not that I'm bitter or anything) walking straight in and down to the toilets without buying a drink. Maybe I'm just getting old, but at times it feels a bit like a catwalk. Hey, maybe that's where they got the name of the pub from!

Anyway, I'm going to down this pint of Gamma Ray and let's get going!

The Cat & Mutton is at the top of **BROADWAY MARKET** ❶, to your left as you exit. If you've never visited Broadway Market before, I thoroughly recommend a stroll down to the canal and back before we get started, especially if it's the weekend when the market proper is on. (If you walked to the pub from Cambridge Heath station you might have already come up Broadway Market, and indeed dropped by the Viktor Wynd Museum, which I mentioned in my first book – probably the weirdest museum you'll ever visit.) Look out for what used to be F. Cooke, which has now become an optician, but still looks like the pie and eel shop it once was!

We're heading the other way, though, into London Fields. Cross over at the zebra by the pub, and then off at an angle to your left is a long straight path, divided into a pedestrian section on the left and a cycling section on the right. We're going to follow this all the way to the other side of the park.

From the thirteenth century onwards this area was used by drovers bringing livestock to London, 'parking' their animals (probably cattle rather than cats) to graze for a bit before heading on to London itself, a few miles on. As you walk up the path you'll see a pebble statue of two such drovers on their way to market. In the 1980s Martin Amis wrote a novel titled *London Fields*... but it was set in west London and had absolutely nothing to do with this park.

You could spend a whole day here, picnicking, watching cricket and swimming in the lido – which is, by the way, an Olympic-sized pool. (It's quite rare in London to find any Olympic-sized pools, let alone outdoor and heated!)

We've just got started, though, so we're marching straight ahead with determination. Eventually the path brings you out onto Martello Street.

Fans of industrial music will be pleased to discover that 10 Martello Street – the big building directly in front of you, with the railings in front of it – is the site of the **DEATH FACTORY** ❷, a recording studio set up by the band Throbbing Gristle in the 1970s. Score yourself some **points** for noticing the pre-1917 street sign indicating that this used to be Tower Street.

Head left along Martello Street. You'll pass the Pub in the Park, but it's too soon for another one, so continue straight ahead under the railway bridge, where it becomes pedestrianised. Keep going as it becomes Hackney Grove and eventually you'll find yourself in a very municipal-feeling area, with **HACKNEY LIBRARY AND MUSEUM** ❸ on your right and **HACKNEY TOWN HALL** ❹, dating from 1937, ahead of you.

The Town Hall replaced the old parish vestry building which we will come to shortly. After 1900, when the parish system got replaced with twenty-eight London Metropolitan Boroughs, the new local authorities tended to want grand new buildings to reflect a sense of civic pride. Look out for the flag on the Town Hall with the Hackney coat of arms on it. You might be able to make out a little church tower above the shield – we'll come to this, shortly, too!

Walk across the square, with the Town Hall on your left, and notice the wonderful 'EMPIRE' sign on the red-brick building in front of you. This is the **HACKNEY EMPIRE** ❺, which was built in 1901 and is yet another one of Frank Matcham's theatres. (He was your go-to man for designing these, having also done the Hippodrome and the Coliseum.)

It's rather famous for comedy, which might explain why there's a statue of Thalia, the Greek muse of comedy and poetry, on the roof. Head to the right, around the corner of the Empire, and left onto Mare Street, where you can get a better look at her above the main entrance. (You'll get an even better view of the statue from the other side of Mare Street.)

Charlie Chaplin, W. C. Fields, Stan Laurel and Marie Lloyd have all graced the Empire's stage; and more recently, Frankie Boyle, Ben Elton, Harry Enfield, Dawn French and Jennifer Saunders.

Between 1963 and 1986 it had become a bingo hall. Mecca, the owners, tried to do some cheapo renovations, substituting the domes on the roof with crappy replacements, but unfortunately they neglected the fact that it was a listed building. They were ordered to replace them again, this time using the correct materials, and it was so expensive that they decided to sell up – so it has reverted back to being a theatre. Happy days.

We'll continue north on Mare Street. Quite soon on the left you'll see the cute entrance to the Old Ship with its mosaic and its tiled signs. I've got another pub in mind, though, so continue on to the **COCK** 🍺 (where I shall try not to talk like one).

As you'd expect from a pub so close to the station, it's very popular with locals and you can even bring your own food, as well as attending their various regular events including 'beer swapping' and cheese nights. (I would refrain from referring to that as the Cock Cheese Night, if I were you...) Score yourself some **points** thanks to their love of pickled eggs – they even hold pickled egg speed-eating contests!

When I was recently in the toilets here a gentleman next to me clearly wasn't observing the Rule of Dan (see page 191) and decided to try and engage me in conversation about the height of the urinals. Apparently they are higher up than usual! (Not something I noticed, as I am 6 ft 6 and they all seem pretty low to me!)

I'll take a pint of Howling Hops, I think, and drink it in their tiny beer garden.

After leaving the pub, turn left to continue up Mare Street towards the railway bridge. Before you reach the bridge, you'll see Graham Road to your left. Now, it's a bit far to walk just for a blue plaque, so we're not going all the way there, but if you were to visit 55 Graham Road you would see that Marie Lloyd, the great music hall entertainer of the nineteenth century, lived there. It would have been an easy commute for her to perform at the Empire. I mention her often in my videos, as I enjoy her double entendres and sing-along classics, such as 'My Old Man (Said Follow the Van)' and 'The Boy I Love Is Up in the Gallery', not to mention my favourite, 'She Sits among the Cabbages and Peas'.

But we're going straight.

Just after the railway bridge, look at the **OLD TRAIN STATION ENTRANCE** ❻ on your left. This building dates from 1870, although the railway first arrived in Hackney twenty years earlier. They had to reposition the station, so what used to be the entrance is now a bar called Oslo.

Bear to your right towards **ST AUGUSTINE'S TOWER** ❼. The original church here was built in the thirteenth century by the Knights of St John, also known as the Knights Hospitaller, but it was rebuilt in the sixteenth century – so what you're looking at is still pretty old!

By 1798 the church had become too small for the growing congregation so they built St John's, which we will come to. However, St John's didn't have capacity for the bells, so despite demolishing the rest of St Augustine's they kept the tower so they could continue to ring the bells here. The bells remained in use here until 1854, when they were removed to St John's following some strengthening work on the new church. If you look at the coat of arms of Hackney you'll see this tower proudly sitting on top of the shield.

Just in front of the tower is the **PARISH VESTRY HALL** ❽, where all the local administration was done. It opened in 1802 but by the middle of the nineteenth century it wasn't really suitable any more, so they built a new one in 1866. That second town hall (since demolished) eventually got replaced by the 1937 town hall, which we walked past earlier.

Confusingly, the stone above the door shows '1900'. That's the year when they re-clad the building and added the 'HACKNEY OLD TOWN HALL' stonework at the top.

The building became a bank and more recently a betting shop – you can still make out the twenty-first-century ghost signs for 'CORAL' – but these days it's a tap room, which I'm not sure qualifies as a pub. (The Rule of Tom on page 191 certainly would suggest it doesn't!) It's run by the company that also runs the Euston Tap, in a similar building outside Euston Station.

Behind the church there are a great many chest-style tombs and family vaults, with some rather well-to-do people buried here. One which is quite close to the tower is that of Francis Beaufort, who invented the wind scale from 0 to 12, ranging from calm to a hurricane. Another tomb (which got lost when they destroyed the main part of St Augustine's) was that of Henry Percy, Earl of Northumberland, who was betrothed to Anne Boleyn before she caught the eye of King Henry VIII. Percy was also the one who arrested Cardinal Wolsey, but all he has now is a plaque inside the new church (don't worry, we'll be getting there soon).

Continue along the pedestrianised section of Mare Street and on the left look at the building above the shops at number 387. It was built in 1845 as a **MANOR HOUSE** ❾ for the Steward of the Manor of Hackney, after his family bought the New Mermaid Tavern on this site. He demolished the tavern so that he could build a big house… which would eventually be turned into a Greggs and a Shoe Zone. If you step back you can almost imagine how it might have looked in 1845.

Walk 15: Hackney | **259**

⑤

Cock

⑧

⑩

⑫

⑮

At the end of Mare Street let's just nip into the **CROWN** 🍺 for a swift half. (Oh go on, go on, go on…) This used to be called Tommy Flynn's, amongst many other names, and was known as a place with plenty of TV screens to watch the big game.

More recently they've taken over what used to be a mobile phone shop next door and renovated that as the Half Crown, which has a slightly more modern feel to it, and they've introduced a quiz night and live acoustic music. Both bits of the pub are good, but I like the original section with its curved frontage, so I'm heading in for a half of Guinness, some Tayto crisps and some good craic.

PUB

Crown

Come out of the pub and turn right into Lower Clapton Road, where you'll come to **ST JOHN AT HACKNEY** ⑩, also known simply as Hackney Church, which I was talking about earlier. In addition to operating as an Anglican church they also put on concerts, with previous performers including Coldplay and Robbie Williams. I expect his song 'Angels' went down quite well. In the grounds are quite a few more of those chest tombs that I mentioned and it's worth a potter about to look at some of the names and statuses of the people buried in them.

Along Lower Clapton Road there are some attractive old buildings which we will come back to, but the first one on the right after the church is a lovely **OLD POLICE STATION** ⑪, built in 1904. Personally, I think they should keep these buildings for their intended uses, but as with many others, the government decided to sell this one off to make some cash. I mean, the police have to go somewhere, so why not here?

Cross over the road and a little further along I recommend having a look around **UMIT & SON** ⑫, where they sell all sorts of film equipment. Film nerds will absolutely love this shop. The proprietor has all manner of old cameras, projectors, VHS tapes, reel-to-reel audio, Super 8, you name it! The VHS rack took me back to more innocent times, when hiring a film required a visit to the Blockbuster video hire shop! He even has a little screening room which can be hired for private viewings. He'll provide popcorn and you can choose one of the films he has on Super 16, or you can bring your own.

After you've enjoyed an exclusive screening of *King Kong* (the uncut version!) come out and turn right, back towards Mare Street, to enjoy a stroll around **CLAPTON SQUARE** ⓭. This was laid out in 1816 as an upmarket residence for merchants, bankers and brokers. When I was growing up, the word 'Clapton' filled me with dread – but I must say, it's a stunning square which does indeed seem suitable as that for which it was intended.

Exit the square via Clapton Passage in the far right (north-east) corner. At the end is where one of Hackney's famous sons lived. As you turn right into Lower Clapton Road, the second shop along, **NUMBER 113** ⓮, is where Joseph Priestley lived (it's a Domino's Pizza at the time of writing). Amongst his other scientific accomplishments, Priestley discovered carbonated water. He said of this place: 'On the whole I spent my time more happily at Hackney than I ever had done before.' That's possibly because he was hounded out of his place in Birmingham for supporting the French Revolution, and Hackney were the only people who would have him! He was even invited to be a minister at the Gravel Pit Chapel, a popular church for dissenters. (Or maybe he just liked Lower Clapton so much because he was living above the pizza shop…) Other famous people who hail from Hackney (but didn't, to my knowledge, live above a pizza shop) include Idris Elba, Sir Alan Sugar and Ray Winstone.

If you look to the right, above number 117 on the corner (currently the Hackney Vet), you can score **points** by spotting the lovely old stone street sign, showing that in 1880 this was known as Clapton Pavement.

Now cross over at the zebra crossing and turn right towards the **ROUND CHAPEL** ⓯, built in 1871 and described as 'one of the finest non-conformist buildings in London'. Previously the United Reformed Church, since the 1990s the chapel has been used as a performing arts centre – but rather childishly, my favourite thing about it is the inscription on the plaque referring to Jesus Christ being the chief cornerstone of the foundation of apostles and prophets. Having a cornerstone in a round chapel amuses me.

I must say, I am really taken by Hackney. It has some lovely houses and excellent shops and cafés. Coming up on the left is a good old second-hand furniture shop, the likes of which I just don't see in my area any more. I've seen a few of these in Hackney and they have really good stuff in them. This one is called **SECOND TIME AROUND** ⓰. Perhaps their 'Established 1998' sign will be pointed out by the Joolz Guides of the future as 'vintage' some day.

Continue and briefly follow Lower Clapton Road as it turns to the right, where you'll see on your left the beautiful Art Deco **STRAND BUILDING** ⓱, erected in 1925 as the Hackney Electricity Demonstration Halls and Offices. Since 1995 it has been flats,

17

20

24

Gun

25

Kenton

which I assume are of the luxury variety – but I have never been inside, so they could be awful for all I know! I doubt it, though.

Further along on the right you'll see **HACKNEY PUBLIC BATHS** ⓲, dating from 1897, also a wonderful building. But we've already seen this bit of road from the other end, so let's go back and turn right down Urswick Road.

Coming up on your right is **SUTTON PLACE** ⓳, where the whole south terrace survives intact from the 1790s. It's a very fine example of a Georgian street, and you can see how the coal would be dropped straight thought the coal holes in the pavement to the cellars beneath. These affluent families would have servants living in the basements who could then access the coal and lug it up to the fireplaces in the rest of the house (a bit like in *Downton Abbey*). *The Hours*, starring Nicole Kidman, was filmed here, and the street was also home to Colin Firth for a while.

The street is named after Sir Thomas Sutton, who was the richest man in England during Tudor times. He was the one who founded the Charterhouse School for poor boys and a charity for unmarried men fallen on hard times. So he was a nice bloke as far as I can tell, although he lived on this site having acquired the land as a result of the dissolution of the monasteries. Oh, and he was also an arms dealer.

Just after Sutton Place is **SUTTON HOUSE** ⓴. Now owned by the National Trust, the house dates from 1535 and was built for Sir Ralph Sadleir, a courtier who worked for Thomas Cromwell and was Secretary of State to King Henry VIII. (Despite the name, Sir Thomas Sutton didn't live here.) Sutton House has been home to merchants, Huguenot silk weavers, sea captains, school mistresses and all sorts through the ages, but it's amazing to think that the oldest residential building in Hackney fell into such neglect that it was actually squatted in the 1980s. What an amazing free address those squatters had! They didn't do too much damage, though, as the magnificent oak-panelled rooms and Tudor fireplaces have survived, making it an interesting place to visit for a peek into how its occupants lived. If you want to explore on your own you can show up on a Friday or Sunday, otherwise you need to book a guided tour.

Just outside the house is the Breaker's Yard, which is now a garden featuring artistic installations inspired by the history of the house and yard. Originally it was for horses and carriages visiting the houses in Sutton Place, but later became a car breaker's yard and garage.

Hackney Brook used to run behind Sutton House and then eastwards, not far from here, but the occupants of Sutton House would have used a nearby well for their water. In those days there was a 'nightsoil path' at the end of the gardens behind the houses in Sutton Place, for the removal of the poos accrued in cesspits. A man called a 'night-cart man' would come in the middle of the night to take it all away… And you thought *you* had a bad job! What must his wife have thought when he climbed into bed next to her?!

Eventually the brook was culverted into a sewer during the nineteenth century and thus one of the worst jobs in history began to die out.

After Sutton House, turn right down Isabella Road and at the end you'll come to the **CHESHAM ARMS**, where we can have a pint (caution: on weekdays they don't open until 4.00 p.m.).

In 2012 the owner of the building closed it and wanted to turn it into flats. Booooooooooh!!!!

Luckily, though, Hackney Council gave it protected status as an Asset of Community Value – and it ended up being voted the best pub in the East London and City area by CAMRA. We'd better check it out, then!

There's a selection of regularly changing beers and ciders, and they don't seem to favour the bigger well-known brands here. Ah, there are board games, too! Okay, I'll have a pint of Oatmeal Pale and see you in the garden with the *Trivial Pursuit*.

Bottoms up.

PUB

Chesham Arms

Turn left out of the pub into Mehetabel Road and at the end turn left onto the path.

Pass under the bridge and continue straight ahead across Morning Lane, into Chatham Place.

On your right is the **BURBERRY FACTORY OUTLET STORE 21**, which has been here since the 1950s. The stock is constantly changing, and you can buy items on a first-come, first-served basis. It's great for picking up a bargain if you're into that sort of thing. Thomas Burberry established his brand in 1856, aged twenty-one – and a strict Victorian he was, too, sacking any female workers who got overly interested in boys! Burberry invented the waterproof gabardine material which became extremely popular in the First World War for trench coats and was also widely used by explorers. Ernest Shackleton wore Burberry clothing on three expeditions to the South Pole, and Burberry received royal warrants from Queen Elizabeth II and her son, King Charles III.

Whoever knew that Queen Elizabeth, King Charles and Ernest Shackleton were chavs? (Non-Brits might need an urban dictionary here…)

Keep going and then turn left into Retreat Place and right into Mead Place.

Actually, I spotted a **STINK PIPE** ㉒ on Retreat Place, further along, which I've marked on the map. You should be able to see it in the distance as you turn this corner. I'm noticing a lot of these along routes near to underground rivers which have been turned into sewers.

On your right, glance over the railings at the cemetery which was the burial ground for the **NEW GRAVEL PIT CHAPEL** ㉓. If you remember, Joseph Priestley was a minister at the Gravel Pit Chapel, named after a gravel pit near Mare Street, which was later referred to as the Old Gravel Pit Chapel. In the early nineteenth century they constructed a new chapel on Chatham Place, which was rebuilt in the 1850s, bombed in the Blitz and then finally, alas, destroyed by the council in 1969 to make way for the housing estate. If the Luftwaffe don't get ya, the local town planners will! As you might be able to see if you are tall enough and the bushes aren't too bushy, they left the graveyard. Perhaps you can even make out some of the names which yet survive, stamped on these lifeless things.

Nothing beside remains. Round the decay of that peaceful plot, boundless and bare, the lone and featureless housing estates stretch far away.

Next turn left into Cresset Road and on the left you'll see **LENNOX HOUSE** ㉔, built in 1937 by J. E. M. Macgregor. It's quite an innovative design, the idea being to create 'a building composed of many separate homes, each having as much fresh air and light as possible, and a real substitute for the garden or yard…together with a sense of privacy.' He also intended to have a covered market beneath the building, the proceeds of which could subsidise the flats above, but that never quite came about.

PUB

Gun

At the end, where Cresset Road meets Well Street, there's a little pub on the corner called the **GUN**. We'll be reaching another pub in just a couple of minutes, but you might like to stop for a quick one here to take advantage of their roof terrace, commanding spectacular views of… Well, okay, there are no points for the view, but I rather like it! It's good for peering down on people below. Let's say it's 'urban'.

'That is Hackney, Madam. Do you mind telling me what you *expected* to see from a Hackney pub roof terrace? The Sydney Opera House, perhaps? The Hanging Gardens of Babylon?!'

The pub itself earns my respect for (at the time of writing) not taking reservations for tables! Perhaps this is something I should make into an official pub rule: no reserving of tables! There's nothing worse than entering a pub full of empty tables and being told they are all reserved.

A pint of Gun it is, then.

WELL STREET

Now turn right into Well Street.

On the left side of the road is my favourite thing about this street, and certainly worthy of scoring **points**. Whilst I'm always fond of a **KING GEORGE VI POST BOX** (25), this one is particularly special, because it has an old stamp-dispensing machine attached. I don't see many of these around any more and again, it's something that reminds me of my childhood so much. One day it will be in a museum… a bit like me.

PUB

Kenton

Next turn left into Valentine Road and soon you'll arrive at the **KENTON**, where our Universally Challenged team sometimes enter the pub quiz on Tuesdays (there's been a quiz here for donkey's years). I feel another pint coming on.

The pub dates to 1858, originally with the full name of the Kenton Arms, which you can still see at the top of the building. Nowadays they describe themselves as a traditional British pub 'with a Norwegian twist' – hence the unusual pub sign of a moose…or is it a reindeer, or an elk?

I'm trying a pint of their 'own pilsner'. They say that Moose Juice is brewed in Belgium but tastes like Norway. It's mighty fine, and if this is what Norway tastes like, I must plan in a trip soon.

Come out, turn left down Kenton Road, then right into Cassland Road and keep going until you see the fabulous **TERRACE** (26) opposite Cassland Crescent. This stretch has been described as the finest example of eighteenth-century houses in Hackney, built in 1792; there are **points** to be had for all the different coal hole covers, too. Look up at the stone pediment, where you'll see the coats of arms of the three developers who built them. The houses opposite were built slightly later, but all in all it's a wonderful street, almost like a film set.

Next turn left into Terrace Road and left again around Church Crescent.

Just after the King George VI post box (**points** to me!) – which also has a box attached for the postman to leave items inside (more **points**, as these are dying out!) – you'll pass **MONGER HOUSE** ㉗ on your left. Originally Henry Monger left money in his will so that in 1670 these almshouses could be built for six poor men over sixty years of age. Although they were rebuilt in Victorian times, they retain some of the original brickwork. What's nice is that they are still used for housing people in need, all these years later.

Follow the crescent round and then enter the churchyard on your right.

ST JOHN OF JERUSALEM ㉘ was built in 1845, to the design of Edward Charles Hakewill. It is said that the Luftwaffe used the church as a handy marker as they flew across Hackney Marshes to bomb the smithereens out of us during the Second World War. In that case, it was a bit foolish of them to bomb the actual church! Nevertheless, that's what they did, and a helicopter subsequently had to be used to lower a new spire into place.

Now cross the church grounds to the front of the church, coming out onto Lauriston Road, where we're turning left. Follow Lauriston Road to the right.

Just before you reach the roundabout which you can see ahead of you, all covered in foliage and flowers, stop for a moment where Southborough Road crosses Lauriston Road.

It almost seems like a roundabout could have been placed here, and it seems odd that two mini-roads should have such a large area at their intersection. The reason that it's so unusually large is because this is where the **TRAMS** ㉙ used to turn around. Originally they would have been drawn by horses, before electricity took over. Look up at some of the dates on the buildings.

As you continue, on the left, just before the roundabout, you'll see the shop which used to be a **COACH HOUSE** ㉚ used by the Metropolitan Tramways and Omnibus Company Limited for their drivers to have a cup of tea and do the crossword.

We're now entering another rather quaint villagey part of Hackney, where I wouldn't be at all surprised to see a Waitrose popping up before long. We've almost finished but if you can't wait for a drink (or a trip to the loo) you could always pop into the Lauriston for a quick one. I'm sad that Mike Gabel no longer does his legendary Hot Breath Karaoke here, but he had to go back to

Canada. Anyone who experienced it will remember it with great fondness. Hi, Mike!

Anyway, I'm carrying straight on, along this very pleasant shopping street, replete with cafés, pushchairs and oat decaf lattes. I also see a couple of original K2 telephone boxes (two of only 1,500 made).

As Lauriston Road starts curving to the left you'll see **HACKNEY JEWISH CEMETERY 31**, opened in 1788 and also known as Lauriston Road Cemetery. You can see over the fence but you'll need an appointment if you want to go inside.

On the other side of the road there's a nice **HORSE AND CATTLE TROUGH 32** just before the amusing **COAL HOLE COVER 33** outside the hair studio at number 107.

These coal hole covers could be very bland or very interesting, and this one is a rather less common example made by – titter ye not – Clark Hunt (which you shouldn't say too fast). Anyway, I like the design of this one, which probably would have cost more, acting as a sort of status symbol.

Right, it's time for our last pint and by lucky hap 'tis but a short crossing of the road to the **ROYAL INN ON THE PARK** opposite.

PUB

Royal Inn on the Park

Back when it was called the Royal Hotel this is where, in 1993, Jimmy Moody, a notorious gangster who rubbed shoulders with the Krays and the Richardsons, was shot dead. He had previously escaped from Brixton prison and fled to Ireland, being described by police as 'extremely intimidating'.

I must say, the Royal Inn on the Park doesn't look like the sort of place to harbour gangsters these days, with their lovely outdoor seating area and their grilled flatbreads, so it just shows how the area has changed. But just in case, we'd better get into character.

Oi, you. *Shut it!*

I'll take a pint of Timothy Taylor's Landlord.

Lovely jubbly.

— Quiz! —

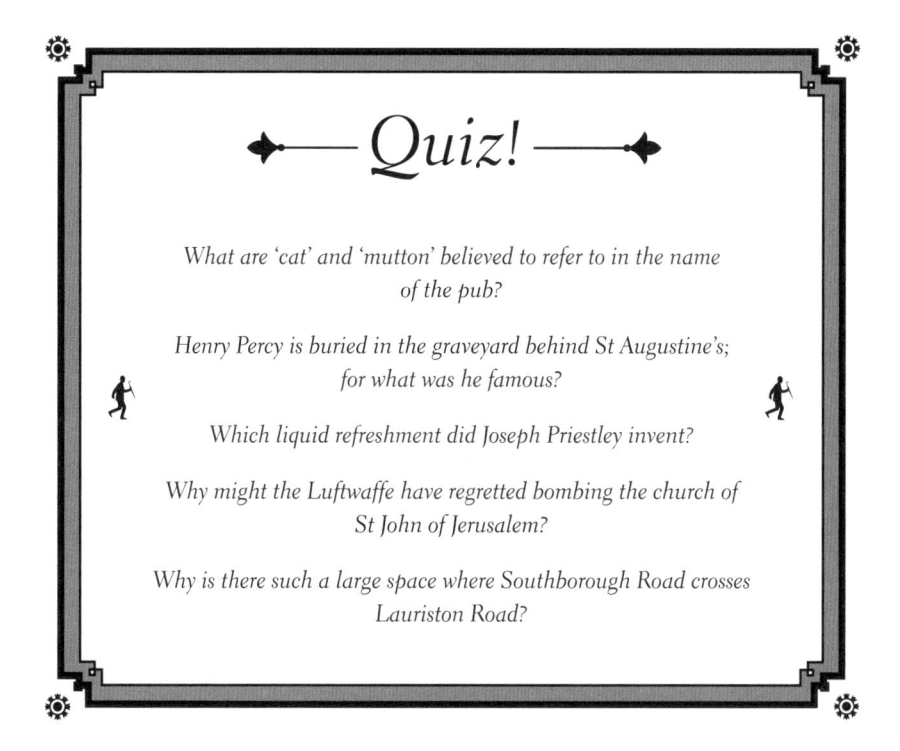

What are 'cat' and 'mutton' believed to refer to in the name of the pub?

Henry Percy is buried in the graveyard behind St Augustine's; for what was he famous?

Which liquid refreshment did Joseph Priestley invent?

Why might the Luftwaffe have regretted bombing the church of St John of Jerusalem?

Why is there such a large space where Southborough Road crosses Lauriston Road?

25. Clapham Grand

15. Bandstand

FALCON

NORTHCOTE

EAGLE ALE HOUSE

ELSPETH ROAD
CEDARS RD
MALLINSON ROAD
BRAMFIELD ROAD
CHATTO RD
AURISTON RD
HILLIER ROAD
THE AVENUE

16 CLAPHAM

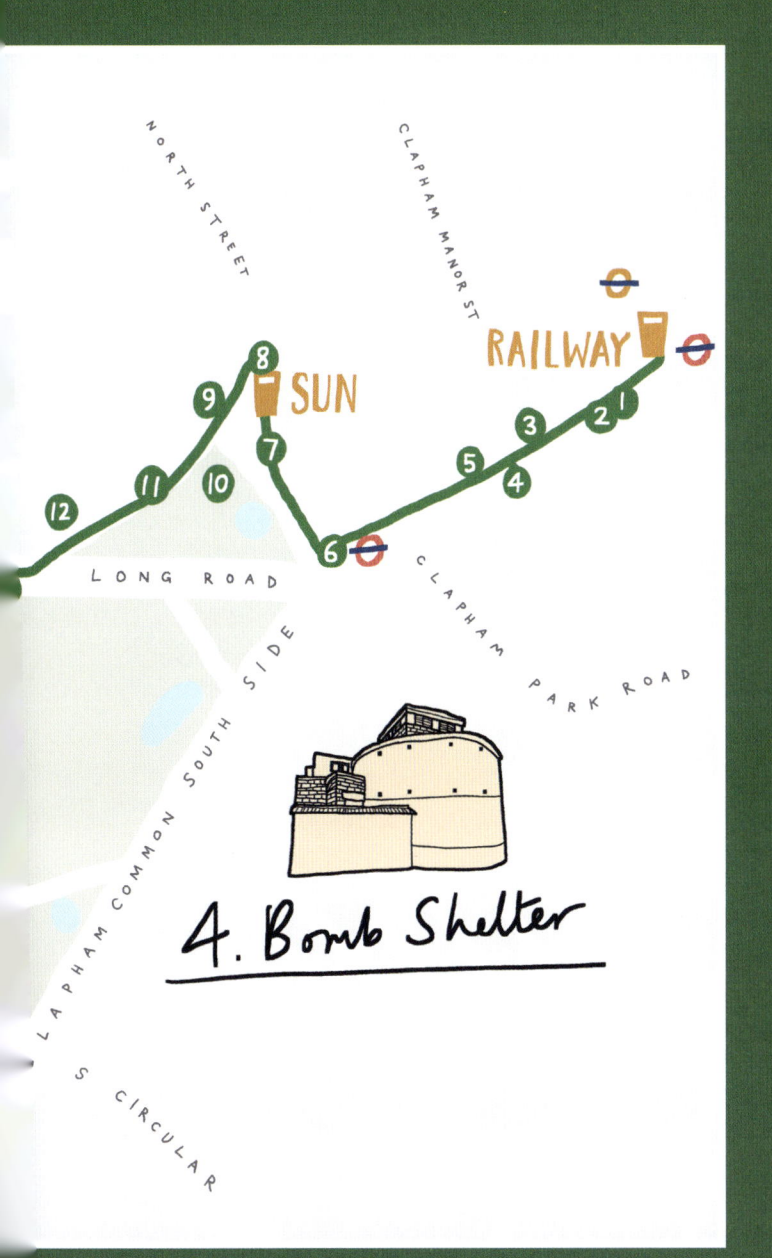

RAILWAY

SUN

NORTH STREET

CLAPHAM MANOR ST

LONG ROAD

CLAPHAM PARK ROAD

CLAPHAM COMMON SOUTH SIDE

S CIRCULAR

4. Bomb Shelter

16 A CANTER ABOUT CLAPHAM

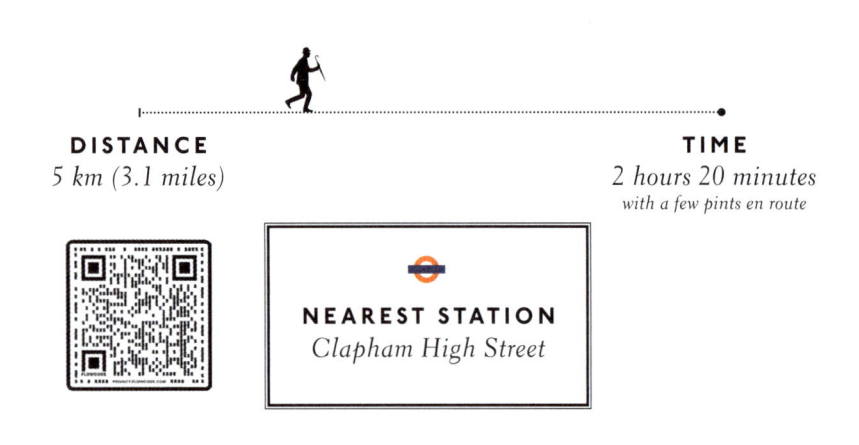

DISTANCE
5 km (3.1 miles)

TIME
2 hours 20 minutes
with a few pints en route

NEAREST STATION
Clapham High Street

PUBS
Railway; Sun; Eagle Ale House; Northcote; Falcon

Pip pip! Here I am waiting at the **RAILWAY** 🍺, which I thought would be a convenient place to start, since it's close to Clapham High Street on the Windrush Line and Clapham North on the Northern Line. It's a pretty spacious Victorian tavern with high ceilings, although the interior has been somewhat modernised. Since it stands on a corner it has windows on two sides, which means I can gaze at people as they go by and keep an eye out for my friends. However, the main thing I'm noticing outside the window is the magnificent stink pipe! Always nice to start a walk by scoring some **points**!

Now you're here I'll polish off this pint and we'll get going.

Turn right out of the pub, walking away from the railway bridge along Clapham High Street, and I'll tell you about Clapham before we reach the main bit.

Clapham's name comes from the Anglo-Saxon *clop*, meaning 'hill', and *ham*, meaning 'village'. So it was a village amongst the hills, which was originally granted by King Edgar to a

PUB
Railway

chap called Jonas, who became Jonas de Clapham in 965 – but then William the Conqueror came along in 1066 and purloined it.

Coming up on your left I rather like the former **TEMPERANCE BILLIARD HALL** ❶ with its curving roof, built in 1911 and until recently home to a firm of architects – but, you guessed it, this is now luxury flats! (I can't be sure whether the beautiful sign has always been there. For many years it looked like the architects had covered it up with their own sign, which would have been an architecturally odd choice if so – although I might be wrong.) I am forever lamenting the sad decline in the number of billiard halls in London; these guys used to have sixteen tables.

Another building I like is coming up on the corner of Tremadoc Road, at **53 CLAPHAM HIGH STREET** ❷. This is currently occupied by solicitors, but was originally a bank. I just like the attention to detail. Look at those beautiful stone figures above the door. Can you imagine anybody bothering with something as intricate as that these days? If you look at the windows on the High Street frontage you can see the old NatWest logos, from the building's final incarnation as a bank. Someone should have told them that the right-hand one is upside down!

Further along, high up on your right, I'm sure you'll appreciate the vintage **GILLETTE ADVERT** ❸ on the side of the building opposite St Luke's Avenue. I often wonder how many more years these will last, but it's hanging in there for now. In fact, there are so many of these old ghost signs around Clapham that you can actually do a Ghost Sign Walk – but not with me… I'm too busy dealing with all the ghosts haunting London's pubs!

A little further along on the left, at the corner with Carpenter's Place, you'll see a round building which was originally the entrance to a **BOMB SHELTER** ❹, dating from the Second World War. Its twin, near Clapham Common station, would have been the other entrance to the same shelter. There's a similar bomb shelter just north of Clapham North station, and another just near Clapham South station, both with twin entrances.

Eight of these deep-level shelters were created across London. Unfortunately, they weren't fully completed until 1942, by which time the Blitz was largely over; however, they were needed again in 1944 with the V-1 and V-2 attacks on London. Life in the shelters was superior to being stuck on a tube platform: you actually got blankets and a lavatory, and war diaries mention people seeing their children walk for the first time and people learning to knit. If people were prevented from entering because shelters were full, fights would break out. One man even attempted to kill his wife during the melee, claiming that she just tripped over!

These days the shelters are mostly used for storing documents and you can go on tours into the depths. At one stage there was a company growing vegetables down here, under LED lights. Funnily enough, the plants were stored in bunks – just like people during the war.

In 1948 when the *Empire Windrush* arrived with hundreds of immigrants from the West Indies, the British government hadn't made enough plans to house them. Many of them ended up staying in these shelters, which I imagine was a far cry from what they were expecting.

Continue along the High Street. Looking up, you can imagine what it was like years ago, before some of these shop fronts were added. You'll pass the lovely Art Deco McDonald's on your right (lovely above street level, anyway!), just beyond which you can still see the remnants of **136 CLAPHAM HIGH STREET** ❺. The shops have taken the place of the front gardens here, so the road would have appeared wider at the end of the eighteenth century when poor old Elizabeth Cook, wife of the explorer Captain Cook, ended up living here after he was killed by the natives of Hawaii. She hardly ever saw him when he was alive, anyway, as he was away so much; but it may have been some comfort that she shared this house with her cousin Rear Admiral Isaac Smith, who accompanied Captain Cook to the South Seas and was supposedly the first European to set foot in Australia. The buildings opposite sprang up later and have the date '1886' on them.

Soon you'll come to Clapham Common station. You might fancy a stop in the Alexandra, just after the station on the left, but I've not built up enough of a thirst yet. I rather like the figures of women above the windows next door to the pub – easily missed if you're staring at your phone, or at this book!

Hop over to The Pavement, which is on the north side of Clapham Common station (if you were at the Alexandra, head back to the junction by the tube to cross over safely). As you follow the curve of The Pavement round to the right, score some **points** for the **HORSE AND CATTLE TROUGH** ❻ being used as a flower bed.

Goodness me, Clapham has changed since I was a boy. All these swanky cafés selling focaccia (although it's nothing like the focaccia you get in Genova!) and decaf mochachinos.

Carry on along The Pavement and keep right when the road forks.

Number 33, with the red door, called the **LODGE** ❼, was used as a fire station from 1868 until the turn of the twentieth century. It was built as one of twenty-six for the newly formed Metropolitan Fire Brigade, but by the start of the twentieth century they needed bigger ones for motorised vehicles and better equipment. They knocked many of the old stations down, but luckily not this one.

Soon you'll find yourself in the Old Town, which is still rather quaint.

Gosh, it seems a pity not to visit one of the pubs here. There's the Rose & Crown on the left (with a cute, smaller than usual, horse trough outside) and the Sun on the right.

They're both good, but today let's head into the **SUN** 🍺, which has been here since Victorian times.

I like the fact that they stay open until midnight, although I do feel a bit like I'm not young, trendy or good-looking enough to be in here. Maybe no one will notice, so while I quaff my pint of Doom Bar and gaze out at the buses parked at the terminus outside, it reminds me of the phrase 'the man on the Clapham omnibus'. I suppose it's a bit archaic now, and I haven't heard it used for a long time – but then again, I'm not often in court. The phrase – used to represent a hypothetical, reasonable man against whom a defendant's conduct could be compared – was said to have been coined by the English judge Lord Bowen during the nineteenth century. It was first used in the wording of an actual judgment in 1903 (after Lord Bowen's death), at which point it became proper legal terminology.

I reckon this pint is good enough for the man on the Clapham omnibus.

Down the hatch!

The houses on the right after the Sun date from 1707, when Clapham was still quite a backwater.

When Vivienne Westwood died many flowers and letters of condolence were attached to the railings of **43 OLD TOWN** ❽, where she lived. She was known as 'the godmother of punk', having created many of the styles and outfits we associate with the Sex Pistols, through her shop on the King's Road, called SEX. I wonder if they'll put another blue plaque up beneath the one for the architect John Bentley, who also lived here.

276 | Rather Splendid London Pub Walks

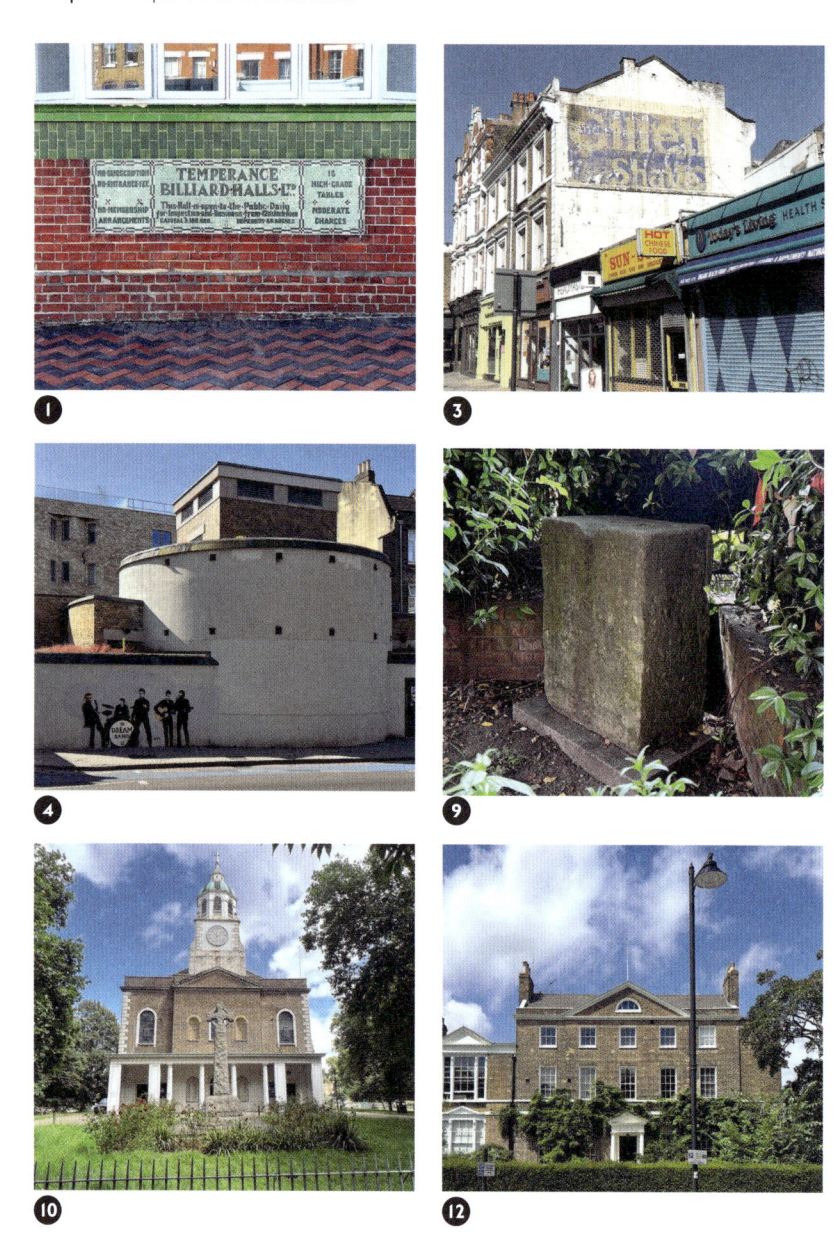

Now, let's turn round and head back towards the Rose & Crown, before crossing over to the right onto Clapham Common North Side.

On the right, at the corner with Orlando Road, is the **OMNIBUS THEATRE** ❾, which was originally built as Clapham Library, opened in 1889. If you sneak into the front garden you'll find what looks a bit like a milestone behind one of the chairs, demonstrating that Clapham was once inhabited by Romans. Well, maybe. The Roman road known as Stane Street certainly passed through here on its way from Chichester to London Bridge, but frankly the stone could have come from anywhere (Historic England, responsible for its Grade II listing, describe it as an altar stone). It was found outside a house on the other side of the Common and bears the inscription 'Vitus Ticinius Ascanius', a man who apparently 'erected it for himself in his own lifetime'. A sort of monument to himself – a bit weird. Anyway, his three Latin names indicate that he was most probably a Roman citizen and free, since slaves (Spartacus, for example) only had one or two names, a bit like Brazilian footballers. Most inhabitants of Britain would not have been Roman citizens.

As you continue along Clapham Common North Side you should be able to see, just inside the park over to the left, **HOLY TRINITY CLAPHAM** ❿. The church was completed in 1776 and came to be associated with the Clapham Sect, a group of evangelical Christians led by the rector, John Venn. Together with William Wilberforce and others, their campaign resulted in the Slave Trade Act of 1807, and ultimately the abolition of slavery altogether in 1833.

Further along Clapham Common North Side are more beautiful old houses, built around 1720. One of these was home to the author Graham Greene, who has a blue plaque at **NUMBER 14** ⓫, and I particularly like the iron ring over the entrance to number 12, which originally might have held a lamp.

During and following the Great Plague many Londoners escaped the City and moved to Clapham for its cleaner air, including Samuel Pepys, who came to live at what is now **NUMBER 29** ⓬ at the start of the eighteenth century. The current building you see (which has a blue plaque for Charles Barry, architect of the Houses of Parliament) was built in the grounds of Clapham Place, where Pepys lived, but which has since been knocked down. By 1800 the area was attracting wealthier people who built these big houses.

Continue to the right, following Clapham Common North Side around. Opposite the junction with Victoria Rise, look out for the listed **MILESTONE** ⓭ just inside the park! **Points**! Well, even more **points** if you can actually read it! It's much too worn out to read all of it, but originally the west side read 'V miles from the Standard in Cornhill'.

Now, as you come to Cedars Road, the building just before it contains a blue plaque for **EDVARD GRIEG** ⑭ – but I feel obliged also to point out the many shenanigans that went on next door at number 46.

For a couple of decades it was owned by Michael Joseph, the South Africa-born photographer who took the inner gatefold shot for the Rolling Stones' *Beggars Banquet* album. Joseph hosted various 'racy' photoshoots here, including one for an Ann Summers erotic lingerie catalogue, as well as filming for a *Joy of Sex* video. Other raunchy moments here have included an orgy scene for a theatrical production of *Spartacus* and Kylie shooting a music video in the swimming pool.

This was all highly publicised when it was put up for sale in 2012, as 'the sexiest house in London', including the claim that the *Beggars Banquet* photo was also an 'orgy scene' (it was actually a banquet…the clue is in the title) and that it was shot here (it was actually shot at Sarum Chase in Hampstead). It's almost as if the owners were trying to sell it for as much money as possible!!

You might want to check the map carefully here, because we'll walk across the park towards the bandstand. Head into the Common via the path which is in a straight line with Cedars Road. When you get to an intersection of paths, follow the one ahead and to the right.

The **BANDSTAND** ⑮ dates from 1890, a year after the locals petitioned London County Council to build it. It was very popular until the 1960s, when I suppose more people started watching TV, so this sort of entertainment was less in demand.

The reason I like it is because you can pinpoint exactly when and where David Bowie wrote his song 'Join the Gang', from his debut album. Thanks to an interview he gave, we know that on 6 November 1966 he got up at midday and went off for a photoshoot at this bandstand. He said he needed coffee, so he sat at the café (which is still here) and said he felt a tune coming on. The photographer left him at the café and when he returned, half an hour later, Bowie had polished off six coffees, baked beans, spaghetti and eggs, and two doughnuts… and he'd completed the song. You can find images of him sitting at the café and posing on the bandstand on t'interweb.

Actually, I was having a bit of writer's block myself as I was writing this, and decided to sit down here for some inspiration. What worked for Bowie can work for me!

By the way, I will award **points** to anyone who manages to find the memorial bench of legendary actor Jeremy Brett, which is in the close vicinity of the bandstand. It happens to be my birthday today and my sister is taking me to a Sherlock Holmes lunch, so it's a coincidence that I should be writing about the actor who was most famous for playing that role. Who's your favourite Holmes? I liked Basil Rathbone.

Now take the path to the south-west, towards Broomwood Road. You should pass a pond to your left. I was once in a photoshoot here, for a billboard advertisement for Embassy No. 1 cigarettes! Just showing my age…

Enter Broomwood Road. I must say, I do like these houses – they're exactly the type of house I'd like to live in. They were mostly built around the late nineteenth and early twentieth centuries, with lovely details like the black-and-white and brown-and-white tiled paths, and decorative tiles beside the front doors. I also like the coal hole covers, directly outside the front doors. You usually see coal holes in the public pavement, but in these roads the coal delivery men would have needed to come through the front gates. I can imagine them getting a bit fed up when it came to delivering to these houses, because it must have taken a lot longer having to access each individual house through its gate.

It seemed to be the fashion for the builders of the time to name their houses, with stylish plaques outside. I like 'Nassau House' – sounds a bit Bahamian.

When you get to the junction with Wroughton Road the house on your left, 111 Broomwood Road, is the site of **BROOMFIELD HOUSE** **16**, where William Wilberforce lived. It was knocked down in 1904 (there's a small plaque on the Wroughton Road side of the present building). To your right you'll see an Edward VII post box, which was presumably put here around the time the houses were built.

Continue along Broomwood Road, noting how it descends into a valley ahead of you, and take the next right, Webb's Road. After the next junction, on the right, look out for the lovely green **STINK PIPE** **17** next to an old street sign. The street sign only shows 'SW' (instead of 'SW11'), like many of the signs around here, indicating that it pre-dates 1917 (unless it's a replica).

The valley we just saw follows the line of the Falconbrook, an underground river that was culverted into a sewer in the nineteenth century. If you read my first book you'll know that these new sewers would get pretty smelly and the fumes could even become dangerous and cause explosions. (Well, we've all tried to light our own farts, haven't we… Or was that just me?)

Around Clapham and Battersea you see a lot of these stink pipes, which carried the farty smelly gas up from the sewers above the Victorian population's heads. That said, sometimes you see them near people's windows if it's a new-build property and the designers didn't check. D'oh! Pooh…

Take the next left down Chatham Road and on the way to our next pub you'll pass some older houses dating from 1863.

The **EAGLE ALE HOUSE** is a lovely little boozer. They have an excellent and regularly changing selection of cask and keg beers from microbreweries across London (this explains the number of kegs you'll often find stacked up outside), and they have a beer garden out the back to drink them in. If you're lucky you might catch a bit of live music – or you can participate yourself, if you're brave, at their regular open-mic night. In 2015 they also laid claim to the honour of having been the first London pub to feature on the cover of the UK-wide *Good Beer Guide*.

I feel like something local… A pint of the Belleville Steam Lager, I think.

Cheers!

Come out of the pub and turn left to continue down Chatham Road, and then turn right into Northcote Road, which follows the line of the Falconbrook.

Now, since this is a book of walks I thought it would be a pity not to take you up such a lovely street and – *whisper it quietly* – it almost makes me want to move to Clapham. This is just a high street, but it's very clean and – how can I put it? – nice… Or, as some people say, 'reassuringly expensive'! It's because of this feeling of safety and affluence that Northcote Road is often referred to as Nappy Valley.

On your right you'll see the deceptively small entrance to **NORTHCOTE ROAD ANTIQUES MARKET** ⓲. If furniture, bric-a-brac, jewellery, homewares, picture frames, chandeliers and mirrors are your thing then I warn you that you could spend hours in here.

All along Northcote Road you'll find plenty of shops, pubs and cafés you can drop into, so you won't go hungry or thirsty.

At the end, near the junction with Battersea Rise, is **NORTHCOTE RECORDS** ⓳. If you're cooler than I am, with more lead in your pencil, and you're here in the evening, they have live bands and a funky night-time crowd. But I'm feeling more sedate, so I'm popping into the

PUB

Eagle Ale House

Walk 16: Clapham | 281

15

17

Eagle Ale House

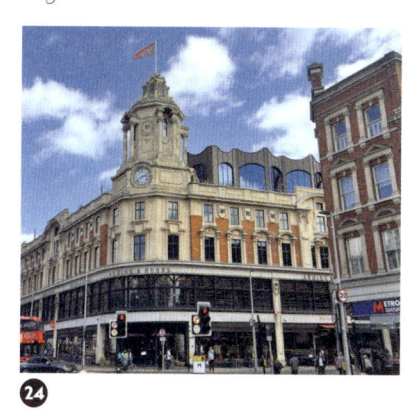

18

24

25

NORTHCOTE 🍺, a couple of doors along, for a quick half.

The pub occupies a perfect corner position with some classic reddish-brown tiles at ground floor level and some charmingly Victorian window lintels on the first floor. These days it's a Young's pub and does what I'd loosely describe as 'high-end classic pub grub', and I've heard that their Sunday roasts are rather splendid.

A half of Proper Job, please!

PUB
Northcote

Oh, did I mention – in the census of 1881, which is the year the pub was established (as the Northcote Hotel), the publican was listed as Spencer Chaplin and the barman as his brother, Charles Chaplin. The Charles in question was Charles Chaplin, Sr. – father of Charles Chaplin, Jr., better known to the world as Charlie.

Confusingly, the world-famous Charlie also had a brother called Spencer… and even more confusingly, Charlie's grandson is called Spencer, too! If you find these connections interesting, you'll enjoy my video all about Charlie Chaplin, which features his grandson and granddaughter.

Come out of the pub and cross Battersea Rise, to continue north into St John's Road. Then turn right into Barnard Road.

The garage area on your left, just behind Marks and Spencer, is where **MI5** [20] used to get their cars souped up in the 1970s. I don't think it was quite like dealing with Q in the James Bond films, adding passenger ejector seats and so on; nevertheless, they were fixed up here. Unfortunately, the facility soon came to the attention of the KGB, so they had to move.

At the end of Barnard Road there's another **STINK PIPE** [21], on Lavender Sweep. Who cares? I'm getting a bit bored of them now, since there seem to be so many around here. However, there is something interesting just to the right of it, at number 85. Look for the word 'SAND' written on the brickwork next to the door; this is a remnant of the Second World War, telling people where to leave sand for the fire wardens!

I must say, I have never encountered any other street with 'Sweep' in its name, so this feels unique. The road was originally laid out as a carriage drive serving four large mansions. These have gone now, but the large house belonging to Tom Taylor, the editor of *Punch* magazine, became known as Lavender Sweep by those many literary figures who used to visit during the nineteenth century. These included Charles Dickens, Lewis Carroll, Henry Irving and William Makepeace Thackeray. The only surviving part of his house is the fanlight which now hangs over the door of number 84, which you'd have to turn right in order to go and find.

John Betjeman describes the road in his poem 'South London Sketch, 1844' – not to be confused with his poem 'South London Sketch, 1944'!

> Lavender Sweep is drowned
> in Wandsworth,
> Drowned in jessamine up to the neck,
> Beetles sway upon bending
> grass leagues
> Shoulder-level to Tooting Bec.

Anyway, we're going left and let's follow the road round to Lavender Hill.

On your right is **BATTERSEA LIBRARY** ㉒, which has a most excellent reference section where I researched some of this walk. It dates from the end of the nineteenth century and has a lovely room with wood panelling and a bright skylight, making it a splendid place to do some work or revise for your exams. The archives upstairs contain a marvellous selection of books about the local area.

We're going to head the other way from the library, west down Lavender Hill, which was made famous in *The Lavender Hill Mob* – one of the Ealing Comedies I mentioned in **Walk 14**.

Before the arrival of the railway in 1838 this area consisted of just a few isolated villas, commercial buildings and fields used for the cultivation of lavender, which was used for perfume. The earliest known reference to the name Lavender Hill was in 1774, when a Mr Porter advertised a reward for the safe return of his pony, which had last been seen in a field on Lavender Hill.

Turn right into Mossbury Road and follow it round to the left.

Stop at **NUMBER 22** ㉓, next to the pottery, and you should be able to make out an old villa from the early 1800s, at a slightly different angle to the rest of the houses, set back a little from the road. When the railway arrived most of the villas got knocked down, despite having gardens described as 'among the best cultivated and most fruitful', but number 22, known as the Chestnuts, survived.

Carry on and turn left at the end.

On the corner of Lavender Hill and St John's Road you'll see what used to be **ARDING & HOBBS** ㉔, which was built in 1876 and was once the largest department store in south London. After a fire in 1909 it was rebuilt and there are still some lovely features inside from the Art Deco period, but now it's been turned into a food hall. It's sad to see all these department stores slowly disappearing, as they were such a large part of my childhood – but I must say, I went to the Prezzemolo & Vitale Italian delicatessen which now occupies part of the ground floor and, by Jingo, do they have some delicious food!

Turn right into St John's Hill and on the left you'll come to the **CLAPHAM GRAND** 25, which was opened in 1900 as a music hall for variety acts. Dan Leno, Charlie Chaplin, Little Tich (with his extremely long boots) and Marie Lloyd – of 'My Old Man (Said Follow The Van)' fame – have all graced its stage. Like so many large theatres, it's also spent time as a cinema and, of course, a bingo hall. Precisely the sort of place that J. D. Wetherspoon would turn into a pub. However, they failed in their attempt to acquire it and so it continues as a live music venue and night club.

Okay, time for another drink, so let's go back towards Arding & Hobbs and head into the **FALCON**.

There's been a pub here since 1733, when it stood on the banks of the Falconbrook, but the current incarnation was built as a hotel in the nineteenth century, with a pub downstairs. The pub's sign, with its golden falcon displaying its wings, is taken from the coat of arms of the Bolingbroke Viscounts, who owned the manor of Battersea in the seventeenth and eighteenth centuries.

This was a popular place for undertakers to drink, as it was on the way back from the local burial ground – so it's rather amusing that one of the landlords in the nineteenth century was a Robert Death. There's even a famous painting of the Falcon by John Nixon which is commonly known as *Drinking at Death's Door* because it depicts drunken undertakers dancing in front of the pub. Due to the pub's proximity to the river, street lamps had to be installed outside to prevent people drunkenly falling into the Falconbrook after a night of revelry.

Otherwise they'd really be up the junction!

With that reference to the song by Squeeze awkwardly shoehorned in, I think I'll have a pint of Doom Bar. It shouldn't take too long to get served, because apparently this pub holds the record for having the longest bar counter in Britain, so I should be able to get my hand on the bar!

*I never thought it would happen
With me and the girl from Clapham*

… and it didn't.

Here's looking at her, anyway.

Cheers.

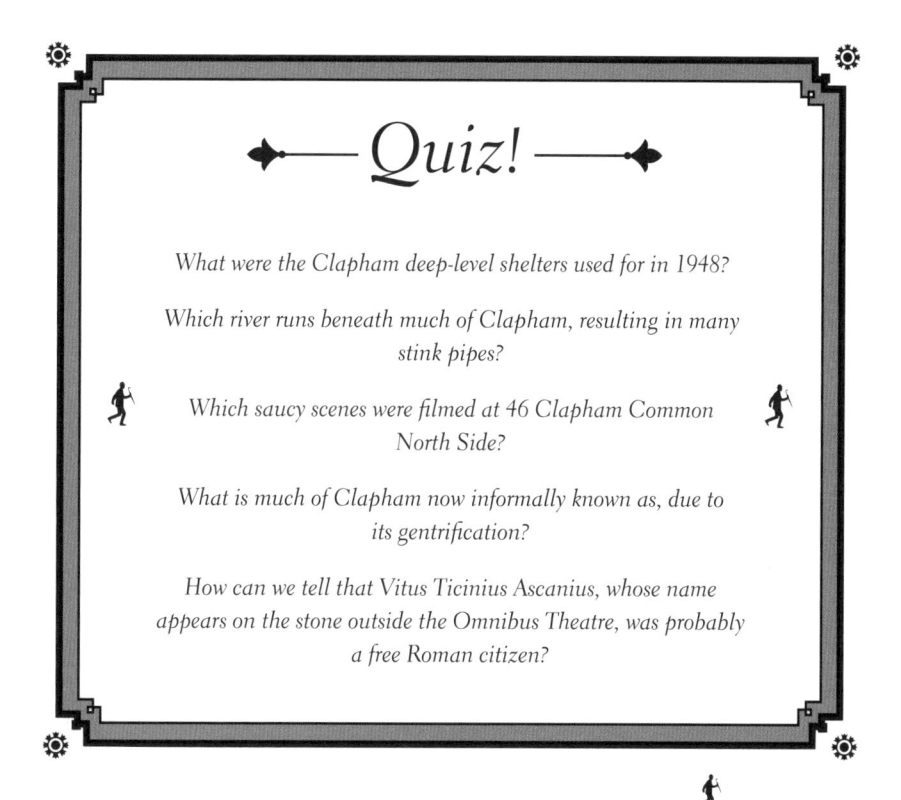

◆— *Quiz!* —◆

What were the Clapham deep-level shelters used for in 1948?

Which river runs beneath much of Clapham, resulting in many stink pipes?

Which saucy scenes were filmed at 46 Clapham Common North Side?

What is much of Clapham now informally known as, due to its gentrification?

How can we tell that Vitus Ticinius Ascanius, whose name appears on the stone outside the Omnibus Theatre, was probably a free Roman citizen?

11. Porchester Baths

PRINCE BONAPARTE

WESTWAY

WESTBOURNE PK RD

BISHOP'S BR RD

PHOENIX

CLEVELAND SQ

LEINSTER

INVERNESS TERRACE

PEMBRIDGE SQUARE

OSSINGTON ST

BAYSWATER ROAD

6. Skanderbeg Bust

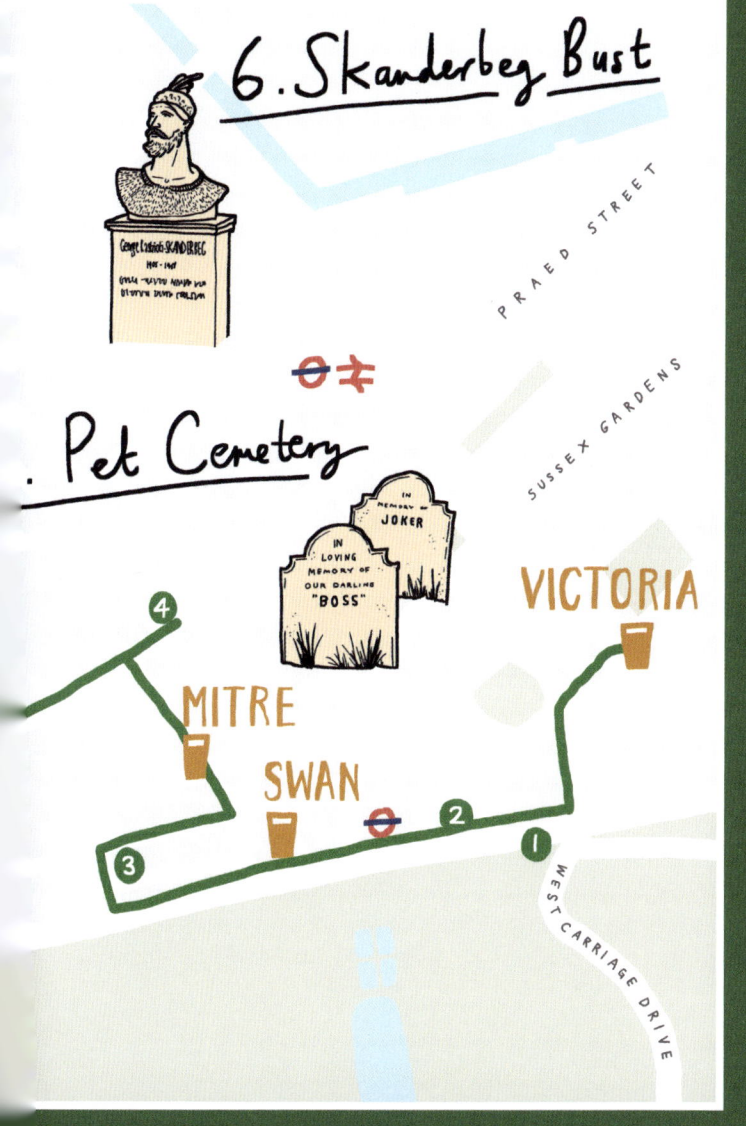

Pet Cemetery

WESTWAY
PRAED STREET
SUSSEX GARDENS
VICTORIA
MITRE
SWAN
WEST CARRIAGE DRIVE

17 BAYSWATER

17 SOME BEERS IN BEAUTIFUL BAYSWATER

DISTANCE
6.6 km (4.1 miles)

TIME
3 hours 10 minutes
with a few pints en route

NEAREST STATION
Paddington

PUBS
Victoria; Swan; Mitre; Prince Bonaparte; Phoenix

Tally ho! We're meeting in the **VICTORIA** on Strathearn Place because it's a glorious pub built in 1837, the same year that Queen Victoria came to the throne – and it's been claimed that she drank in here, too. Many of the features have been preserved from the nineteenth century, such as the etched mirrors and mahogany interior, so it's easy to imagine Charles Dickens (yes, him again!) sitting by one of the windows writing *Our Mutual Friend* (which is what he did, apparently).

There's plenty of Victoriana all over the place, whilst the upstairs is decorated with pieces taken from the Gaiety Theatre in the 1950s. Most importantly, however, it was here in 1966 that a young David Bowie, who had only just changed his name from David Jones, held a launch party to promote his new single 'Can't Help Thinking About Me'. Apparently, the journalists were only interested in him and ignored the rest of his band, The Lower Third. They went their separate ways after the single was released (it flopped in the charts).

PUB
Victoria

A pint of Fuller's ESB, please, and let's be off.

When you leave the Victoria, walk down Stanhope Terrace (to the left beyond the mini-roundabout) and turn left into Brook Street. Cross over Bayswater Road and head to the railings to the right of the park-keeper's cottage, at Victoria Gate.

If you're nine feet tall you can look over the hedge, but otherwise just poke your nose through the railings and in the garden you'll see many cute little gravestones. This is the **PET CEMETERY** ❶ which was established around 1880 by the park-keeper, Mr Winbridge. Originally he just agreed to bury a friend's dog here – but when a dog belonging to Sarah Fairbrother (she was the 'illegal wife' of the Duke of Cambridge) got squished by a carriage, Winbridge, who was their former servant, brought him into the house, where he died; so Winbridge agreed to bury him, too. After that it became rather fashionable, with over a thousand pets being laid to rest here, including cats, dogs, parrots and monkeys. It got a bit full and they stopped around 1903.

George Orwell described the pet cemetery as 'perhaps the most horrible spectacle in Britain' – although I must say, I've seen worse!

Continue west along Bayswater Road, past the cluster of **FOUR TELEPHONE BOXES** ❷. There isn't an official collective noun for these, so I put it to my subscribers, who came up with the following suggestions (amongst many others).

A clamour of call boxes? A phluster of phone boxes? A charm, a directory, a natter, a clarion?

What do you think it should be?

Continue past Lancaster Gate tube station and you'll get to a redundant drinking fountain on your left. Across the road you'll see the **SWAN** 🍺. I'm nipping in for a very quick half, although I know we've only just got started!

The Swan was rebuilt in the nineteenth century, but the oldest record of a pub on the site is from 1721, when it formed part of the Flora Tea Gardens, with its skittle alley and other entertainment. This was one of the last coaching inns, or stage posts, on the way to London, where coaches carrying the mail could rest their horses. It's claimed that the famous French highwayman Claude Duval had his last drink here in 1670, on his way to being hanged at Tyburn Gallows (further east, where Marble

Arch is today). This, however, would be unlikely: the route to Tyburn Gallows was usually from Newgate, in the east, and then along Oxford Street. If the story is true, though, it would make this pub even older than they say! I like the fireplace and the floral themes relating to the tea gardens (which got flattened so they could build all the big houses).

PUB

Swan

By the way, Claude Duval was certainly an interesting character. He had worked as a stable boy for the English royals when they were in exile. He then came to London and started robbing people along Holloway Road – but he was said to shun violence, and instead would tie his victims to a tree. He once promised only to take half a gentleman's loot on the condition that his lady would dance with him. This led to a famous painting of the incident and spawned the myth about highwaymen being chivalrous and romantic. He's buried at St Paul's Church in Covent Garden.

Leave the Swan and continue along Bayswater Road. You'll soon come to Lancaster Gate (the street, rather than the tube station, which we've already passed). Don't take this first right, but continue along to the second right, which is also part of Lancaster Gate, where you should see a church spire to your right.

These terraces, along with Christ Church, were part of the 1860s redevelopment on the site of the Flora Tea Gardens and were named after the actual gate to the park opposite (in honour of Queen Victoria, who was the Duke of Lancaster, not the Duchess – strange though it sounds).

The church suffered dry rot in the 1970s and was mostly destroyed, apart from the tower, so they turned it into flats.

THE COLUMBIA HOTEL ❸ on the right is where Ethiopian Emperor Haile Selassie is said to have stayed during his exile from the Italian invasion of Ethiopia in the 1930s. He became known as Ras Tafari (*ras* meaning 'prince' or 'duke' in Amharic, with Tafari being his original first name) and ended up becoming the spiritual leader of the Jamaican Rastafari movement. Many claimed that he was descended from the Queen of Sheba and Solomon the Wise and was the Second Coming of Christ!

In 1941 he was reinstated as Emperor of Ethiopia and I read somewhere that this was his headquarters during his exile years. Then again, a bloke down the pub told me that Haile Selassie lived in Bath during his exile, but I suppose he must have spent time in London, too.

During the 1990s the Columbia gained a reputation as a rock 'n' roll establishment due to its popularity with various bands, including Blur and Oasis – whose song 'Columbia' was inspired by the hotel.

In front of the church turn right, keeping the Columbia to your right. Walk east and then at the end turn left into Craven Terrace and you will soon see the **MITRE**, dating from 1859, where we can sneak in another drink.

It's called the Mitre because of its wedge shape on the corner, resembling a bishop's hat. You might recognise it from one of the scenes in Woody Allen's film *Scoop*.

They've got a wonderful Victorian dining room on the first floor, which is worth a peek even if you're not eating; and if you're looking for a cocktail, you'll find a secret speakeasy bar in the basement, known as Old Mary's. (Well, it can't be that secret if they have signs for it outside.) Why is it called Old Mary's? Naturally, the pub is said to be haunted! Mary was the mistress of Lord Craven, who used to own the building, and she was found murdered in the scullery. Whether you believe in ghosts or not, it's an interesting vaulted space.

I'm wearing my new trousers and I don't want to get any ectoplasm on me, so

PUB

Mitre

I'm sticking to the ground floor, where I'll take a pint of Beavertown Neck Oil.

Cheers.

Turn left out of the pub and walk past all the quaint lovely shops along Craven Terrace.

Turn right at Craven Road and stop when you reach the entrance to Upbrook Mews, on your left.

The blue plaque is for **TOMMY HANDLEY** ❹, who was one of those fast-talking old-school comedians. He starred in a very successful radio series in the 1940s called *It's That Man Again*. He's not so well known these days, but the show spawned many catchphrases that we still use today, including 'TTFN', which stands for 'ta-ta for now', and the exclamation 'D'oh!', which was later picked up by Homer Simpson. (Some people have suggested that the latter was first used by James Finlayson in the Laurel and Hardy films, but his was a longer, more drawn-out

'Dooooooooooooooh', rather than the short one used by Handley in *It's That Man Again*.)

'Can I do you now, sir?' Fnarr, fnarr.

As you face the plaque, turn to your left and retrace your steps along Craven Road, and then follow it across the junction as it becomes Craven Hill. There are some lovely houses and beautiful squares along here, although the section of Craven Hill Gardens on your left near the end is surrounded by that old mesh fencing that was used for a lot of schools in the 1970s, but you don't tend to see these days. I'm told that is perfectly normal to see it in America but over here it's dying out and reminds me of my school days trying to climb over it.

I think the Luftwaffe must have missed this area.

At the end of Craven Hill turn right and stop at what ought to be **23–24 LEINSTER GARDENS** ❺ on your left. When you look at the façade you'll see that all the windows are greyed out. This is because these are not houses at all – they're just a wall which was built by the railway company. Beneath here run the District and Circle line trains, but they didn't want to ruin the aesthetic of the buildings (especially as the locomotives were originally steam engines, belching out clouds of steam in the gaps between tunnels) so they built this false façade to blend in.

Let's go round to the other side and you can see what I mean. Head back along Leinster Gardens the way you just came, and then turn right into the narrow section of Craven Hill Gardens. Now turn right again into Porchester Terrace and just after number 23 on the right you can see the back of the 'houses' we just saw (and if you're tall enough you can see over the wall down to the railway tracks).

Carry on straight, past yet more lovely houses, and when you reach Porchester Gardens turn left.

On the corner of Inverness Terrace you'll see a bust of George (Gjergj) Kastrioti, known as **SKANDERBEG** ❻, the fifteenth-century Albanian hero who led resistance to the Ottoman Empire. In 2012 the Albanian community wanted something to commemorate 100 years of Albanian independence. It took them a while to decide on this location for him, because there were already so many statues around London. Eventually it seemed this spot was available, so this is where he resides.

Continue along Porchester Gardens to the next junction and turn left at the Prince Alfred. (I'm continuing past, but stop in for another drink if you like!)

You're now on Queensway, which used to be known as Black Lion Lane when Queen Victoria was born at Kensington Palace, but because she often used this

Walk 17: Bayswater | **293**

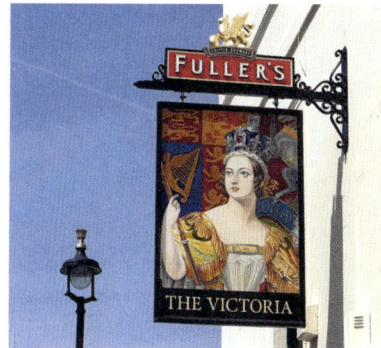

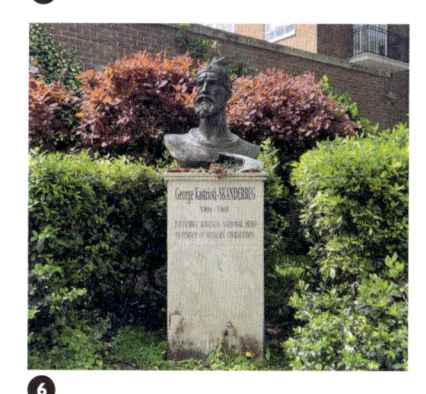

Victoria

❶

❷

Swan

❻

❾

road it later became known as Queen's Road and then Queensway.

Look up to your right before you pass Bayswater tube station and you'll see a lovely old **GHOST SIGN** ❼ advertising safety razors and blades, with a little girl shaving her father's face. You might have to stare at it a while to make it out. Rather him than me!

Keep going along Queensway and on the right (just before Queensway tube station) you'll see an overhang with the words 'QUEENS MEATliquor', looking like it might be the entrance to a cinema. This is actually an **ICE RINK AND BOWLING ALLEY** ❽. I always thought it a strange place to have an ice rink – beneath a residential building – but it's the oldest in London, dating from the 1930s, and was the first place to televise ice-skating on the BBC. They still rehearse for *Dancing on Ice* here sometimes (unless they've canned that show now).

Now turn around and retrace your steps back up Queensway.

After passing the Prince Alfred again you'll come to the huge building on the left that is – or rather, was – **WHITELEY'S** ❾. The original Whiteley's, said to be London's first department store, started around the corner in Westbourne Grove, but it moved here in 1911. William Whiteley was a penniless draper's assistant from Yorkshire who arrived here in 1863 with only a few pounds, but managed to build up his business into one of the biggest department stores in London (it would have been a bit like Harrods still is today), where you could buy anything 'from a pin to an elephant'. It served royals and nobles from around the world; it's where Eliza Doolittle gets her dress in *Pygmalion* (and is similarly mentioned in the film adaptation *My Fair Lady*).

It all ended quite badly for William Whiteley, though, because in 1907 a fellow called Horace Rayner came into his office claiming to be his son and demanding a job. When Whiteley told him to go and get knotted, Rayner pulled out a gun and shot him dead!

It's quite possible that Rayner was in fact his estranged child, as his mother often told him, 'Any time you're in trouble, go to see your real dad, William Whitely!'

At Rayner's Old Bailey trial he said he had asked for a job nicely, and that his father had been ever so mean. Amazingly, he was acquitted through public sympathy, because his dad was so cruel. So apparently that justified Rayner shooting him dead. Things were strange in those days. Yikes!

The department store itself closed down in 1981, and in later years it was converted into a big shopping centre. More recently the building has been redeveloped again, to contain a luxury hotel and luxury flats alongside luxury shops – or should that be luxury 'boutiques'? They've even changed the name slightly, to The Whiteley, which probably counts as a luxury name.

Keep going and to your right you'll see the lovely old Art Deco **QUEENS CINEMA** ⑩, built in 1932, which is now flats. Cross over and keep going straight up Queensway past the public toilets. (Yes, I know… Actual public toilets which are still open. Rare as hen's teeth!) At the end you'll find the **PORCHESTER BATHS** ⑪. Now called the Porchester Centre, together with its adjoining Porchester Hall and Paddington Library all the way round the corner to Porchester Road, this contains a beautiful example of a 1920s Turkish baths complex, with hot treatments, cold plunge pools and a swimming pool – as well as an events space where they filmed the scene in *Monty Python's The Meaning of Life* in which Mr Creosote projectile-vomits into a bucket before exploding. Delightful. I do recommend a visit to their facilities, which are pretty much the same as they were a century ago.

Now return the way you came and turn right into Westbourne Grove.

I can recommend coming back one evening to enjoy an Austrian meal at the **TIROLER HUT** ⑫, on your left, which was opened in 1967 by Josef – who is still there now, in his eighties – playing the accordion and yodelling, to the delight of his customers. Amongst the celebrities who have enjoyed a bratwurst or schnitzel here are Muhammad Ali, Kate Moss, Hugh Grant, Boris Becker, Claudia Schiffer and Joolz from Joolz Guides!! It's great fun and you'll make friends for sure. Prost!

Just after the Tiroler Hut on the left is a parade of shops which all used to comprise the original Whiteley's. This street has changed a lot over the years, demonstrated by the fact that in John le Carré's novel *Smiley's People* the Estonian general, Vladimir, lives in a dingy flat here. There aren't too many of those around these days.

Continue on Westbourne Grove and turn right into Monmouth Road. At the end, just to the right, there is a little pathway called Kildare Passage leading through to Kildare Gardens just ahead.

Walk through the gardens and then along Kildare Terrace, and I must just point out that I'd love to live in this street. What a delightful little enclave.

Turn right into Talbot Road, then right at Westbourne Park Road and then right again into Alexander Street.

As you enter Alexander Street, glance up to your right and you'll see all the previous street signs. It looks like they changed the name of this one from Sunderland Terrace.

NUMBER 32 ⑬ is where Stiff Records was founded by Dave Robinson and

Jake Riviera in 1976, with their motto 'If it ain't Stiff it ain't worth a f***!'

Stiff Records were responsible for signing some of the most influential bands of the 1970s. They released what was regarded by many as the first punk single, 'New Rose' by The Damned. Also on their label were Elvis Costello, Ian Dury and the Blockheads, Madness and, briefly, Motörhead – although I think Lemmy decided to go elsewhere, despite hanging out here in the offices a fair bit. There's a great documentary you can see on YouTube in which many of these stars of yesteryear are all running out of the shop and onto a bus parked in this street. The houses looked a lot more run-down than they do now. It was all like that in the 1970s!

Now return to Westbourne Park Road and follow it to the left, keeping St Stephen's church on your left.

I should point out that if you walk to the end of this road you will come to the Westbourne, a pretty trendy pub where I once saw Robbie Williams. But instead we're turning left into St Stephen's Gardens, and then left again when we reach Chepstow Road.

The flat on the corner of the square, **29 ST STEPHEN'S GARDENS** ⑭, is where Michael Caine's character lives in the film *Alfie*, with Annie (Jane Asher). I also like to think that this could be 'the remote corner of Bayswater' where, in Oscar Wilde's *The Importance of Being Earnest*, the perambulator carrying Jack was found abandoned.

Continue along Chepstow Road and we'll rest our feet awhile in the **PRINCE BONAPARTE** 🍺 on the left, built in 1850. Somehow this pub seems to attract good-looking young Europeans who are more cheerful and enthusiastic about life than me, and unless it was my imagination, a lot of French people in particular. Can it be due to the name? Anyway, it's an upmarket gastropub which is pretty modern and spacious inside. Again, I like these pubs with lots of windows!

I think I'll have a quick half of Dark Star Hophead.

Santé.

Carrying on down Chepstow Road you'll pass **NUMBER 58** ⑮, which, appropriately, has a lizard as a door-knocker. This was where Peter Rachman, the notorious slum landlord of the 1950s and 1960s, had his brothel.

Rachman's approach to being a landlord

PUB

Prince Bonaparte

Walk 17: Bayswater | **297**

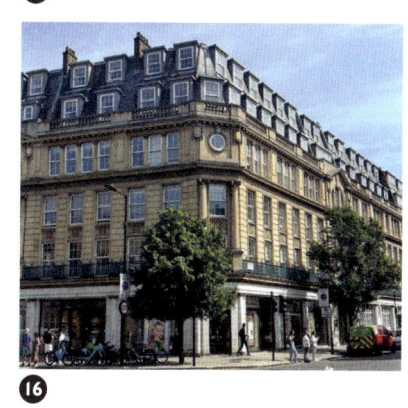

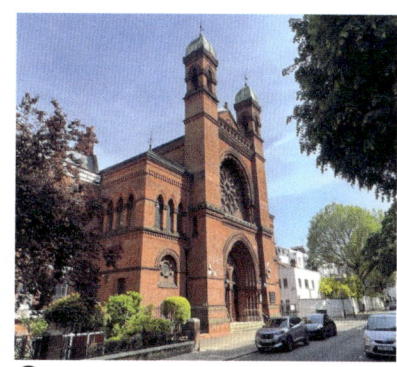

was to squeeze too many people into tiny bedsits and charge them too much. Then when they couldn't pay he'd threaten them by turning off the water and sending thugs round with scary dogs. Pleasant-sounding chap.

Carry on and at the junction with Westbourne Grove look across at the large corner building on the left with the green balcony and 'B' within the ironwork.

In the 1860s this was the site of a **COLD STORAGE FACILITY** (16) founded by Samuel Bradley – where people could store away their fur coats during the summer. In 1896 his sons turned it into the Bradley and Sons Arctic Fur Store, which became the biggest furrier in Europe, selling driving gloves, coats, goggles and all sorts. It was so popular that the Churchills shopped here, as did the royal family. In fact, it's said that due to the fading memory of Queen Mary (wife of George V) they changed the phone number to Bayswater 3456 just so she could remember it!

After the Second World War it went into a bit of a decline and then it got turned into flats, named Baynards House, where Richard Harris used to live with his wife. You might not be surprised to hear they were difficult tenants!

Continue over the junction, and when you get to **57 CHEPSTOW PLACE** (17) you might want to take a selfie outside the house used in the publicity photo for the cult film *Withnail and I*. It looks like they've refurbished it a bit, but it's still recognisable as the place where Richard E. Grant and Paul McGann sat on the steps outside. The horrendous kitchen where they discover 'matter' in the sink was upstairs…

Turn left into Dawson Place and then left again into Prince's Square, which leads to Leinster Square. Take the second turning on the right and walk alongside the gardens to the end, where we're crossing over to **28A LEINSTER SQUARE** (18).

This contains the basement flat where Sting first lived (with his then wife) when he moved to London. In fact Trudie (his future wife) was living very nearby and this is where they met. It was probably cheaper in those days.

Turn right and follow the road south until you see the magnificent **GREEK CATHEDRAL OF ST SOPHIA** (19) on the corner of Ilchester Gardens and Moscow Road. Also known as the Greek Orthodox Cathedral of the Divine Wisdom, it was consecrated in 1882 and if you can have a look inside it really is terrific, with lavish gold mosaics and religious artwork.

It's funny that the roads nearby are called Moscow Road and St Petersburgh Place, because in the James Bond film *Goldeneye* Natalya comes to this church to meet Boris – but in the film it's a church in St Petersburg, Russia!

Carry straight on, into St Petersburgh Place, and you'll pass **ST MATTHEW'S CHURCH** ㉑, built in 1880, and then the **NEW WEST END SYNAGOGUE** ㉑, built in 1879, one of the oldest synagogues in Britain, and Grade I-listed for its Anglo-Jewish architecture.

Hmm… Time for a medium dry vodka martini, so let's turn left at Orme Lane and then left again, into St Petersburgh Mews. At the end turn right and head into the **PHOENIX** 🍺 on Moscow Road, using the Rule of Ted (see page 166; it was the closest pub!).

PUB

Phoenix

Forget the martini, I'll take a pint of IPA. The name's Guides. Joolz Guides.

Chin chin.

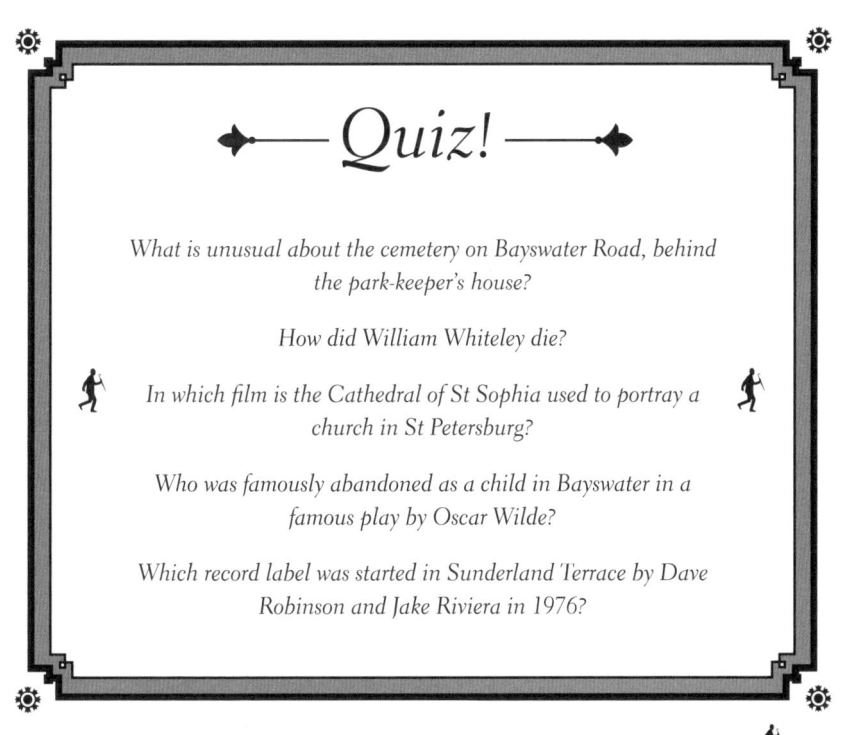

✦ — *Quiz!* — ✦

What is unusual about the cemetery on Bayswater Road, behind the park-keeper's house?

How did William Whiteley die?

In which film is the Cathedral of St Sophia used to portray a church in St Petersburg?

Who was famously abandoned as a child in Bayswater in a famous play by Oscar Wilde?

Which record label was started in Sunderland Terrace by Dave Robinson and Jake Riviera in 1976?

18. Drinking Fountain

HUMBER ROAD

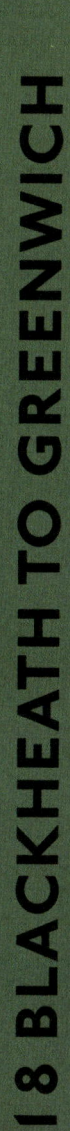

23. Flamsteed House

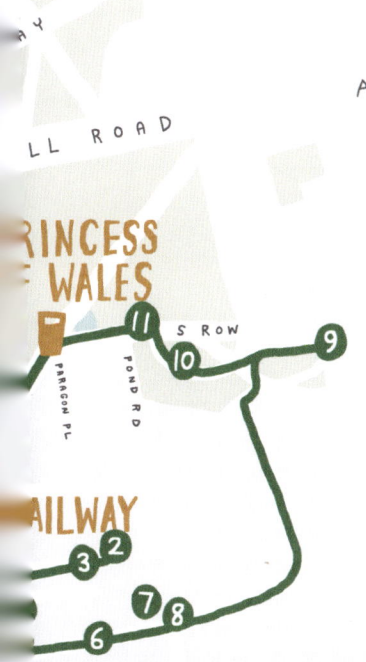

A 2

9. Morden College Gatehouse

18 BLACKHEATH TO GREENWICH

18 A QUAINT SAUNTER FROM BLACKHEATH TO GREENWICH

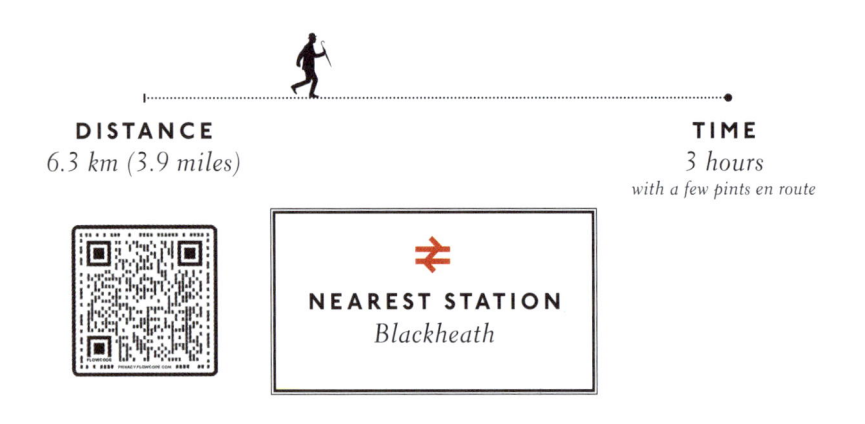

DISTANCE
6.3 km (3.9 miles)

TIME
3 hours
with a few pints en route

NEAREST STATION
Blackheath

PUBS
Railway; Princess of Wales; Crown; Hare & Billet; Plume of Feathers

Well met! I thought the **RAILWAY** would be a suitable starting point, since (as you might guess from the name) it's so close to the train station and pretty convenient from London Bridge, Cannon Street or Victoria. The Railway also has both a courtyard beer garden and a roof terrace, for those days when the sun is shining…unlike when I last visited. Gonna down me this pint and we'll get going.

The first thing that strikes you on leaving the pub is how quaint Blackheath Village is, with a number of well-preserved buildings which survived the Second World War. Look across the road to the right, at the corner of Bennett Park: this used to be **SWIMMING BATHS** ❶ from the 1860s, and later a Lloyds Bank. At the time of writing the main part of the building had remained unoccupied for quite a while due to all sorts of complications with planning permission – because they actually have an old swimming pool in the basement, which is protected.

I always find it interesting looking at redundant relics that survive on buildings like the train station. What now constitutes the left-hand entrance looks as though it must have, at some point, had a front door of sorts, possibly for the station master or some other official. There is an old-style doorbell on the right, and a hole at the bottom of the wall, which would have contained a foot scraper to remove the mud from your boots, but now it contains lots of cigarette butts.

Apparently the heath itself, which we shall come to, acquired its name because of the darker colour of the grass and soil compared to that of the surrounding fields. Some people say it's because many victims of the Black Death were buried in mass graves here, but frankly the grass just looks green to me. When we get there you can decide if you can see any difference.

From the station, cross the road and walk to the right. Then turn left down Bennett Park, which has a charming street sign fashioned out of wood. At the end of this pleasant residential street is number 47, the **BLACKHEATH ART CLUB** ❷ – which has now been turned into flats, of course.

Blackheath Art Club was built in the 1880s. Soon after the First World War it ceased being a club and eventually passed into the hands of the GPO Film Unit, whose job it was to make promotional films for the Post Office. By the Second World War it was being used to make morale-boosting propaganda films. Today it's a rather splendid-looking place to live.

Now come back again, passing on your left, between numbers 30 and 28, the cute **MINI BLUE PLAQUE** ❸ remembering Bertie the legendary street cat. He was fluffy, ginger and friendly, and sometimes got the bus around Blackheath!

Turn left at the end of Bennett Park and walk up the hill past the quite exquisite **BLACKHEATH HALLS** ❹, a music and cultural venue built in 1895, with its wonderful reliefs and artwork on the side of the building. Did you also spot the King George V post box on the other side of the road?

Now, there's a bit of a walk ahead of us, so it's a good opportunity to work up an appetite before the next pub.

Turn left into Blackheath Park, which is a stunning street lined with impressively grand houses dating back to the 1820s.

The first thing I noticed was at the beginning of the street: a lovely semicircular **LITTER BIN** ❺ with wooden slats down the side. I'm sure residents of Blackheath probably think I'm mad, but this is something I haven't seen since my childhood. Blackheath seems to retain a number of features like this which, whilst not being ancient, are certainly no longer commonplace 'down our way'!

Look out for **NUMBER 10** ❻ on your right, which rather sticks out like a sore thumb, being one of the few modern houses amongst the older properties along this stretch. It took quite a feat by its architect, Patrick Gwynne, to gain planning permission in 1968 and opinion is divided on it. I think it looks like the *Thunderbirds* hideout!!

I won't point out too many things along here but this is, after all, a book of walks, and I must say this is an extremely pleasant stroll, making one feel like one is in a country village.

Keep going past the church of **ST MICHAEL AND ALL ANGELS** ❼, completed in 1830. Strictly speaking, we're actually in Kent here and the tall spire is known as the 'Needle of Kent', although I confess I can't tell the difference between this and any other spires!

Sometimes on a street corner around here you'll see a white stone resembling a milestone, like on **THE CORNER OF FOXES DALE** ❽, but these are just bollards to prevent carriages mounting the corner as they turn. No **points** for these! That said, what is remarkable is the number of different bollards you get in Blackheath. Once you start noticing them you can't stop. They have become very 'bollard trigger-happy' here, with numerous inexplicably placed bollards all over the place. I even spotted two in the driveway of number 4 earlier, and then various different shapes and sizes strewn along this road and throughout Blackheath, often not matching.

Continue straight and just after Papillons Walk the street curves around to the left. Follow Blackheath Park around the curve (don't go straight on) past yet more extremely desirable, charming cottages which remind me of old Will Hay films.

Despite the beauty of the surroundings, what catches my eye along here are the concrete lampposts, which resemble the old bus stops which seemed to disappear in the 1980s. Maybe they're common in other parts of Britain, but it's unusual to see these in London nowadays. They really take me back to the 1970s, when I would often sustain injuries by scraping against their rough surfaces… Most of the lampposts in Blackheath carry some sort of parking warning. If you spot a lamppost *without* an officious notice on it you get **points**!!!

As you continue Blackheath Park becomes Morden Road Mews (there's a sign which might make you think that Morden Road Mews turns off to the left, but keep going straight ahead). I feel sorry for the postal workers and delivery drivers around here because there is no rhyme or reason to the numbering system. The houses at the end seem to start at number 11, and I'm not sure what happened to the first ten houses.

At the end, after crossing the railway and reaching a wooden gate, turn right and then left into Morden Road.

To your right is a red-brick building and a gated entrance which, strictly speaking, I shouldn't send you through, since this is the entrance to a care home, although you do get a better view that way. If they let you in it's worth walking up the driveway; otherwise, follow the railing on your right and you'll come to another gate and a pathway, with a green footpath signpost for Sir John Morden Walk. It's left open for pedestrians these days but the 'kissing gate' is more like those which you see in the countryside to prevent livestock getting through – a hangover from the days when sheep and cattle would pass by here.

The magnificent **MORDEN COLLEGE** ❾ is not a school, as you might think, and although it looks like the work of Sir Christopher Wren, it was built by his master mason, Edward Strong. The charity was founded by Sir John Morden in 1695 as a home for 'Poor Merchants and such as have lost their Estates by accidents, dangers and Perrills of the Seas or by any other accidents ways or means in their honest endeavours to get a living by means of Merchandizing'.

Sir John Morden was a successful merchant and committee member of the East India Company who had moved to Greenwich to escape the Great Plague and Great Fire of London.

His friend Daniel Defoe wrote that he 'had it from his own mouth' that Morden was 'to make apartments for forty decay'd merchants, to whom he resolv'd to allow 40£ per annum each, with coals, a gown (and servants to look after their apartments) and many other conveniences so as to make their lives as comfortable as possible.'

Apparently, being over the age of fifty qualified a person as suitably 'decay'd', which doesn't make me feel too great about myself – but fifty is the new forty, after all.

The two figures standing over the entrance are Sir John Morden and his wife, Lady Susan, and it still functions as a care home today. If you are able to have a look around, you'll find it truly stunning – it doesn't look like it's over three centuries old. Look out for the sundial, with the motto 'SIC UMBRA SIC VITA', meaning 'Thus the shadow, thus life' (a cheerful reminder of how few summers we get to spend on this theme park spinning through space).

Inside there's a fire engine dating from the 1750s.

But look, don't go barging in unless you have permission.

Now return to the red-brick gatehouse and head up toward the crescent of late eighteenth-century houses called the **PARAGON** ⑩. I like how each house has a stone mounting block outside on the pavement to help the residents get into their carriages. (At least I think that's what they are.) If you needed a bit more height there is a bigger one in the middle on the grass, which resembles a small flight of stairs leading to nowhere. A little further along there is also a boundary stone in the grass with the letters 'G. P.' on it, referring to Greenwich Parish.

These are amongst the most magnificent houses I've seen in London, when you take into consideration the view too, and I'm rather enjoying this walk, even if I'm getting increasingly jealous of the occupants of these tremendous abodes.

At the end turn left into South Row past **CATOR MANOR** ⑪, with its Latin inscription reading 'NIHIL SINE LABORE', meaning 'Nothing comes out of doing no work'. It sounds more like something you would find on the door of a workhouse – but this wasn't a workhouse.

John Cator, whose family crest is above

PUB
Princess of Wales

the door, was a timber merchant who did rather well for himself amassing a fortune through hard work, with which he developed a lot of the houses around here.

I'm sure there is a much more functional and boring explanation for the zigzag chimney on one of the adjoining buildings (you might have to cross the road carefully to see it), but I have heard chimneys were built this way to prevent witches flying down them! It's a fun story and certainly good enough for Joolz Guides, although I don't know what Father Christmas thought of it.

Well, I have to say we've probably earned a pint after all that walking, so let's drop into the **PRINCESS OF WALES** 🍺, coming up on the left, which was named after Caroline of Brunswick, the wife of King George IV, who lived across the park. (She's the one who, upon his first sight of her, caused George to have to call for strong brandy on account of her displeasing looks.)

In 1871 they selected the team for the first England rugby international

Walk 18: Blackheath to Greenwich | **307**

1

5

9

11

Princess of Wales

12

fixture here and the pub has been long associated with Blackheath rugby club. It's pretty modern inside and is popular especially in the summer for outdoor drinking.

It's a brisk day and the bleak winds do sorely ruffle. That strong brandy sounds like a good call, actually. Make mine a double.

Cheers!

Come out of the pub and turn left, then bear right along Royal Parade. They've made it a bit confusing for pedestrians here: you can use the zebra crossing just after the pub, then walk along the grass for a bit, crossing Prince Charles Road; or you can continue along the same side of the road as the pub and then cross over a bit further down where Royal Parade turns off.

I like the imposing view of Blackheath Hospital looming over the buildings if you look to the left down the hill. Oh, I see another cattle trough over there, being used as a flower bed. We're back in Blackheath village and it really is picturesque.

On your right is **ALL SAINTS CHURCH** **12**. As you continue along this stretch, known as 'Washerwoman's Bottom', since it's where servants would beat carpets and hang laundry out to dry, I can definitely recommend a visit to the **BOOKSHOP ON THE HEATH** **13**, coming up on the left corner. There are

PUB

Crown

some wonderful second-hand books about the local area, as well as other gems, and it's a very peaceful and lovely space overlooking the heath. I recently picked up an excellent book of London paintings here.

The **FOUNTAIN** **14** across the road was erected to commemorate the sixtieth year of Queen Victoria's reign, in 1897 – but, of course, it doesn't work.

Now turn left down the hill. Before nipping into the Crown for a quickie, just have a little snoop in **COLLINS SQUARE** **15**, which is a delightful little street past the pub. It's just to get more of a flavour of what a charming neighbourhood this is, not that you need it.

I must say, I do like a pub with a piano. The **CROWN** has been here since the sixteenth century, when it was a coaching inn. These days it's much modernised and has an upstairs restaurant, allowing more space for us serious drinkers downstairs.

I'll have a pint of Spitfire.

Here's mud in your eye.

Turn left out of the pub and head up Tranquil Vale. When you see an opening on your left, that's Lloyds Place. Head over to the wonderful houses on the far side, **GROTE'S BUILDINGS** ⓰, built in the 1760s and commanding spectacular views of the heath.

The little plaques up on the walls are not fire insurance plaques, as you might think – but you still get **points** for spotting them, because they are property markers, indicating that this land has belonged to the Morden Estate since 1695 (the folks who built the lovely retirement home we saw earlier).

Follow Lloyds Place back round to the main road and turn left on Hare and Billet Road, where you'll come to the **HARE & BILLET** 🍺.

Oh, go on then, we'll have another quick one. Just so we can gaze out over the windswept heath through the rain. One can imagine doing the same when this was just an isolated coaching inn on the heath in the 1600s, feeling relieved to have escaped one of the highwaymen who were notoriously operating along here.

In 2014 a visit to this pub by the MP for Lewisham sparked a saucy debate in Parliament! He was in the pub when he was underwhelmed by being served Henderson's Relish, instead of Lea and Perrins Worcester Sauce, and almost spat out his cheese on toast. Outrageous!

The sauces do look pretty similar, both with brown liquid and orange packaging, and I must admit I hate it when establishments try to fob me off with an alternative to Heinz tomato ketchup. The MP accused Henderson's of 'parasitic packaging' during a debate in the House of Commons on intellectual property. This sparked a furore, with many celebrities weighing in.

Everyone knows that Lea and Perrins contains anchovies and Henderson's doesn't! Actually, I didn't know that… but on my last visit I would have been more upset at the price of the fish and chips, personally – although the service was very friendly and the food was good, at least. When I showed up at lunchtime it did feel more like a restaurant than a pub, in all honesty.

Another thing that makes this pub stand out is that, remarkably, it's *not* haunted! I know!

That said, the road outside is haunted, by a poor woman from the eighteenth century, who hanged herself on an elm tree because her lover didn't show up to meet her. Seems a bit drastic, especially in those days. Maybe he got held up by a highwayman or got served the wrong sauce and was busy lodging a complaint.

Cheers. Down the hatch.

Turn left out of the pub and walk along Eliot Place.

I tire of saying it, but there are yet more magnificent houses here. I particularly like number 6, with one of those old doorbell ringer pull-things (I think that's their official name), and Eliot Vale House, which is another beauty. I mean, I thought Hampstead takes some beating, but this gives it a run for its money.

When you reach the King Edward VII post box on the corner of Pagoda Gardens, turn left and look at the extraordinary house on the right.

THE PAGODA **(17)** was built in the late 1700s in this Chinese style, which is rather unusual for the area. It was later leased to the Prince Regent (who became King George IV) and used as a summer house for Caroline of Brunswick, no doubt so that he could get rid of her. (He wouldn't even let her attend his coronation!)

Go back up to Eliot Vale and turn left. Then turn right into the Orchard.

Walk to the end of the Orchard, where it meets Mounts Pond Road, crossing over to head across the heath, bearing slightly to your right. You'll have to cross Hare and Billet Road before continuing further across the heath. You're heading for the corner of Goffers Road and Shooters Hill Road.

Down the years Blackheath has been the location of many important events.

Further along to the left, you might just be able to see a **DRINKING FOUNTAIN** **(18)** in the distance, where Shooters Hill Road meets Cade Road and Wat Tyler Road. You can walk over to it if you wish; it's a little out of the way, but what is remarkable about it is that it actually works!

In 1381 Wat Tyler gathered the peasants here during the famous Peasants' Revolt. Later, in 1450, it was here that Jack Cade camped with his followers during the Kentish rebellion against King Henry VI. Apparently Cade declared himself Lord Mayor of London by crossing London Bridge and striking the London Stone with his sword, before being driven back over the bridge and killed. A pretty short stint as self-appointed mayor!

Head towards a small, light bluish-grey wooden shack, which is the **BLACKHEATH TEA HUT** **(19)**. Amazingly, this has been going since 1924 and is the only business licensed to serve refreshments around here. It has become quite a popular meeting place, especially for bikers, who can get a nice, uncomplicated cup of tea with a bacon roll here. None of this fancy frappucino nonsense. The table even has holes in it, functioning as makeshift cup holders, to stop your drink blowing away. It can be a bit of a life-saver on a long walk, actually.

The road the Tea Hut stands next to is Goffers Road, which is most probably a reference to the fact that the first golf course in England was here, on Blackheath. Although golf had existed in Scotland for many years, it was only when King James VI of Scotland ascended to the throne as King James I of England in 1603 and came to London that he insisted on an English version of 'a good walk spoiled' (as Mark Twain is said to have described the sport). Since he was staying at Greenwich Palace this seemed like a suitable place for it, although Royal Blackheath Golf Club has since moved to Eltham.

Cross over Shooters Hill Road into the start of Charlton Way and enter Greenwich Park through the gate between the two bins on the right.

Once through the gate, stick to the left-hand path and on your left you'll come to the remains of **MONTAGU HOUSE** ㉐, demolished in 1815. Originally it was the home of the Duke of Montagu,

and, for two years, a remarkable fellow called Ignatius Sancho.

Sancho was born enslaved on a ship around 1729 and was gifted to three sisters who lived on the other side of Greenwich Park. Occasionally they would be visited by the Duke of Montagu, who befriended Sancho to the extent that when Sancho got sick of his treatment at the hands of the sisters, he ran away and ended up as butler to the Duke.

It's a remarkable story, but among his many achievements Sancho ended up becoming an extremely witty and eloquent writer, an accomplished musician and composer, and the first Black man to vote in an English Parliamentary election. He even had his portrait painted by Thomas Gainsborough. They've recently opened up an Ignatius Sancho Café on the other side of the park.

Later Montagu House was yet another one of the residences of Queen Caroline of Brunswick. You can still see her bath in the grounds here, which they excavated.

It's a pity the house has been destroyed, but there is another Georgian house just a little further along. The **RANGER'S HOUSE** ㉑ was used in the Netflix series *Bridgerton* – you often see fans of the show getting their photos taken outside. These days the building houses art exhibitions.

17

19

21

23

24

25

Keep straight along the path and when you see the Royal Observatory over to your right, leave the path and start walking towards it. You can't miss the building with a red ball on top.

Oh, the sculpture on your left is **KNIFE EDGE** ㉒ by Henry Moore.

Now, I'll be honest: I don't want to talk about the Observatory and these buildings in this walk, because they should really be seen in conjunction with a general Greenwich walk, in which there is so much to discuss that I'd need another chapter or two! That said, I do like the ball on top of **FLAMSTEED HOUSE** ㉓. Every day since 1833 this ball has been dropped at 1.00 p.m., signalling to the ships on the Thames to adjust their chronometers, so they can take accurate astronomical readings. Although it's not necessary these days, they still do it to please tourists, of which there are a great many here.

You might wish to go and explore these buildings, but for this walk we're just going to wander up to the top of the hill to take in the magnificent view of the **ROYAL NAVAL COLLEGE** ㉔, designed by Christopher Wren. This is one of my favourite views in London (except when the aliens landed their spaceship here in the Marvel film *Thor: The Dark World*).

Most people tend to be looking at the view and don't stop to wonder about the statue which has pride of place here. It's one of the most prestigious locations for a statue, as far as I can tell. This is **GENERAL JAMES WOLFE** ㉕, who died during the capture of Quebec, which ultimately ensured that Canada remained British and not French. Readers of my first book will know about the bell which the French garrison failed to ring in time to warn of the attack of the British, who were scaling the cliff. It ended up in a church in Tottenham.

As you face London, turn to your right and walk straight, perpendicular to James Wolfe.

Soon you'll come to a fenced off tree which is lying on its side, known as **QUEEN ELIZABETH'S OAK** ㉖.

This was planted in the twelfth century and formed part of the grounds of Greenwich Palace (which no longer exists). King Henry VIII and Anne Boleyn were known to have danced around it, and their daughter, Elizabeth I, picnicked beneath its branches. Well, so the legend says. People always seemed to be dancing around trees in those days, but I must say, I have never done so myself. They say that it was hollow and was even used to imprison people behind a huge door which was attached to the trunk.

I wonder if that's where Shakespeare got the idea for Prospero's line, 'I will rend an oak and peg thee in his knotty entrails, till thou hast howl'd away twelve winters.'

Anyway, by the 1870s the tree eventually died – and I might go a similar way if I don't get a drink soon. The shadows grow tall, the sky bruises, and we shall be forced to camp.

Let us repair to the Plume of Feathers.

Head down the hill and out of the exit to the right of the Queen's House and National Maritime Museum, onto Park Vista.

Turn right and you'll walk past a plaque in the wall indicating that you are crossing the **PRIME MERIDIAN** 27, or zero degrees longitude.

Look out also for the rather beautiful recessed post box in the wall. I haven't seen many of these marked from King Edward VII's time, so you get **points** for spotting this.

The **PLUME OF FEATHERS** has been here since 1691 and is the oldest pub in Greenwich. Whilst you get plenty of tourists here, it's a real locals' pub with a very warm and cosy atmosphere, and the service comes with a genuine smile. It gets busy on Sundays for their roasts, so you might want to book if you're eating, or you can just try your luck, like me. Nautical memorabilia occupies almost every inch of wall space and Toby jugs hang from the ceiling, giving this a genuinely English flavour.

PUB

Plume of Feathers

They've retained a proper carpet in here, which I like, and you can probably bag yourself plenty of pub paraphernalia **points**… Are those horse brasses I see above the fireplace?

This is a good place to rest our feet, sit by the fire and exchange tales of youth, drunkenness and frivolity.

I'll take a pint of Harvey's Best. Here's to being single, drinking doubles, and seeing triple.

Chin chin!

— Quiz! —

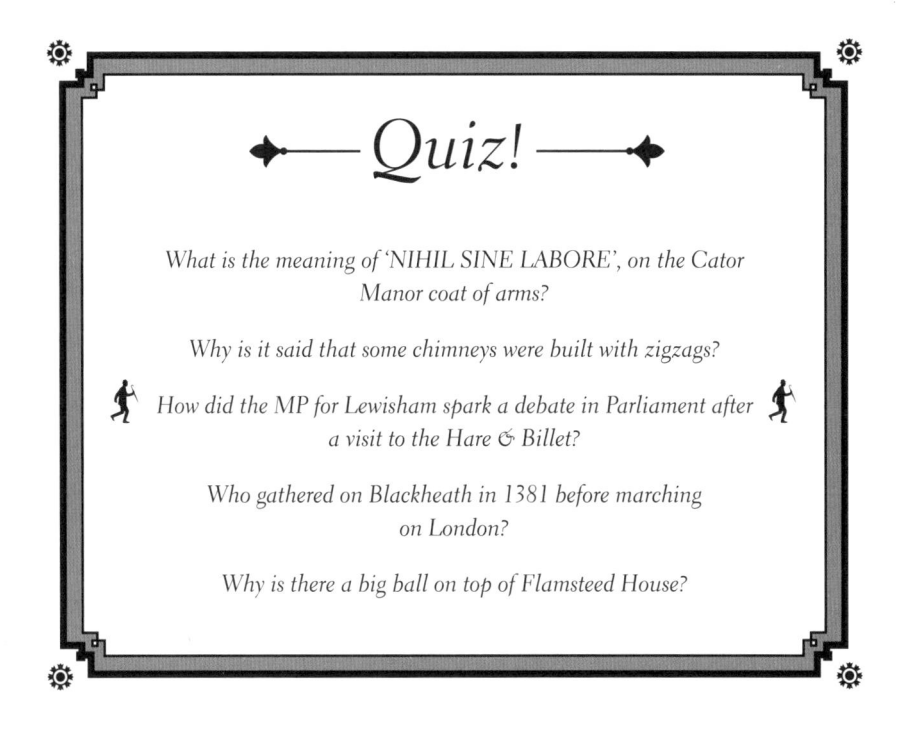

What is the meaning of 'NIHIL SINE LABORE', on the Cator Manor coat of arms?

Why is it said that some chimneys were built with zigzags?

How did the MP for Lewisham spark a debate in Parliament after a visit to the Hare & Billet?

Who gathered on Blackheath in 1381 before marching on London?

Why is there a big ball on top of Flamsteed House?

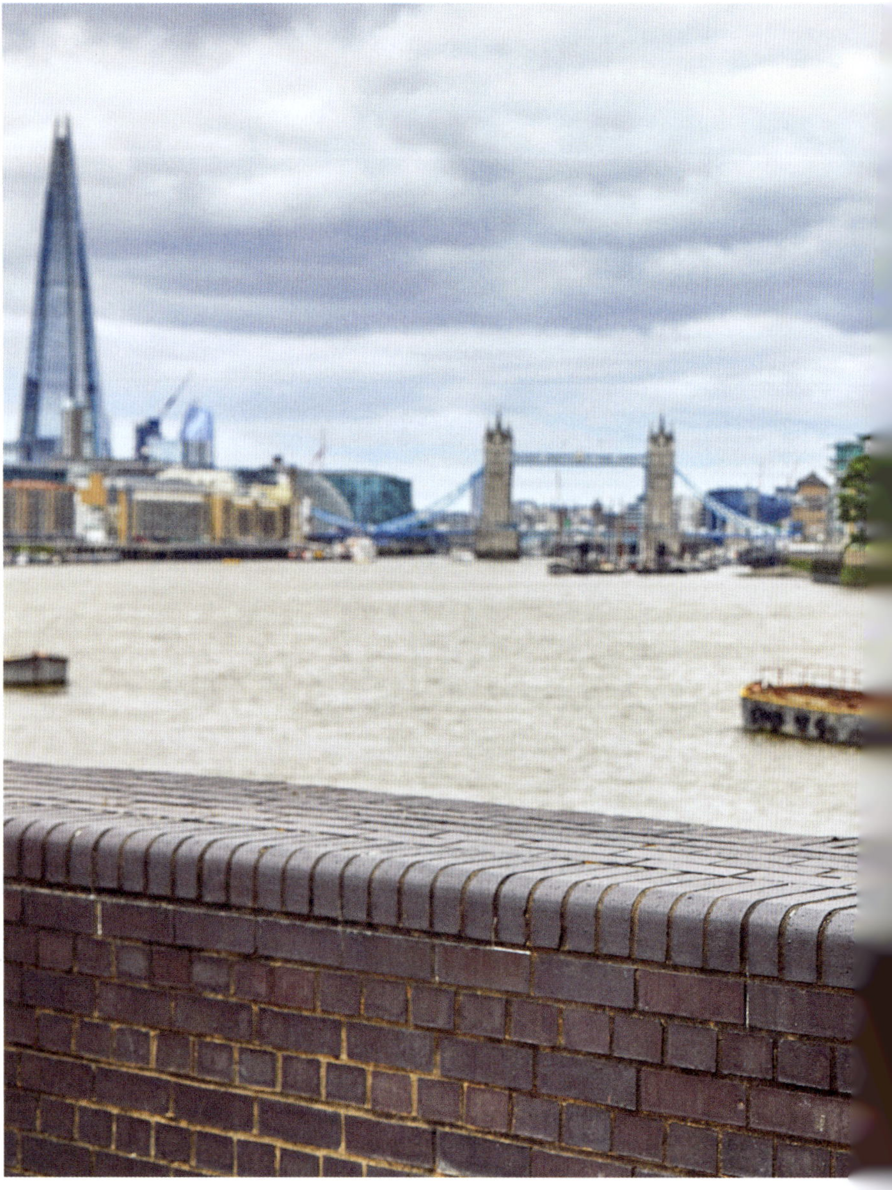

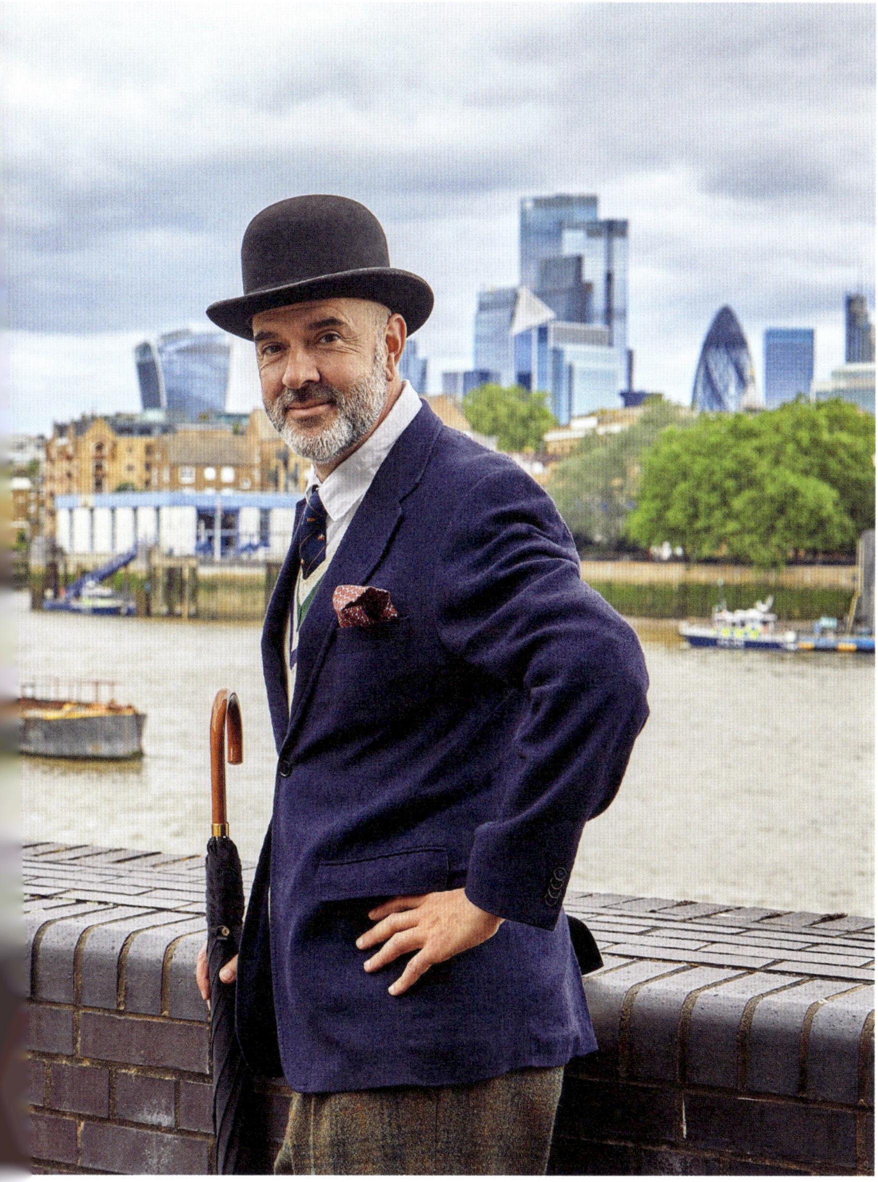

ACKNOWLEDGEMENTS

Laura Willis: for sticking by me and still being my friend after all you had to go through getting my first book off the ground. Neither book would exist without you!

Sarah Lavelle: thank you for offering me a second book, after all my diva behaviour!

Robert Timms: going absolutely above and beyond again! Your research, hard work and attention to detail have been invaluable.

Dimitri Sachkov: thanks for your help with Maida Vale.

Laura Barnard: thanks for the wonderful maps!!!

Katherine Case: thank you for putting all this together so efficiently.

Luke Albert: for the splendid photos of moi.

Luke Bird: for the eye-catching cover design.

Ralph Tilt, Joanna Brown, Paul Moody, Ted Hughes, Dave Gorman and Dan: thank you for the pub rules.

Harry Adès: thanks for your pub rule and paraphernalia knowledge.

Tom Adeney: thanks for your pub knowledge and advice.

Monica and Steve Buttling-Smith: for some excellent Crouch End knowledge.

Yen Nguyen: thank you for a memorable evening at the concert on the houseboats overlooking Tower Bridge, and for your help with Rotherhithe.

Lou Psyche: for the poems, songs, pub knowledge and generally being a massive part of Joolz Guides!

Alex Edward: for confusing everyone by being called Simon and being such an instrumental part of Joolz Guides.

Most of all, a massive thank you to all my subscribers and people who have watched my videos!! Without you Joolz Guides is nothing!

Acknowledgements | **319**

For my mummy

Quadrille, Penguin Random House UK,
One Embassy Gardens, 8 Viaduct Gardens,
London SW11 7BW

Quadrille Publishing Limited is part of the Penguin Random House group of companies, whose addresses can be found at global.penguinrandomhouse.com

Penguin Random House UK

Copyright © Julian McDonnell 2025
Photography © Luke Albert 2025
Maps © Laura Barnard 2025

Julian McDonnell has asserted his right to be identified as the author of this Work in accordance with the Copyright, Designs and Patents Act 1988

Penguin Random House values and supports copyright. Copyright fuels creativity, encourages diverse voices, promotes freedom of expression and supports a vibrant culture. Thank you for purchasing an authorized edition of this book and for respecting intellectual property laws by not reproducing, scanning or distributing any part of it by any means without permission. You are supporting authors and enabling Penguin Random House to continue to publish books for everyone. No part of this book may be used or reproduced in any manner for the purpose of training artificial intelligence technologies or systems. In accordance with Article 4(3) of the DSM Directive 2019/790, Penguin Random House expressly reserves this work from the text and data mining exception.

Published by Quadrille in 2025

www.penguin.co.uk

A CIP catalogue record for this book is available from the British Library

ISBN 9781837832798
10 9 8 7 6 5 4 3 2 1

Managing Director Sarah Lavelle
Editor Robert Timms
Design Manager Katherine Case
Design Concept Luke Bird
Photographer Luke Albert
Maps Laura Barnard
Head of Production Stephen Lang
Production Controller Sabeena Atchia

Colour reproduction by F1

Printed in China by C&C Offset Printing Co., Ltd.

The authorised representative in the EEA is Penguin Random House Ireland, Morrison Chambers, 32 Nassau Street, Dublin D02 YH68.

Penguin Random House is committed to a sustainable future for our business, our readers and our planet. This book is made from Forest Stewardship Council® certified paper.

MIX
Paper | Supporting responsible forestry
FSC® C018179